ALLAN PINKERTON

ALLAN PINKERTON

The First Private Eye

JAMES MACKAY

CASTLE BOOKS

For Elly and Benny

This edition published in 2007 by
CASTLE BOOKS ®
A division of Book Sales, Inc.
114 Northfield Avenue
Edison, NJ 08837

This edition published by arrangement with and permission of
John Wiley & Sons, Inc.
111 River Street
Hoboken, New Jersey 07030

This publication is designed to provide accurate and authoritative information in regard to the subject matter covered. It is sold with the understanding that the publisher is not engaged in rendering legal, accounting, or other professional services. If legal advice or other expert assistance is required, the services of a competent professional person should be sought.

Library of Congress Cataloging-in-Publication Data:

Mackay, James A. (James Alexander)
    Allan Pinkerton: the first private eye/James Mackay.
        p.   cm.
    Includes bibliographical references and index.
    1.   Pinkerton, Allan, 1819-1884. 2. Dectectives-United States-Biography. 3.
    Private investigators-United States-Biography. 4. Pinkerton's National Detective
    Agency-History. I. Title.

HV7911.P4675M33   1997
363.28'9'092-dc21
[B]

97-21271

ISBN-13: 978-0-7858-2235-6
ISBN-10: 0-7858-2235-6

Printed in the United States of America

Contents

Introduction

Pinkerton as a name synonymous with protection and security is a household word the world over; so, too, is the expression 'private eye', which derives from the unblinking, unflinching eye adopted by Allan Pinkerton in 1850 as his trademark, along with the slogan 'We Never Sleep'. His was an eye which could register the salient details of a person or a situation in a twinkling. In the Chicago underworld of the 1850s Allan Pinkerton soon came to be known, simply, as the Eye. His watchful eye was omnipresent; nothing escaped him. Today, Pinkerton's Security Services tend to place more reliance on Radar Eye, developed by its electronics division, but the principle remains the same.

Considering how well known the Pinkerton name is nowadays, it is remarkable how vague, contradictory and incomplete has been our knowledge of Allan Pinkerton the man. Even his date of birth has been mis-stated in every publication until now, and virtually every detail concerning his antecedents is wrong. Much of the blame must rest on his own shoulders, for many of the facts concerning his life were derived from his reminiscences, written shortly before his death. Previous biographers were only too ready to accept Allan's statements at face value without checking them. Worse, they were often careless and contradictory, so that untangling the web of confusion has come to resemble one of the cases which Allan Pinkerton himself unravelled.

In all conscience there was enough that appeared contradictory in the life and character of Allan Pinkerton without making the situation worse. Was he the fugitive from justice which he liked to make out? To be sure, he was one of the leading, most uncompromising, figures among the physical force Chartists in 1839–42, and his part in the Newport Rising of 1839 would have earned him a stiff sentence of transportation to Botany Bay had the authorities been apprised of it. Earlier writers have conjured up the picture of a clandestine marriage and the fugitive bride and groom being smuggled aboard ship to escape the clutches of the law; but the marriage of Allan Pinkerton and Joan Carfrae in Glasgow Cathedral, after due proclamation of banns on three consecutive Sundays, belies this. The only criminality involved was the marriage itself, for Joan was only fifteen years of age at the time, though she may have misled Allan into thinking that she was three years older.

Even the ship on which they sailed to the New World, the details of their shipwreck and subsequent movements in Canada, have been shrouded in mystery and contradiction. Similarly, the details of their six children have never been given till now; indeed, their names, dates of birth and death have been presented in a vague, chaotic manner, if mentioned at all. Allan's early life in America, the year in which he solved his first case, even the date at which he established his famous detective agency – all have been the subject of controversy.

These points pale into insignificance, however, in the face of the half-truths or complete distortion of the facts concerning Allan's political outlook. It has long been fashionable to condemn Allan Pinkerton as the one-time labour agitator who turned against his class, but much of the opprobrium heaped on his head was posthumous. Allan died in 1884, eight years before the tragic Homestead Strike which resulted in terrible bloodshed. The popular image which lingers to this day is that the Pinkertons were strike-breakers when, in fact, they were acting within the law in the protection of industrial premises against a violent mob ten times their number. Allan Pinkerton himself had laid down very clear guidelines in 1850; his Protective Patrol, as the uniformed security guards were originally known, were strictly warned against labour espionage or interfering in any way with the right of working men to strike. There is, in fact, abundant evidence that Allan never deviated from the radical liberal ideals of his youth. To condemn him on the grounds that he himself became an employer of labour, and hobnobbed with the great American capitalists of the mid-nineteenth century, is as unjust as it is simplistic.

The other glaring charge levelled against him is that of causing the unnecessary prolongation of the American Civil War. Had General McClellan pressed home his assault against Richmond in the spring of 1862 the war would have been ended within months, instead of dragging on for a further three years, with appalling loss of life and untold hardship on both sides. That he did not is usually explained away on the grounds that he was sadly misled by Allan Pinkerton, his intelligence chief, regarding the numbers of Confederate troops opposing him. This, again, is a simplistic view of the peninsular campaign, which is as unfair to McClellan as it is unjust to Pinkerton. The copious and extremely detailed intelligence reports, amounting to thousands of pages, are preserved in the Library of Congress and the National Archives and give the lie to the canard that Pinkerton may have been a good detective but was a poor intelligence analyst; yet the myth persists, and is repeated *ad nauseam*.

Allan Pinkerton had to put up with controversy all his adult life, but he never shrank from doing battle with his enemies and assailants, criminal or political. The young firebrand who trounced the moral force Chartists on the rostrum or fought gangs of Tory thugs in the street battles of the 1830s was the same fearless incorruptible who earned the grudging respect both of the official police and the criminal fraternity of Chicago. In the Byzantine world of Washington during the Civil War he came up against devious politicians, scheming generals and the sinister forces of the greedy, ruthless and corrupt – not to mention Confederate spies and Southern sympathisers.

In many respects the Civil War marked the high point of his career, yet in the post-war period Pinkerton's National Detective Agency expanded as the country flourished, population exploded and communications mushroomed. The fast and furious development of the United States took place against a background of mounting lawlessness. The forces of law and order operated only at county or state level and were often untrained, inept and corrupt – wholly inadequate for the maintenance of law and order on a national scale. In this vacuum the Pinkertons provided a vital service, combating the fast-moving outlaws and criminals on their own terms. This was the era of the Wild West, when Allan Pinkerton took on such outlaws as the Reno brothers, Jesse James and his gang and the Youngers. Often Pinkerton and his agents were caught between the outlaws and the vigilantes, seldom able to rely on local lawmen. Just as there was a great deal of misplaced sympathy for the James boys in their home state of Missouri, so too the Pinkertons would encounter considerable hostility in bringing the Molly Maguires, an Irish terrorist organisation, to justice. The Mollies were unprincipled scoundrels who terrorised and intimidated the English, Welsh and German miners in Pennsylvania, and reacted just as ferociously against fellow Irishmen who crossed them. Yet, today, the Molly Maguires are often held up as martyrs of the labour movement, and the man who pursued them relentlessly to the gallows is denigrated as a traitor and turncoat to the Chartist ideals of his youth. The plain fact is that the Molly Maguires were gangsters and hoodlums without any redeeming features, condemned at the time by the Catholic Church and the trade union movement alike. The view of them as politico-religious martyrs barbarously suppressed by a private police force is only one of the more ludicrous pieces of historical revisionism in recent years.

On one score alone most writers appear to agree and that is on Allan Pinkerton's implacable hatred of slavery and his dogged, not to say fanatical, adherence to the abolitionist cause. Though very little is known of his clandestine activities as a 'foreman' of the so-called Underground Railroad in the late 1840s, his uncompromising attitude is far better documented in the period after 1850 when, in the wake of the Fugitive Slave Act, this most upright of lawmen quite calmly broke the law by helping John Brown and others to get runaway slaves out of the country to freedom in Canada.

Firm views on the rights of man and the basic principles of democracy, inculcated when he was hardly out of his teens, never left Allan Pinkerton, whatever his detractors may have implied. Yet the man who had fair and liberal views regarding the people in his employment could be a domineering, unreasoning tyrant in his own home. He had a rigid, often harsh code by which he lived his own life, and it never crossed his mind for a moment that his family might not necessarily share his views. It is not known, for example, whether his sons William and Robert had any choice about coming into the business and both terminated their studies abruptly to join their father. Admittedly, there was a war on, and Allan argued that they were better with him, at the battlefront, than running away from home to enlist, as so many other boys did, blinded by the romance and glamour of war.

Similarly, as a husband, Allan showed very little evidence of the tenderness and consideration which a wife might have expected, yet Joan appears to have deferred to his wishes in every respect. Where his sole surviving daughter was concerned, however, Allan showed himself in a bad light, doing everything in his power to blight her happiness and prevent her from marrying the man of her choice. Yet this domestic tyrant who treated his own womenfolk like chattels was also the man who recognised the rights of women in the workplace. As early as 1856 he employed female detectives, half a century before they were recruited by the New York Police Department. Interestingly, in this regard, Allan had a bitter battle with his sons and other senior executives of the Agency in the 1870s and 1880s when they conspired against the old man and tried to have the Female Detective Bureau disbanded. Allan himself stoutly defended his policy, arguing that women detectives could often worm secrets out of suspects in situations debarred to male operatives.

A cooper by trade, Allan Pinkerton might have spent his entire working life making barrels had he not stumbled across something in the summer of 1846 which roused his suspicions. An uninhabited island with a blackened patch in a copse where someone had recently lit a fire might not have seemed out of the ordinary to most people; but to the young cooper who had gone there to cut saplings for barrel-staves it was a portent of wrong-doing. Later in life, this sixth sense enabled him to anticipate a crime even before it had happened. In itself, it was not conclusive; but to this was allied a persistence that refused to be worn down by disappointment. On several occasions Allan returned to the island at night and a damp, cold, lonely vigil, before his patience was rewarded. This combination of sensing something not quite right, together with dogged tenacity and unbounded patience, paid off when he was the means of arresting a gang of counterfeiters. This led to 'a little job in the detective line' which, in turn, resulted in Allan's appointment as a part-time deputy sheriff. From this he progressed to full-time deputy sheriff in Chicago, then the first (and only) detective on the Chicago police force, and finally to setting up his own North-West Detective Agency in 1850.

This was the first organisation of its kind in the western hemisphere. From the outset Allan handled criminal cases of all kinds, from murder and arson to insurance fraud, but resolutely refused to undertake divorce work. In 1861 he foiled the plot on the life of President-elect Lincoln and, putting the resources of the Agency at the disposal of General McClellan, set up the first military intelligence service in the United States. It would be true to say that he was the father of the Secret Service, although that body was developed separately, and outside his control, a year later, with unfortunate short-term results.

The organisational ability which young Allan Pinkerton had shown in the Chartist movement in Britain was developed in the formation and expansion of the Detective Agency which, after the Civil War, was virtually a national police force, albeit a private one. Not for nothing was Pinkerton's widely known as America's Scotland Yard, and its services often called upon by other governments to combat international crime, long before Interpol was established.

With no formal training in the detection of crime, Allan Pinkerton was a natural. He devised many of the techniques of surveillance and infiltration which are now in common use everywhere. He was quick to exploit such new technology as the railway and the telegraph in mobilising the forces of law and order against interstate crime, and at a very early stage utilised photography by creating a Rogues Gallery of mugshots, accompanied by detailed records and descriptions of criminals and suspects.

The organisation which Allan Pinkerton started in 1850 with a staff of two, in a tiny office in Chicago, now has 250 offices in twenty countries worldwide, and 50,000 employees. Pinkerton Security Services, as the present-day name implies, is now mainly concerned with security of business and industrial premises. Transportation continues to be an important part of the company's role, although nowadays aviation security is predominant. An important aspect of the firm's commercial work consists of vetting over a million job applications per annum. Specially trained officers, experts in communications, crowd control and fire-fighting, are employed in the special events division. The detective aspects, currently handled by Pinkerton Consulting and Investigations Services, account for only about four per cent of the business, but they continue to provide global industry and commerce with corporate investigations, executive protection, asset security and crisis management.

Only the scale has changed over the years; the general principles which Allan Pinkerton enunciated almost 150 years ago remain as valid as ever.

In writing this book I have had the assistance of many people on both sides of the Atlantic. In chronological order I am indebted to the staff of the Mitchell Library in Glasgow, one of the finest municipal libraries in Europe. Oddly enough, the Glasgow Room, where I might have expected a wealth of material pertaining to one of the city's greatest sons, yielded almost nothing; but the files of the newspapers of the late 1830s and early 1840s, the *Herald*, the *Weekly Herald*, the *Northern Star* and, above all, the *Scottish Patriot*, proved to be a goldmine, not only in reporting the movements and activities of the Chartists and the various breakaway groups but in recording the meetings and even the speeches of Allan Pinkerton and his associates. The Mitchell Library also boasts a number of Allan Pinkerton's own books; all of these have autobiographical elements, although, by the nature of the way in which many of the later books were 'ghosted', their contents have to be treated with considerable caution.

The Mitchell Library's Family Room, containing both the Mormon micro-fiche of parish records and microfilms of the records themselves, enabled me to shed light on the origins and antecedents of the Pinkerton and Carfrae families. There are still Pinkertons in Glasgow, and I am indebted to Roy Pinkerton, now of Edinburgh, for useful information on other members of the family. Much of the previous writing on Allan Pinkerton's boyhood was derived from Edgar L. Wakeman, a friend of the Pinkertons in Chicago, who made a pilgrimage to Scotland in 1889, some five years after Allan's death, and allegedly sought out facts from friends, relatives and casual acquaintances. Out of this research Wakeman distilled an article which appeared in several American newspapers in September 1889 but nothing stated therein has stood the test of time or more objective research. The staff of Strathclyde Regional Archives produced invaluable data on Clyde shipping records which enabled me to solve the mystery regarding the ship on which the Pinkertons sailed to Canada. To my very good friends John Maclean and Martin Christie, respectively Deacon-Convener and Clerk of the Coopers' Guild of Glasgow, I am indebted for information regarding the most famous member of their profession.

Farther afield, the National Library of Scotland in Edinburgh and the British Library in London yielded copies of Allan Pinkerton's books, several of which are regarded as major rarities. It has been estimated that the eighteen books bearing his name run to over three million words, a formidable amount of reading. To the staff of these libraries I am, as always, indebted for their unfailing courtesy and efficiency. The Public Record Office, London, contains a great deal of material dealing with the Chartist movement, and provided me with useful information on Allan Pinkerton's associates, notably George Julian Harney. This also threw up some intriguing connections between the Chartists and the anti-slavery movement, which had a significant bearing on Allan Pinkerton's later career. I am grateful also to the librarian and curator of the municipal museum in Newport, Gwynedd, as well as the staff of the South Wales Police Museum at Bridgend, Mid Glamorgan, where records and relics associated with the Newport Rising (including maps and transcripts of the subsequent treason trials) are preserved. For useful information on Pinkerton's activities in 1839–41 and his movements in Cumbria, Dumfriesshire and Ayrshire, I am indebted to David Lockwood of Dumfries Burgh Museum and Alastair Johnston of the Ewart Library, Dumfries. Jan Kelso of Mauchline also turned up details of Julian Harney's wife and her family.

For information regarding the Pinkerton National Detective Agency I must express my thanks to various members of Pinkerton Security Services, notably Thomas W. Wathen, Chairman of the company, and Denis R. Brown, President and Chief Executive. To the man on the spot, Bill Dunne, MM, Director of the Glasgow office of Pinkerton's, I must record special thanks for his unfailing help and enthusiasm throughout this project. In particular, I am indebted to the staff of Pinkerton's, on both sides of the Atlantic, for the illustrations used throughout this book, as well as access to archival material now held at world headquarters in Encino, California.

Over a period of several years I have been making regular visits to Washington DC to study the Pinkerton letter-books, journals, day-books, correspondence and reports preserved in the National Archives and the Library of Congress. Apart from the Pinkerton manuscripts, I have also taken the opportunity to study the McClellan papers, a rich and relatively untouched treasure of material, as well as the Herndon-Weik collection which includes the copies of Pinkerton records made at the behest of William Herndon, Abraham Lincoln's law partner. Other material has come from the collections of the Chicago Historical Society, the Illinois Central Railroad collection in the Newberry Library and the Lamon papers in the Huntington Library, San Marino, California. To the staff of these libraries and institutions who gave of their time to steer me in the right direction and answer my importunings by correspondence over the past ten years, I must record my gratitude. Finally, special thanks are due to my long-suffering wife Renate, who ploughed through seemingly interminable copies of the *Radio Times* to track down details of the film in which Christopher Reeve of *Superman* fame played the part of the stocky little Glasgow detective.

JAMES MACKAY
GLASGOW, 1996

The Gorbals
1819–38

Metropolitan detectives can trace a thief over the entire kingdom – if he
does not get to the Gorbals of Glasgow.

SIR JOHN FIELDING (1722–80)

Few place-names in the United Kingdom are as well known as the Gorbals, and none possesses such a pejorative ring. Yet the reputation for lawlessness and the worst slums in Europe is both simplistic and undeserved. This district, lying on the south bank of the River Clyde, was first settled in the fourteenth century. At the time when the first stone bridge was erected across the river from the city of Glasgow, the Gorbals was uninhabited, apart from St Ninian's Hospital founded by Lady Lochow. This was a leper colony, into which were decanted the unclean of Glasgow where they were left to languish until they died, conveniently segregated from the city by the broad river.

This was an area directly administered by the See of Glasgow; indeed its very name betrays its ecclesiastical origins, for *garbale* in medieval Latin signifies a tithe or teind. By 1571 leprosy was a thing of the past and in that year the Archbishop of Glasgow feued the land to Sir George Elphinstone, a merchant and former lord provost of the city, who had the hamlet of Gorbals erected into a burgh of barony and regality. When times were prosperous Sir George built himself a fine mansion near the centre of his little burgh, but he fell on hard times and was forced to sell it to the city. Gorbals was then parcelled out between the Trades House and the trustees of Hutchesons' Hospital, a connection reflected in the unimaginative names of Tradeston and Hutchesontown in use to this day.

In 1661 Gorbals was annexed by Glasgow, despite being a burgh in its own right. For many years it was governed, not by its own provost, but by a Glasgow bailie. Perhaps this anomalous position encouraged the loose character of the place in the ensuing century. The Gorbals, at the far end of the Old Bridge, was a place where the writ of the lord provost seemingly did not run. By the 1790s it was a bustling little town of some five thousand inhabitants, where there was a public house or licensed spirit dealer for every twelve families, although this took no note of the unlicensed shebeens and drinking dens.[1] Writing in the *First Statistical Account*, the Revd William Anderson, minister of the Gorbals, commented sombrely that 'the number of children of depraved parents, thrown on the public without anyone to take care of them, almost exceeds belief. A great proportion of these children are brought up in ignorance, in idleness and vice, without the fear of God and very little of man.'

The Gorbals was 'the haunt of the Glasgow prostitutes and their bullies or fancy-men', banished from the city itself. One report, published in 1816, estimated that on average the girls were paid a shilling for their services, but robbed their clients of half a crown. Heavy drinking went on in these brothels, while many pubs were barely disguised fronts for prostitution.[2]

The Gorbals was a place where the honest citizens of Glasgow went to let their hair down. A great deal of the evil reputation of the place stemmed from this fact, and was largely perpetrated by Glaswegians themselves. One minister who passed through the Gorbals on a Sunday commented on the fact that, on one side of the Main Street, he could hear the sounds of praying and psalm-singing, but on the other the worst profanity and blasphemy issued from the drinking dens. Douce burghers and their families, returning from the parish church near the river, had to dodge the drunks staggering in the gutter. Decent artisans lived cheek by jowl with drunkards and strumpets. Drunken brawling might have been commonplace, but serious crime was actually rare.

There was another aspect to the village. Much of the heavy industry of the district was located there, ever since the 1660s when the first coal-mine was opened up. In the eighteenth century the Gorbals attracted many factories and workshops, a speciality of the district being fine firearms. In 1793 the majority of the honest inhabitants earned their living as handloom weavers. They were the aristocrats of labour, hard-working, industrious, generally well educated by the standards of the day, and with an independent turn of mind.

Most of the houses in the Gorbals were single-storey thatched buildings, but at the centre of the burgh, clustered round the Cross, were three-storey tenements of rubble stone. The quaint and picturesque but tortuous Main Street running north and south was the principal thoroughfare. Even by the Glasgow standards of the time the humble tenements of the Gorbals, many of them thatched, were mean and squalid in the extreme. The tawdriness of the scene was relieved only by the baronial tower of the mansion of the Elphinstones on one side of the Cross and the imposing height of the Ark, a five-storey tenement with a slated roof which dwarfed its neighbours.

In 1800 Main Street was still broad enough to permit the passage of wheeled carts, but within thirty years additions and extensions, mostly rickety wooden structures and ramshackle lean-tos, had reduced it to the point where pedestrians could barely pass one another. As for the labyrinthine loans, courts and vennels running back from the Main Street, turning and twisting crazily in all directions, they eventually became so congested that their flimsy wooden upper storeys virtually met across the alleyway and all but blotted out the grimy daylight. It is hardly to be wondered at, as Sir John Fielding wryly noted, that a criminal could vanish into this warren without trace.

As the nineteenth century dawned, however, there was a polarisation of Gorbals society. In 1800 James Laurie obtained the feu of land in the west of the burgh and began laying out broad streets on a grid plan. In these streets, named Carlton, Oxford, Portland, Norfolk, Bedford, Cumberland, Devon and Cavendish after the great aristocratic families of England, were erected fine, modern tenement blocks which, for a time, became very fashionable and attracted a few of Glasgow's well-to-do merchants, but Laurieston, as the area was known, had the chief effect of withdrawing the respectable inhabitants from Main Street, Kirk Street, Buchan Street, Malta Street and Rutherglen Loan which formed the old Gorbals. As one writer noted, 'The land tenure of the old Gorbals, and its limited area for parochial management, necessitating high poor-rates, had the effect of hindering the transfer and improvement of heritage, and the result was the general dilapidation of property, crowded by the labouring classes, a large proportion of whom were paupers.'[3]

The streets of Laurieston were made relatively safe for this middle-class populace when, in 1808, the Gorbals got its own police authority. For almost two decades this part of the burgh at least was actually quite respectable, but in the old Gorbals the respite from lawlessness was brief. Trade and industry slumped at the end of the Napoleonic Wars. Widespread destitution in rural areas, particularly the Highlands, drove thousands of desperate people into the towns and cities seeking work in the new heavy industries based on coal and iron that developed in the 1820s. Dixon's Blazes, a vast complex of iron foundries and steel mills erected in 1824 on the south side of the Gorbals, became a powerful magnet for the displaced and the dispossessed. Between 1793 and 1835 the population of the burgh rose from 5,000 to 35,000, and then doubled again in the ensuing fifteen years, without any significant increase in the area occupied.

Irish immigration began in the 1820s; even by the time of the 1841 Census it was found that seven out of ten inhabitants of the Gorbals had been born in Ireland, but this was as nothing compared with the dramatic influx from that island as a result of the potato famine a few years later. By 1841 very few of the original Scottish residents were still in the burgh, most having migrated across the river into Glasgow itself. The Irish influx was viewed with horror by the inhabitants of the city and there are countless racist references in the newspapers and periodicals of the period to the barbarian hordes, the Huns and Vandals who were wrecking the Gorbals, infesting its already overcrowded and crumbling buildings, spreading filth and disease. 'When once these Milesians of the lower class make a settlement, we are told it is nearly as difficult to expel them as to hunt rats out of a city drain,' commented Senex.[4] Sanitation was rudimentary, with communal ashpits and dungsteads in the back-courts, though urine was assiduously collected and rendered down for use in calico-printing. There were few wells in the Gorbals and most people drew water for all purposes from the Blind Burn, virtually an open sewer. The very air itself was heavily polluted by the smoke belching from a thousand factory chimneys, not to mention the sulphurous fumes emitted day and night from Dixon's Blazes.

One of the oldest families in the old Gorbals were the Pinkertons. As far back as the parish records go (early seventeenth century), it appears that Pinkertons had been living in the Gorbals and the neighbouring burgh of Rutherglen, in which they attained some eminence as provosts and deans of guilds. The name comes from a tiny hamlet south-east of Dunbar on the east coast of Scotland. People of that name were, by 1600, living in Prestonpans near Edinburgh and, a little later, in Kilmarnock, south of Glasgow. In 1638 Allayne Pinkertoune married Margaret Davidson in Little Govan[5] and was the progenitor of the Gorbals branch of the family which, for several generations, worked at the burgh smithy. The smithy and farrier's workshop were located in Malta Street, in the courtyard of one of the oldest buildings in the burgh, erected by a Quaker named George Swan in 1687. Half a century later John Campbell, a blacksmith and farrier, became the occupant and finally purchased the premises from Swan's descendants in 1749.[6] Campbell's only child, a daughter, married a Glasgow merchant named Falconer and the building remained in the hands of their descendants until 1849 when it was demolished as unsafe. For almost a century the Falconers let the front of the building as a public house, but in the yard at the rear they owned the smithy which gave employment to several generations of Pinkertons.

On 4 August 1727 George Pinkerton married Anna Murdoch.[7] Their son James, born in March 1735, married Margaret Love on 16 February 1759 and two years later Margaret gave birth to her first son, also named James, whose descendants live in Glasgow to this day. A second son, named William, was born on 4 January 1767. George, born two years later, died in infancy, but a second George, born in September 1771, lived to a ripe old age. The youngest son was Allan, born in 1779 and who, in due course, became a blacksmith like his father. William Pinkerton, on the other hand, became a handloom weaver and, like so many others of his calling, had acquired some education and the ability to think for himself. A big man, just over six foot tall (which was well above average height for the time), he had a dour, saturnine nature. A century later the notion would get about that William and his wife were pious and deeply religious, but their famous son would explode that myth by saying that, in fact, they were atheists who had little to do with organised religion, except in so far as they were obliged to have their children baptised in the parish church. This is, indeed, borne out by an entry in the Gorbals parish records. On 30 July 1792 William Pinkerton and Isabella Stevenson acknowledged before the Kirk Session that they were married in the previous April. At that time marriage in Scotland could be the merest formality 'by habit and repute', but the Kirk liked to keep things tidy, hence the summons of the young couple to acknowledge publicly that they had been living together as man and wife for several months.

By Isabella Stevenson, William Pinkerton had three daughters and four sons. The eldest child, born on 12 February 1792, was a daughter christened Love, from her grandmother's maiden surname. The eldest son was James, who was born on 10 April 1796 and named after his paternal grandfather. Mary was born on 13 May 1798 and Janet on 11 May 1800. William came into the world on 6 February 1803, followed two years later by a son who died at or soon after birth, and lastly Andrew, born in 1807. Family legend has it that Isabella Stevenson died giving birth to her last child; this cannot be verified as the Gorbals burials registers prior to May 1807 are no longer extant, but from the absence of her name after that date it may safely be assumed that she died some time previously. The fact that Andrew was never baptised seems to bear this out. His birth was not recorded in the parish register, although his death four years later was.

For some time William Pinkerton carried on alone, attempting to raise his large brood single-handedly in a two-room apartment on the top floor of the tenement at the corner of Muirhead Street and Rutherglen Loan near the decrepit Elphinstone mansion, although it is highly probable that his widowed mother, who lived in one of the closes of the Main Street just round the corner with her unmarried son Allan, played her part too. But on 11 November 1811 little Andrew succumbed to measles. The loss of his youngest child must have been a hard blow for William. He himself would soon be forty-five, a good age in the Gorbals; but he was in the prime of life and had a good job which, thanks to the wars with France, brought high wages. By that time all three daughters were working in James Thomson's cotton mill farther up Muirhead Street and contributed to the family budget; only James was a ne'er-do-well who could never keep a job for long and preferred the company of the louts and hooligans who congregated at the Cross. Whoring and hard-drinking when he was barely out of his teens, James would break his father's heart.[8]

William came to the conclusion that his younger son and namesake, now rising nine, needed the steadying influence of a mother. Love, who had been filling that role, was now almost twenty and would probably soon leave home to get married, and in a few years the other girls would be off his hands too. The idea of remarrying appealed to William so he cast around for a likely bride. One of the older hands at Thomson's cotton mill caught his eye. At thirty-three, Isabella McQueen might be classed as an old maid; at that age she could no longer afford to be choosy. No details of their courtship, if there was any, have survived, but it seems that Isabella merely moved in with William.[9]

William and his second Isabella might have been atheists, as their son claimed, and had no regard for attending church or going through the ritual of marriage, but when it came to the issue of their casual union they dutifully conformed. Their first son, John, was born in March 1813 and duly baptised in the parish church. Baby John, however, died of teething fever on 7 February 1814. The first surviving son was Robert, born on 12 March 1815. Two years later came Allan, named after his uncle who witnessed the baptism on 13 April 1817; but on 11 October 1818 this toddler died. The cause of death entered in the parish register was laconic in the extreme – 'decline'. The fourth and last child born to Isabella McQueen was likewise christened Allan.

Myth, legend, distortion of the truth and controversy would surround this Allan all the days of his life, and this pattern was established from the outset. The birth of Allan Pinkerton, as given by all previous writers,[10] was 25 August 1819. In fact the Gorbals parish registers show that he was actually born on 21 July and *baptised* on 25 August when he was little more than a month old. The infant was christened, not in 'the high vaulted baptistry of the Scotch Baptist Church'[11] but at the font in the neo-classical parish church. This fine building in Carlton Place, with its Doric columns and Grecian friezes, had been erected only in 1811 when the Gorbals was at the height of its prosperity, and its lofty steeple boasted the first bell cast in Glasgow. The minister who baptised all of William Pinkerton's eleven children except Love was the Revd James McLean, who had come to the parish at the age of thirty-two in 1793 and continued to serve until his death forty years later, by which time his congregation had risen seven-fold. The parish church, situated on a pleasant elevation overlooking the Clyde, was a familiar landmark of the area until the 1950s, when it was swept away in the wholesale demolition of the Gorbals. Its site is now occupied by the oppressively fortress-like buildings of the Sheriff Court of Glasgow and Strathkelvin.

If Allan Pinkerton were to return to his birthplace today the metamorphosis of the parish church would not be the only shock. The tenement at the corner of Muirhead Street and Rutherglen Loan survived only till the end of the nineteenth century when it was a victim of the redevelopment east of the Cross which resulted in the creation of Ballater Street, the broad highway running east and west, a block north of the old Rutherglen Loan, itself transformed into Old Rutherglen Road. Muirhead Street was subsequently renamed Inverkip Street, but of this narrow back street, one block east of Main Street (now Gorbals Street) there is now no trace. It, too, was demolished in the 1950s. Part of the site has never been redeveloped, and today is waste ground covered by tall trees more than forty years old, but the north end, where Isabella Pinkerton and her step-daughters once laboured in Thomson's Mill, is now occupied by the Glasgow Central Mosque, completed as recently as 1984, with its multi-faceted golden dome and tall, slender minaret.

While he was growing up in the Gorbals, Allan was acutely aware of the Irish invasion which totally transformed the burgh. The existing tenements were, for the most part, sound structures, many of which would survive until the holocaust known euphemistically as the Comprehensive Development Area which hit the Gorbals in the 1950s; but by the 1840s these tenements had become teeming slums, their apartments divided and sub-divided into 'single-ends' into which crowded Irish labourers and their numerous progeny. In one such single-end, measuring seven by fifteen feet, nine adults were recorded as living in 1848.

By the end of the century the Irish had, by and large, moved on and upwards, their place taken by refugees from the pogroms of eastern Europe. For seventy years the Gorbals was effectively a ghetto whose shops were inscribed in Hebrew, where seven synagogues were packed every Shabbat, and Yiddish was the language of the crowded streets. After the Second World War the Jews migrated southwards, to the affluent suburbs of Giffnock, Whitecraigs and Newton Mearns. In the 1950s and 1960s decayed and sound housing was indiscriminately swept away, and only the elegant Georgian houses of Carlton Place remained. As part of the CDA project (the largest in the United Kingdom at that time) tower blocks were erected in 1965–70 to rehabilitate the Gorbals. The fact that they were designed by Sir Basil Spence did not make them more aesthetic or habitable and, in turn, they have now been razed to the ground, making way for infinitely more pleasing apartment blocks. Today the Gorbals has a predominantly Pakistani population.

The sight of the mosque to the north of his old home would not be the only thing to astonish Pinkerton today. Where the corner tenement in which he was born once stood there is now the impressive headquarters of the Procurator Fiscal for Glasgow and Strathkelvin, the Scottish counterpart of the District

Attorney in the United States. Seeing his old home thus transformed into the bastion of law and order for the west of Scotland, Allan would doubtless permit himself a sardonic grin.

Regrettably, no statue or monument to its most celebrated son has ever been erected in the Gorbals, though at the time of writing (1995) a memorial mural is being designed for the Adelphi Street walkway along the south bank of the Clyde. Perhaps some day a modest plaque on the wall of the Procurator Fiscal's building may record the fact that the founder of the world's greatest private detective agency was born on that spot and spent the first twenty years of his life there.

Allan Pinkerton could not have chosen a worse time to come into the world. The series of wars with France which had lasted for almost a quarter of a century (1793–1815) were followed by a slump and the general stagnation in trade which caused widespread unemployment among the working classes of Glasgow and the Gorbals. The distress of the workers in 1819 was so great that the conscience of the middle and upper classes was pricked and a fund speedily raised £9,653 which was distributed among 23,190 persons. As if this were not bad enough, the city and suburbs were severely afflicted by an outbreak of typhus fever that summer, causing 171 deaths.

Crop failures and changing technology combined to cause widespread distress and discontent in the year of Allan's birth. The first was unpredictable but the latter had been a long time in development. In 1787 the cotton manufacturers of Glasgow had proposed to reduce the price of weaving, as a result of which many of the handloom weavers stopped work, marched in demonstrations through the streets of Glasgow and destroyed a number of webs in the Drygate and Calton. Provost Riddell called out the military and in the ensuing fracas three men were killed near the Hangman's Brae, and several others were wounded. During the French Revolutionary period (1789–93) unrest smouldered and mutual antipathy between the weavers and the cotton manufacturers increased. In a bid to reduce their reliance on the workers, the manufacturers sought ways and means of mechanising the various textile processes. In 1774 the Revd Dr Richard Cartwright had invented the power-loom which would eventually transform the textile industry. In 1789–90 several of these looms were installed in the hulks moored in the Thames estuary and driven by convict labour. James Lewis Robertson acquired a power-loom in 1793 and installed it in a cellar in Argyle Street, Glasgow, using a Newfoundland dog walking in a drum or cylinder to drive it. Within a year there were forty power-looms in the Glasgow area, used to weave calico for printing. In the ensuing decade hundreds of looms, powered by water or horses, were installed all over the city and suburbs. By 1807 Archibald Buchanan had devised a machine which combined the warping, dressing and weaving processes. This, coupled with the use of steam-power a few years later, totally revolutionised the industry. Tweeds (1809), checks (1810), figured goods (1818) and even lappets (1820) were woven by machines which became bigger, faster and more powerful with every passing year.

The result was that thousands of handloom weavers were thrown out of work, the same cloth being more efficiently and much more cheaply produced by machines tended mainly by girls at a fraction of the old handloom weavers' wages. Unemployment reached an all-time high in 1819. In vain the city magistrates created temporary work for upwards of six hundred men, in breaking stones and paving roadways. A further 340 weavers, superintended by James Cleland, the Gorbals bailie, were employed in landscaping Glasgow Green. While this privileged few worked diligently with pick and shovel, thousands more marched past with radical banners and attended monster public rallies on the Green.

William Pinkerton, at the age of fifty-two, became part of the statistics. A few years earlier, he had been earning as much as fifty shillings a week, but for some time past his wages had been falling steadily and latterly he had been taking home as little as ten shillings. He experienced the bitter humiliation of seeing his daughters Love, Mary and Janet supplanting him as the main bread-winner, for the girls, working a six-day week, thirteen hours a day, were earning more in Thomson's Mill. In June 1819 Love, now twenty-seven, finally got married at Cumbernauld, a village in Stirlingshire some miles north-east of Glasgow. Her husband, Andrew Weston, was a coal-miner and therefore in a form of employment which was unlikely to be threatened by mechanisation, at least for the foreseeable future.

One of the many myths surrounding the Pinkerton family is that William became a sergeant in the Glasgow police,[12] but a search of the records pertaining to this force, which was raised in 1800 as the first of its kind in Britain, shows this to have been untrue. In fact, William Pinkerton pulled strings and secured employment as a trusty at the City Gaol. Prior to 1807 the town gaol had been located at Glasgow Cross, but its thirty-two cells were by that time hopelessly inadequate to serve the populous counties of Lanark, Renfrew and Dumbarton as well as the city and its suburbs. The new gaol, containing 122 cells, was erected close to the River Clyde at the western end of Glasgow Green. Interestingly, the statistics show that, of the 1,388 prisoners incarcerated in 1830–31, no fewer than 630 were debtors, while only 758 were classed as 'delinquents' held on criminal charges.[13]

This may not have been the most congenial employment imaginable, but it provided a steady wage and gave William a certain standing in the community. The gaol had what the tenement in Muirhead Street had not – indoor sanitation of the most advanced kind, in the form of a water closet on every landing, as well as pure, filtered water supplied from the new Glasgow Water Company's pipes. The City Gaol was regarded as something of a pioneer in penal circles, much lauded for the two cells, with ante-rooms, insulated from the rest of the establishment, where persons under sentence of death could be held securely *without irons* until such time as they were led out for execution on the gallows opposite the entrance to the Green.

William Pinkerton crossed the river every day to go to work at the gaol. He had a choice of routes: either he could walk up Main Street and cross by the Old Bridge, then turn right along Clyde Street to the gaol, or he could walk along Rutherglen Loan to Crown Street, then across the temporary wooden bridge which stood right beside the gaol and the entrance to Glasgow Green. Either way was no more than a few minutes on foot.

Contrary to widespread belief, Glasgow was not such a den of iniquity in this period. Between 1765 and 1830 only eighty-four men and five women were publicly executed at Glasgow; given the dramatic rise in population after that time, the number of executions was modest, eleven men and one woman being hanged in 1831–34 (six for murder, one each for rape, hamesucken or assault and robbery, and three for burglary).

Potentially more serious than the occasional murder, however, was the general unrest of the district since the end of the Napoleonic Wars. Unemployment due to changing industrial conditions was aggravated by large numbers of men demobilised from the army and navy and unable to find work. These were men who remembered the slogans of the French Revolution and the writings of Tom Paine. Talk of the Rights of Man was commonplace and there were rallies, marches and demonstrations demanding the reform of Parliament, cheaper bread and the repeal of the Corn Laws, and the right to join trade unions and to strike for better wages and working conditions. In October 1816 a vast throng estimated at over 40,000 gathered in James Turner's field at Thrushgrove and demanded the redress of grievances. Although this crisis fizzled out, Glasgow and its environs remained in a dangerously unstable condition, and a report the following year to the Houses of Parliament alluded to Glasgow as 'one of the places where treasonable practices prevailed to the greatest degree'.

While Earl Grey was sceptical of this, suspecting paid informers and *agents provocateurs* at work, the situation deteriorated. During the autumn of 1819 a corps of special constables, recruited from the middle classes, was raised to patrol the streets, while a regiment of cavalry was quartered at the barracks and held on constant alert. The rebellion, long-expected, erupted on Monday, 2 April 1820, when the working men of Glasgow downed tools. Men were drilled openly on the Green and the most fantastic rumours were flying around. Fifty thousand French troops were daily expected to help the movement (despite the fact that France itself was then in the grip of a Bourbon reactionary government) and there was even a report that five thousand French troops would be taking control of the Cathkin Braes, overlooking the city, at any moment. In fact, only desultory attempts at armed revolt were made, significantly by bands of handloom weavers in some of the outlying villages. There was one half-hearted foray, farcical but bloodless, known to posterity as the Battle of Bonnymuir, which resulted in the seizure of eighteen men and their subsequent trial at the High Court of Edinburgh for high treason. Andrew Hardie (grandfather of Keir Hardie, the first socialist MP and leader of the Labour Party) and John Baird were executed as the ringleaders, the others being transported for life. In Glasgow, the Radical leader James Wilson was tried and convicted of high treason. The barbarous sentence was that he be hanged by the neck until dead, then beheaded and his body quartered for public exhibition. The last part of the sentence was mercifully remitted, but some twenty thousand gathered in silence to witness the spectacle of the hanging, followed by the decapitation performed by a medical student, masked to conceal his identity.

After this grim spectacle, the mood of the Glasgow working class was sullen but subdued. Prince Leopold, later King of the Belgians and favourite uncle of Queen Victoria, was offered the freedom of the city but declined the honour, and when King George IV came to Edinburgh in 1822 (the first reigning monarch to visit Scotland since 1651) he pointedly excluded Glasgow from his itinerary. Later that year there was a major riot in which a merchant's house was looted. The ringleader was Richard Campbell, a handloom weaver whose crime was regarded as all the more heinous because he had previously been a police officer. To emphasise the seriousness of the affair, Campbell was sentenced to fourteen years' transportation, but before leaving Glasgow he was paraded through the city, bound to a cart, and given twenty lashes at each of four locations, south of the gaol, at the foot of the Stockwell, at the head of the Stockwell and finally at the Cross in front of a vast throng which winced collectively as Campbell groaned loudly before the eightieth stroke.

This had the salutary effect of cowing the populace, but it was the last time that a public whipping was held in the Glasgow streets. Although 1826 was a year of poor harvests and crop failures, the decade as a whole was one of peaceful progress and a gradual up-turn in trade. It was also the period when the right to strike was finally conceded (1825) and the traditional restrictions on Catholics were lifted (1829). There were no riots or disturbances in Glasgow or its suburbs throughout this period, giving the lie to yet another Pinkerton myth. Allan himself, many years later, seems to have originated the story that his father (in his role as police sergeant, no doubt) had been killed during a political riot. . .

One version of this story alleges that William was killed in a riot when Allan was eight, which would have placed the incident in 1827. While accepting that William died when Allan was around this age, Horan[14] added, 'A legend that has hardened by repeated telling has the older Pinkerton suffering fatal wounds in an uprising, but a search of the Glasgow police records fail (*sic*) to uncover such an incident'. Oliver Wendell Holmes, on the other hand, unequivocally accepting that William was a police sergeant, stated, 'When Allan was ten years old his father, on duty during Chartist riots, was so severely injured that he never walked again. Four years later he died.'[15] Aside from the fact that Chartism did not come into existence till the late 1830s, this version places the death of William Pinkerton in 1833. A search of the Gorbals death registers, unfortunately, does not resolve the matter, for no record of William's death is contained therein. There is, however, a gap in the register, between January 1830 and December 1831, so it seems likely that William died at some time in that period. This, at least, would accord with the version given by Lavine, who stated that Allan 'was barely ten when left fatherless'.[16]

Of Allan's childhood only meagre details have survived, and these, recalled by the man himself more than half a century later in a series of letters to his son Robert written intermittently between 22 May 1879 and 28 April 1883 shortly before his death, are imprecise and impressionistic rather than factual.[17] From this source we glean that Allan's half-brothers were 'unruly' but that William Pinkerton 'refused to be ruled by them'. James, the eldest son, was hardly mentioned at all, apart from the intriguing comment that he almost broke his father's heart. He led a rather aimless life until 1824 but in March that year, at the age of twenty-eight, he married Mary Cochran. By her he had two daughters – Isabella Stevenson (named after his mother) on 26 October 1828, and Love Cochran born on 17 November 1835. Little Isabella, however, died of a fever in March 1832.

One brother, according to Allan, 'enlisted as a soldier but after a few years had to be bought off (*sic*)'. This was, in fact, his half-brother William who did, indeed, enlist in the 42nd Regiment in which he served for several years as a private soldier. Whether he was bought out, or was demobilised at the end of his contracted term, cannot be ascertained, but by 1833 he was back in Glasgow and serving in the city's police force. He resided at 148 Stockwell Street and eventually attained the rank of sergeant, so perhaps the myth confused him with his father, although William Junior was not wounded, fatally or otherwise, in any Chartist riot.

Allan stated incorrectly that his half-sisters left home in their teens to get married. Love was past twenty-seven when she married Andrew Weston, and Mary was twenty-five when she married Thomas David Steuart on 20 December 1823. According to Allan, one sister married 'a head waiter in a

Glasgow restaurant' and this appears to fit Steuart's description, but Allan seems to be in error where the third sister was concerned. This unnamed girl is said to have married a butcher, yet Janet, at the age of twenty, married Hugh Murray on 2 June 1820, at which time he was a bricklayer in East Campbell Street in Glasgow itself.

Allan recalled his childhood as 'completely filled with the tensions of two families existing in a few rooms', but by March 1824, when he was only four and a half, all of William Pinkerton's first family were married or dead, and of the second family only Robert and Allan himself remained. As James, the feckless member of the family, was the last to settle down and leave home, there is probably an element of truth in Allan's recollection of the tension at home, but it would be unrealistic to place too much emphasis on it as a lasting influence on his character.

In the matter of education Allan had rather more schooling than his previous biographers have supposed. William Pinkerton, who had acquired his education the hard way by being largely self-taught, placed great store by formal teaching. In an era when Scots, both boys and girls, had a far higher standard of general education than their counterparts in England and Wales, and certainly in Ireland, both sexes were taught as a matter of course to read and write. In later life Allan, apart from being a copious letter-writer and compiler of voluminous case notes, would personally produce at least four of the eighteen volumes bearing his name and dealing with his most famous cases. The four books incontrovertibly his own work contain useful reminiscences and are written in a pleasant style indicating the breadth of the author's general knowledge and wide vocabulary. At various periods Allan was taught by Robert White and John Milne, near neighbours of the Pinkertons, who conducted a school in Rutherglen Loan.

Allan's education was interrupted by his father's death, about 1830, when he was past the age of ten. This may seem a very early age at which to give up formal schooling but, given the educational system of the period, with its emphasis on the three Rs, Allan would by that time have had a good grounding. The rest would be up to him. The internal evidence of his own prolific writings suggests an avid reader from boyhood. He was singularly fortunate to be living in a city where there was an abundance of cheap or free reading matter; there were numerous circulating libraries from which books could be borrowed at a halfpenny a time, while apprentices and operatives had the use of the vast Mechanics' Library.[18]

Allan's first job was as an errand-boy for Neil Murphy, a friend of his father, who had a lucrative business at 4 Wilson Street in the Candleriggs, as a harness-maker, pattern-drawer and agent for Jacquard looms. Allan would later recall working 'from dawn to dusk for pennies' but it is untrue to say that he was engaged by Murphy as an apprentice, as he was too young. After work he would wait at the corner of Muirhead Street for his mother, coming home from Thomson's Mill. It is significant that one of the few specific details remembered from this unhappy period was of Isabella bringing home a precious egg for tea.

According to Allan's autobiographical letters, he found pattern-making 'a dreary existence', so when he was old enough to seek an apprenticeship and learn a trade, he himself took the decision, at the age of twelve, to become a cooper. The choice of barrelmaker was probably dictated by the fact that his Uncle John (his father's youngest brother) had been a cooper, with premises at 34 Saltmarket.[19] John Pinkerton died about 1806, so was unable to help his nephew get started in the trade. Instead, Allan bound himself to William McAulay whose workshop was conveniently located at 123 Main Street, Gorbals.[20] In later years Allan would vividly recall that memorable day, 26 December 1837, when 'at Richard O'Neil's Public House, opposite King William's statue', the eighteen-year-old apprentice received his journeyman's card as a member of the Coopers of Glasgow and Suburbs Protective Association.[21] This simple ceremony at Glasgow Cross, doubtless sealed in O'Neil's best ale, launched the young barrel-maker on the great adventure of life.

◆ 2 ◆

The Young Militant
1839–42

Hark! listen to the trumpeter,
He sounds for volunteers!
Rise, helots, rise, unite your strength,
Shake off your slavish fears!

CHARTIST HYMN, 1839

In the country at large, 1837 was memorable for the accession of a teenage princess as sovereign of the United Kingdom. In Glasgow, however, people of all classes were far more concerned by a resurgence of industrial unrest. Parliamentary reform had come at last, in 1832, but the results fell far short of what the ordinary people desired. To be sure, large industrial towns such as Greenock now had their own MP, but the vote continued to be a privilege enjoyed by the propertied classes. Within two years, the radicals who had campaigned so ardently for the Reform Act were on the march once more. In 1835 a vast throng gathered on Glasgow Green to cheer Daniel O'Connell who, having secured Catholic emancipation, was now working for an extension of the franchise to the working classes. O'Connell was ably supported by the Revd Patrick Brewster of Paisley Abbey, who thus earned the censure of the Synod of Glasgow but endeared himself to the workers of the city. Out of this came the National Radical Association which declared a boycott of both Whig and Tory shops. It was a case of 'a plague on both your houses' and the working classes now began to seek political representation which was not tied to either of the traditional parties.

Britain as a whole had a prosperous year in 1836, with full employment, good wages and a quiescent working class; but by March 1837 there was a decided down-turn in the economy. Exports declined sharply and merchants were often compelled to sell their goods at a loss. In April the cotton manufacturers came up with their own drastic solution to the problem and once more sought to cut wages in the mills – this time by a swingeing fifty per cent. Thousands of Glasgow mill hands downed tools and went on strike. The right to strike had only been grudgingly conceded a few years previously, though trade unionism received a severe setback in 1834 when the Tolpuddle Martyrs were sentenced to transportation for trying to form an agricultural union.

No one could have imagined that the Glasgow Cotton Spinners' dispute would drag on for so long. The cotton mills were silent for fourteen weeks, before the starving workers were forced to give way without having achieved their aims. This was bad enough, but in September a vindictive establishment, led by the Sheriff of Lanarkshire, Archibald Alison, a High Tory who regarded unions as 'a moral pestilence', singled out the five members of the Spinners' union committee for trial at the High Court of Edinburgh, and the following January they were arraigned on charges of illegal combination, administering unlawful oaths, conducting union business in secret, assault and intimidation, fire-raising and the murder of a 'blackleg'. The more serious charges were thrown out, but they were convicted on the conspiracy charge and sentenced to seven years' transportation. Although this was a comparatively lenient sentence by the standards of the time, the overtly political nature of the prosecution provoked an immediate outcry and Glasgow was in a dangerous ferment for several months. In the words of Sheriff Alison, Glasgow was in a state of insurrectionary fever. The Spinners' Five were frequently likened to the Tolpuddle Martyrs, and as commercial depression deepened into a winter of discontent, the workers were convinced that the state, hand in glove with the factory-masters and coal-owners, was moving against them. To make matters worse, Daniel O'Connell chose the Spinners' case to attack trade unionism and demanded a parliamentary enquiry into their character and organisation. O'Connell appeared to have changed sides, and where he had been cheered only months earlier his name was now reviled.

The situation was aggravated by the implementation of the New Poor Law which withdrew outdoor relief and forced the unemployed into workhouses where they laboured long and hard for starvation wages. The workhouses, grim bastilles erected in every town, soon became a symbol of dread and hatred.

This coincided with the birth, at Birmingham, of a new political movement in which various radical elements combined to form the Birmingham Political Union. Having launched their campaign for reform, the Birmingham radicals looked for a suitable place to bring their aims and ideals before the public at large. In April 1838 John Collins was sent north. No missionary was ever fired with such passion and zeal for his cause; no missionary made so many converts in such a short space of time. A 'Grand Demonstration' was planned for 21 May on Glasgow Green, to be followed by a soirée later on. Delegates from two hundred trade unions, workshops and factories in the Glasgow area unanimously resolved to come forward with their flags, banners and music.

The appointed day, a Monday, was cold, wet and windy, but all public works came to a standstill as seventy trade unions, led by forty-three bands, marched in a procession that stretched for more than two miles. Amid the three hundred banners of the trade unions could be seen the colours of the Anti-Corn Law League and even a tattered flag which had been carried by the Covenanters into battle at Bothwell Brig a century and a half earlier. Young Allan Pinkerton, now a journeyman cooper, was swept up in the heady atmosphere and sang as lustily as any as he marched with the members of his union. At the Green the procession came to a halt. According to the Tory newspapers, some 30,000 'operatives' assembled in the drizzle; the Radical press put the number at 200,000. The true figure was somewhere in between, but the throng of men and women, gathered from the towns and villages within a ten-mile radius of Glasgow, must have been an impressive sight. The cold and the wet were forgotten as Allan, and thousands like him, fell under the spell of such orators as Thomas Attwood and John Collins from Birmingham, the Revd Dr Arthur Wade from Warwick and Patrick Murphy from the London Working Men's Association. Loud and prolonged cheers greeted the chairman, James Turner, the best-known of the Glasgow radicals and a veteran of earlier struggles.

The demonstration was noteworthy for its orderliness and discipline. Press reports commented on the peaceful behaviour of the men and the large number of 'well-dressed females' who accompanied them. Attwood emphasised that on their side they had no strength, save the justice of their cause. Where Glasgow led, forty-eight other towns and cities would follow. Once forty-nine delegates of these towns had met in London, he would like to see the House of Commons reject their petition! If Parliament rejected their petition then they would petition again, and again. Then they would resort to a general strike – a 'sacred month' – until their wrongs were removed.

For two weeks the west of Scotland was gripped by political excitement. There was a solemn pilgrimage to Elderslie, Renfrewshire, which was believed to have been the birthplace of Sir William Wallace, the thirteenth-century patriot,[1] and a monster rally at Paisley. Attwood returned to Birmingham on 23 May but his apostles made triumphant visits to Kilmarnock, Stirling, Perth, Dundee, Cupar, Dunfermline and Edinburgh; by the time the Birmingham deputation had left Scotland, a great mass of the working classes had become familiar with the People's Charter and its six points: annual parliaments, universal suffrage, vote by secret ballot, abolition of the property qualification for Members of Parliament, payment of MPs and equal constituencies. Within

Parliament itself, a handful of Radicals led by Daniel O'Connell eloquently argued the case, but the Whigs and Tories closed ranks and strenuously opposed it.

Considering that all but the first of the six points have long since become accepted, it is difficult from the modern standpoint to appreciate the passion which the People's Charter engendered. To the working classes it embodied their political creed and was their hope of salvation; to the aristocracy, the gentry, the commercial sector and the middle classes as a whole, however, it smacked of revolution. Those who preached the people's rights were feared and detested.

Middle-class fears of imminent revolution were greatly exaggerated. In fact, the initial enthusiasm of the workers soon evaporated, despite visits to Glasgow of Dr John Taylor and Feargus O'Connor in July 1838. Significantly, the numbers who turned out to hear these demagogues were far fewer than had attended the May rally. Below the surface, though, there were important developments. The West of Scotland, with its strong Covenanting traditions, soon witnessed the growth of Chartists' churches, where Chartist hymns were sung and Chartist sermons preached. At the height of this politico-religious movement a score of Chartist churches flourished in and around Glasgow, foreshadowing the Great Disruption that rent the established Church of Scotland in 1843.

Allan Pinkerton had little interest in the religious aspects of Chartism, but he was soon deeply involved in political activity. Highly intelligent, possessed of immense self-confidence, he had 'a guid conceit of himself'. He read voraciously, took a keen interest in schemes of social reform, trade unionism, improved hygiene and better housing, and passionately espoused the causes of temperance and the abolition of slavery. In light of his subsequent career, the last-named deserves closer examination. The British government, at the promptings of William Wilberforce, passed an Act in 1807 declaring the trade in African slaves illegal, though many years elapsed before the trade was actually stamped out. This did not improve conditions for existing slaves and it was not until 1833 that slavery, as such, was abolished in the British colonies. Slave owners were not only handsomely compensated, but a transitional seven-year period followed, during which slaves progressed gradually through indentured labour to full liberty. In the late 1830s there was abundant evidence of the plantation owners dragging their feet, and the plight of the slaves in Jamaica and Barbados was constantly in the newspapers. Ironically, many of the middle-class philanthropists who took up this cause so ardently were industrialists blind to the appalling conditions of the men, women and children employed as 'wage slaves' in their own satanic mills and factories.

Having completed his apprenticeship with William McAulay, it must have been a bitter blow to Allan to find himself cast adrift. For almost seven years he had laboured long and hard to perfect the art of making casks, barrels and kegs. He took a pride in his craft and looked down on wrights and carpenters; after all, it mattered not whether their joints fitted precisely, but a barrel that was not absolutely watertight was useless. Any hopes Allan might have had about being kept on by McAulay after completing his apprenticeship were dashed. The cooper's son Alexander was coming to the end of his own apprenticeship and there would not be room for two journeymen in the cooperage, especially with business so poor.

At the New Year of 1838, therefore, Allan went 'on the tramp'. For four years he had a nomadic existence, travelling the length and breadth of Scotland and northern England, mostly on foot, wherever he could find work. Sometimes he would find employment for several weeks with a brewery or distillery; at other times he would migrate to the coastal towns when the need of barrels for the packing of salted herring was at its height. Coopering was seasonal work and the demand fluctuated wildly. Often Allan would sleep rough, unable at times to afford the twopence that would secure a cot in the meanest lodgings. When he was working, he tried to save as much as he could and send money to his mother, now unemployed and not in the best of health.

Periodically he was back in Glasgow, lodging with his mother in Muirhead Street. At the end of 1838, at a time when Radical activity was actually at a low ebb, Allan joined the Glasgow Universal Suffrage Association. As its name implied, this body agitated for the grant of the vote to all men and women over the age of twenty-one. Pinkerton himself was barely nineteen at the time but soon made his mark. People who recalled the young cooper many years later would describe him as being of medium height, but with powerful shoulders and muscular arms from swinging the ten-pound hammer used to drive the staves into the iron hoops of barrels. He was regarded as quiet, sober and serious-minded, the feature which struck people on first acquaintance being his frank, open countenance and cool, penetrating blue-grey eyes. Normally taciturn, he would become quite animated when arguing one of his favourite causes; then those icy grey-blue eyes would light up with passion.

Chartism, it soon emerged, was all things to all people. As the initial momentum of the movement to gain political change by peaceful demonstration and monster petition died down, factiousness emerged. O'Connell, O'Connor and Murphy were not the only Irishmen to play a prominent part in Chartism, but soon the side issue of Home Rule for Ireland arose and threatened to divert the Chartists from their main goal. Under the influence of Father Mathew and his temperance movement, there was considerable agitation against the demon drink (yet another tool of the masters for enslaving the workers), but many men argued just as forcibly against 'signing the pledge'. Chartism attracted a great many cranks and eccentrics who proclaimed their own peculiar brand of socialism. There were geographic factors, and in Scotland there developed a power struggle between Edinburgh and Glasgow. Ironically, Glasgow, as a hotbed of Chartism, was more highly regarded south of the border than it was in the east of Scotland.

Matters came to a head on 5 December 1838 when delegates of the Scottish Radical Associations, summoned by John Fraser and Abram Duncan to a conference in Edinburgh, hotly debated ways and means of renewing the campaign. Fraser, a Johnstone schoolmaster, and Duncan, a Glasgow wood-turner who later became the Chartist minister of Arbroath, roundly condemned the insurrectionary methods of J.R. Stephens and Feargus O'Connor and argued that only by 'moral force' would the movement succeed. Fraser and Duncan were in the minority, and at a monster rally on Calton Hill shortly afterwards, their moral force resolutions were vehemently repudiated by the Revd Patrick Brewster, a humourless preacher in the finest hellfire tradition, who argued that the time had come to apply 'physical force'. Several associations recoiled at the violence of the Calton Hill resolutions, and Brewster's leadership of the movement took a severe knock as a result.

Nevertheless, after Calton Hill, the Chartist power base shifted from Edinburgh to Glasgow, reinforced by the emergence in July 1839 of the *Scottish Patriot*, initially the press organ of the Glasgow Chartists but soon the powerful mouthpiece for Scottish Chartism as a whole. A charismatic leader emerged that summer in the form of Thomas Gillespie, secretary of the Glasgow Universal Suffrage Association, who organised a formidable delegate conference held at Glasgow in August. Thanks to the organisational skills of Gillespie and his lieutenants (including Allan Pinkerton), this conference voted overwhelmingly in favour of direct action, although there was some dissension as to what form that might take. It was generally agreed, however, that agitation must be kept on the boil until 'some favourable accident' arose to bring about universal suffrage.

An immediate outcome of this conference was the establishment of a Central Committee for Scotland, with a permanent secretariat funded by district associations. Of the fifteen members of this Committee, only John Duncan of Edinburgh lived more than six miles from the centre of Glasgow. Six of its members were directors of the Glasgow Universal Suffrage Association, including Allan Pinkerton, who had been elected to this position at the beginning of September 1839. Six of the others were officials of associations in the suburbs or neighbouring burghs; but both they and the two remaining members were often prominent in the meetings of the Glasgow Universal Suffrage Association. It is hardly surprising that Aberdeen and

Edinburgh, the main centres of the moral force movement, regarded the Central Committee for Scotland as 'the Glasgow Committee'.

Within a matter of months even this Central Committee began to be weakened by factiousness. The majority strove to preserve an air of respectability by promoting the non-violent character and moral idealism of Chartism. In this regard geography was on their side for Scotland, in that era before the railway network was fully established, was relatively remote from Birmingham or London. It had its own press, and English newspapers (especially the more Radical publications) did not circulate there to any extent. Thus the Glasgow Chartists, in the main, sought to promote an alliance with middle-class Radicals, like Hume, Roebuck and Sturge, and distance themselves from O'Connor and his followers.

The Central Committee, however, fell between two stools. They failed to interest more than a handful of the middle-class Radicals who had previously belonged to the Glasgow Political Union (active in the campaign for parliamentary reform in 1831–32), and soon alienated the younger firebrands within their own ranks. While the Central Committee concentrated on sending out Chartist missionaries to the colliery villages and mill towns of Lanarkshire and Renfrewshire, and organised Saturday evening concerts, socials and dancing classes in Glasgow itself, the young hotheads of the movement, led by Allan Pinkerton, plotted direct action.

At this time Allan first came under the spell of George Julian Harney. Though not much older than Pinkerton (Harney was born at Deptford, London, on 17 February 1817), he was light years ahead in his political development. He had briefly been a cabin-boy aboard ships of the Royal Navy but poor health, in the form of congenital quinsy and partial deafness, forced him to give up the sea. Instead he became a pot-boy in a London pub and then assistant to Henry Hetherington, a prominent figure in the National Union of the Working Classes who published several socialist papers. At a time when there was a fourpenny tax on newspapers and periodicals, Hetherington defiantly published unstamped papers, for which both he and his assistant were sentenced to terms of imprisonment on several occasions. These spells under the harsh regime of Coldbath Fields Prison turned the frail young Harney into a dedicated agitator on the far left of the working-class movement. Harney had a much broader vision of the socialist utopia than most of his counterparts. A close friend of Karl Marx and Friedrich Engels, he sought to internationalise the workers' struggle, and Marx and Engels would later sneeringly refer to Harney in their correspondence as 'Citizen Hip-Hip-Hooray' on account of his indiscriminate espousal of many disparate causes; but in 1839 Harney was one of the few Chartist leaders who could see beyond the purely parochial level.

In the spring and summer of 1839 there were sporadic uprisings, to use the government term for them; but in fact they were minor disturbances of a purely local nature, invariably perpetrated by Tory thugs in the first instance, as they violently broke up Chartist meetings, and easily crushed by magistrates aided by the military. The Chartist speakers, as well as the rank and file of the movement, were at first determined not to be drawn into retaliation against the mob violence of their opponents, although the ugly incidents, at Devizes and Trowbridge in April, for example, showed them that sooner or later force would have to be countered by force.

Of greater significance was the emergence of a more avowedly extremist press that year. Feargus O'Connor's *Northern Star* roused the working classes in the north of England, but in April 1839 Harney and J.C. Coombe brought out the first number of the *Democrat*, the most extreme of all the Chartist papers. From the outset, Allan Pinkerton was an avid reader of this unstamped penny weekly, and his militancy in general, and admiration of Harney in particular, were formed by it. While confessing that he was 'uneducated in the usual meaning of the term', Harney had a natural talent for polemics. In the style of Communist propaganda a century later, Harney studded his writings with emotive words and phrases, constantly repeated, with a subliminal effect on his readers who were regaled with 'rodomontade flaying bloodstained kings', 'tyrant aristocrats', 'persecuting priests', 'the vile shopocracy' and 'scoundrel-cannibal usurers'. One of Harney's closest confidants was a Major Beniowski who had fled from Tsarist vengeance after taking part in the abortive insurrection that swept Poland in 1830–31. With his military expertise and, more particularly, his practical experience, Beniowski played a central role in the insurrection which was being planned to erupt in London towards the end of the year, 'in the long dark nights before Christmas', in conjunction with risings in other parts of the country. Twenty towns were to be seized by 100,000 armed Chartists, who were being organised pyramidally in groups of ten with a Council of Five at the top. It was later averred that a Russian fleet stood ready to sail for England to aid Beniowski when he began the insurrection in South Wales.[2] Apart from the similarity to the scare about French troops coming to the aid of the Scottish Radicals in 1819, this story was ludicrous in view of Beniowski's enduring hatred of all things Russian, but it reflects the paranoia and xenophobia in official circles at that time.

The 'physical force' men in Scotland, among whom Allan Pinkerton was emerging as leader despite his tender years, came to the conclusion that Scotland was too remote for an insurrection there to have any impact on Britain as a whole and as a consequence they enthusiastically pooled their resources with the general insurrectionary movement. During the late summer and autumn of 1839 Harney toured the far north of England, making a series of inflammatory speeches. Allan Pinkerton, who would in old age admit that at this time he was 'the most ardent Chartist in Scotland', appears to have met Harney for the first time at Newcastle upon Tyne and taken an immediate liking to the slightly built, sandy-haired fellow who, despite the enormous and disfiguring tonsillar abscess which occasioned him considerable pain, impaired his hearing and made swallowing difficult, yet overcame his painful handicap and by his powerful oratory could hold a large crowd rapt.

Between July and the end of October, secret workshops in Newcastle were busy manufacturing thousands of iron-shod pikes, the preferred weapon of insurgents at the time, and a highly sophisticated network of communications was established, linking Northumberland to Glasgow, Birmingham and South Wales.[3] The 'favourable accident' which the physical force men had long been seeking had now occurred.

Henry Vincent, 'the young Demosthenes of English Democracy',[4] had joined the Chartist movement at the outset and swiftly emerged as a golden-tongued orator of remarkable powers: 'Wherever he appeared his fervid declamations awakened every sympathy of the heart . . . His thrilling tones, as he depicted the burning wrongs of the toiling classes, fanned their passions into a flame which no after prudence could allay.' Vincent had been attacked by Tory mobsters at Devizes in April, thrown into gaol at Monmouth (22 April), re-arrested on a charge of sedition at London the following month, and then freed on bail to await trial. While briefly at liberty he made a dangerously inflammatory speech at Bath: if the demands of the people, embodied in the Charter, were again rejected by Parliament, all should arm themselves under his leadership. Vincent was again arrested and taken across the county boundary to Monmouth Castle where he was in due course brought to trial and sentenced to twelve months in the castle dungeons. Vincent was feared by the forces of law and order, not only as a demagogue but as the editor of the *Western Vindicator*, a weekly which was immensely popular in Wales and the west of England. Although Vincent languished in Monmouth Castle, his friends continued to bring out the newspaper until December 1839.

The plight of Henry Vincent roused the militant Chartists to a fury, and secret plans that autumn were formed for his release by armed force. That, at least, is the accepted version, although the actual course of the rising in South Wales that November has never been satisfactorily resolved. The discrepancy between the avowed aim of the uprising and the place where the showdown took place has confused one previous biographer into thinking that Monmouth Castle was in Newport,[5] when in fact it is some twenty-three miles to the north-east. If armed Chartists had been intending to spring Vincent from his prison, they would surely have marched on Monmouth. That they chose instead to descend on Newport implies that they were intent on making a mammoth demonstration in sympathy. What took place at Newport on the morning of Monday, 4 November 1839, was bloody and tragic enough, but it cannot be construed as an insurrection. Yet the Newport Rising it was called at the time and it has since passed into history by that name.

In South Wales itself the people were in a state of sullen discontent. The coal-pits of the Welsh valleys had been a hotbed of unrest for years, intimidation by the bosses being matched by the terrorist activities of the secret gangs known collectively as the Scotch Cattle. Vincent, serving a twelve-month sentence, was held up as a martyr, and became a focal point for working-class resentment that went far beyond Wales and the West Country. Ironically, the *Monmouthshire Merlin* carried a report, on Saturday, 2 November, that Chartism was extinct: 'the forbearance of the government is rapidly destroying Chartism without making victims of the deceived or martyrs of the deceivers'. On the very next day the militant Chartists began their march on Newport.

Why Newport, rather than Monmouth, was the target, has never been satisfactorily explained. There had been wild rumours flying around for some time, so much so that the competent authorities in the end chose to ignore them to a large extent. That some sort of incident had been planned for a while and was by no means a spontaneous affair was borne out by the fact that Chartists had been subverting the local garrison. That autumn a company of the 45th Regiment had been posted to the town. The majority of the rank and file were young Irishmen with less than two years' service. It was later alleged that they had been treated to drinks in the alehouses of Newport and promised half a crown a day if they deserted. Only two soldiers eventually took up the offer but after a few days in the hills they returned to barracks.

More serious was the evidence that pikes and other weapons were being forged in the smithies of Newport and elsewhere, and that bullets were being cast in rough moulds. In a mining community, gunpowder was easily obtained without attracting attention, but firearms were more difficult to procure. Nevertheless, there is abundant evidence that muskets and pistols were purchased.

Even today the sequence of events and the actions of the ringleaders are obscure and confusing.[6] The leader of the rising was John Frost (1784–1877), a middle-class Radical who had actually been mayor of Newport in 1836–37 and had had the duty of proclaiming the accession of Queen Victoria. His transformation, within two years, into one of the most hated and reviled men in the kingdom was nothing if not dramatic. It was Frost's misfortune to be overtaken by events and other factors outside his control. He was a delegate to the National Convention in which he was prominent among the moderates. As recently as 28 September 1839 he had written to the authorities in mild and measured tones urging that Vincent's treatment at Monmouth should be more lenient 'as the agitation had now subsided'.

Yet, less than a week later, he hurried up the valleys to a meeting at Nantyglo because of a rumour that the miners were about to rise in arms to liberate Vincent. The meeting was held at the public house of Zephaniah Williams, and Frost tried to persuade his audience that a rising would be the height of folly, but he was shouted down by William Jones, a rabble-rouser, out-of-work actor and part-time tavern-keeper. This public meeting was followed by a second, held in secret, at another pub a mile away. A heated discussion raged most of the night, Frost urging a monster rally of moral support for Vincent, instead of the armed insurrection favoured by the others. No agreement was reached and the meeting ended in uproar. The more militant workers, inflamed by months of talk of physical force, were now hell-bent on violence.

Frost's movements in the ensuing weeks have long been the subject of controversy, but it is on record that he was in Lancashire in October and may also have been in County Durham and Northumberland. Reports that a rising in South Wales was planned for 4 November were certainly circulating as far afield as London and Newcastle by 28 October. During that month the Chartists of South Wales were at fever pitch, and the dispute between the moral and physical force elements became increasingly bitter. Although meetings were held in secret it was inevitable that they were infiltrated by government informers. To what extent the demonstration was transformed into insurrection by the activities of *agents provocateurs* is a matter of speculation. Significantly, these meetings were frequently addressed by Jones and Williams, but Frost was conspicuous by his absence. On Sunday, 27 October, however, Frost told his friend Dr William Price that the rising was to take place on the following Sunday night. Frost was 'deeply agitated; he wept like a child and talked of heaven and hell', said Price. But it was now too late to turn back.

The final meeting took place in secret at the Coach and Horses inn in Blackwood on the afternoon of Friday, 1 November. The meeting was attended by leaders of Chartist lodges, not only from Monmouthshire and the immediate vicinity, but also from as far afield as the Forest of Dean. It cannot be verified that Allan Pinkerton, the delegate of the Glasgow physical force men, was actually present on that occasion although he later implied that he was. By now John Frost had composed himself, and was resigned to playing his part as leader of the insurrection. The outcome of this meeting was that upwards of five thousand men, mostly armed with pikes and stout clubs, would advance on Newport on Sunday night in three contingents, one from Blackwood under Frost, the second from Nantyglo and Ebbw Vale under Williams and the third from Pontypool led by Jones. All three were to rendezvous at Risca, six miles north-west of Newport. Captains were elected over every ten men, and the thickset young cooper was placed in command of the Glasgow squad assigned to John Frost's column.

Sunday morning was dull and cloudy, with intermittent rain which did not augur too well for the desperate enterprise. Jones had left his home before daybreak and by seven o'clock had reached Abersychan on horseback. There he found his men mustering in the village taverns in the chill dawn half-light. He ordered them to go to the racecourse a mile below Pontypool, assuring them that Zephaniah Williams had a good supply of muskets and pistols for them. They were to set out for Pontypool at two o'clock and were advised to pressgang all whom they encountered, partly to swell their ranks and partly to prevent anyone from informing the authorities of what was afoot. Placards had been prepared which were to be posted in Newport the following day, in the name of John Frost as President of the Executive Government of England. This may well have been no more than a figment of Jones's fertile imagination, for no such treasonable placards were ever found after the event.

Jones later went up the valley and across to Nantyglo to confer with Williams, then he crossed over to the Sirhowy valley and about three in the afternoon was seen riding at full tilt through Tredegar in the direction of Blackwood. There, the Chartists had met in the morning and again in the afternoon and arranged their final meeting for six o'clock.

With all this to-ing and fro-ing it was inevitable that the authorities were soon aware that something was afoot. The valleys were buzzing with rumours, and the Lord Lieutenant wrote that day to the Home Secretary saying that there was a plan in the hills to descend on the towns and destroy property. Colliery managers and ironmasters, mostly English incomers, fled with their wives and families from Ebbw Vale and Abersychan, spreading panic and alarm as they went. In the afternoon John Frost himself went to the Coach and Horses to finalise his plans. He paced up and down outside the inn, clad in a rough greatcoat and a bright red cravat. At seven o'clock Jones rode up and conferred briefly with him; and shortly afterwards a stranger in a glazed hat appeared and told Frost that the soldiers in Newport were all Chartists and would join the uprising as soon as the contingents reached the town.

Thus reassured, Frost mounted his horse and gave the signal for his men to move out. The streets of Blackwood thronged with armed men and the congestion was intense. Women and children were crying, the rain was now a steady downpour, and the chaos was total. Frost fired a shot, the signal to move, and the motley crowd shouldered pikes and began to trudge out into the murky night. So great was the crowd that they could not all go the same way. Pinkerton and his men followed Frost himself, taking the mountain road over into the Ebbw Valley, and then turned south to Abercarn. By midnight Frost and the leading ranks of his ragged column had reached their primary objective at Risca. Progress was painfully slow, as the insurgents toiled along a badly made road in the teeth of a vicious storm in almost total darkness.

Planning such an operation probably looked simple on paper; in reality it was a fiasco from start to finish. At Risca, Frost's column rested as well as they could in the appalling circumstances and waited for the other contingents to catch up. Inevitably the marchers had tarried at the alehouses and taverns *en route* and, despite the injunctions of their leaders, many of them were drunk and riotous by the time they reached Risca. In the end, only a part of Jones's contingent joined Frost; it appears that Jones himself had turned back to chase up the stragglers and consequently by the time he eventually reached Risca the uprising was over.

Some time in the early hours the contingent from Ebbw Vale, led by Zephaniah Williams, staggered into Risca. The Chartist army, now soaked to the skin, their gunpowder in a state of semi-liquidity, trudged on as far as Cefn in search of shelter. The rest of the night, the main force was strung out along the road, camped in Risca and the Welch Oak as well as Cefn. During the night both Frost and Williams continually rode backwards and forwards between the Welch Oak and Cefn, exhorting their men. As dawn broke Frost gave the order to advance as far as a place called Pye Corner. Here he ordered the men armed with guns to move to the front rank, the pikemen behind them and the others, armed with pitchforks, crowbars, sledge-hammers and miners' mandrils, to take the rear rank.

From Pye Corner the vast rabble, Frost's men in front and the Williams contingent in the rear, advanced into Tredegar Park and along the mineral tram-road. After the dreadful weather of the night, Monday dawned bright and sunny, more like a summer's day, which must have raised the spirits of the bedraggled and mud-spattered Chartists. In the Park they tried to get into proper ranks, Williams giving the unmilitary order to 'rank themselves tidy'. From the Park the Chartists, led by Frost on horseback and kept in step by Jack the Fifer, slowly descended on the town. The vast, shambling army proceeded slowly up the lane past the Friars to the turnpike on Stow Hill, and came to a halt in front of the Westgate Hotel at the corner of Commercial and High Streets.

Not surprisingly, news of the Chartist approach had thrown the town into a panic. The Lord Lieutenant, Capel Hanbury Leigh, had detached a corporal and four privates of the 45th Regiment to guard his own house, a selfish act which earned him a great deal of opprobrium later. The mayor of Newport was Thomas Phillips, an old and deadly adversary of Frost, a corrupt and crooked lawyer with whom Frost had clashed on more than one occasion. On this momentous Monday, however, Phillips showed his mettle. Over five hundred special constables were hurriedly sworn in the previous day and most of the known Chartists in the town itself were rounded up, some being held at the Westgate Hotel and others consigned to the workhouse, under heavy military guard. About six o'clock on Sunday evening Phillips had sent out two men on horseback to reconnoitre the Risca road. They returned five hours later, one with a pike wound in his leg, to report that the Chartists were encamped less than six miles away. The mayor then sent an urgent message to Bristol, by way of Beachley Ferry, demanding troops; but the Bristol magistrates said that they had none to spare. Troops were eventually despatched but their steamboat ran aground and it was not until nine o'clock on Tuesday morning that these reinforcements reached Newport.

When the Chartists were observed in Tredegar Park, Mayor Phillips summoned troops from the workhouse where they were guarding the prisoners. Captain Stack despatched Lieutenant Gray with two sergeants and twenty-eight privates to the Westgate. They arrived soon after eight o'clock and after some delay were ordered to take up positions in a public room at the front of the hotel. They had barely got into position before the Chartists appeared. Frost's army came at a brisk trot down the hill with considerable uproar. A few of them tried to enter the hotel through a wicket gate at the rear but the majority gathered on Commercial Street at the front.

What then took place is confused and uncertain. The Chartists chanted, 'Give us up your prisoners!' to which the special constables responded, 'No, never!' There ensued a scuffle, in which a constable tried to seize a Chartist's pike. Windows were smashed, and a few Chartists ran into the lobby of the hotel. A shot was heard inside the hotel, though who fired first was never identified. At any rate this was the signal for a ragged volley from the Chartists in the street. The windows of the front room, occupied by the soldiers, were heavily shuttered and, though bullets struck the glass and hit the ceiling, no real damage was done. Phillips ordered the troops to load their muskets with ball cartridge. Both the mayor and Lieutenant Gray removed the shutters at considerable risk to themselves; indeed, Phillips was shot in the arm and the hip, sustaining serious injury. Gray immediately ordered his troops to open fire. Instead of firing over the heads of the Chartists, the soldiers discharged their deadly volley straight into the crowd at point-blank range. Then they fired into the hallway for upwards of ten minutes, slaughtering the unfortunate Chartists who had previously gained entry to the hotel.

At the first volley the Chartist army dropped its weapons and fled in wild disorder. The only spirit was shown by a one-legged man who coolly fired three times at the hotel. The description of him was none too clear, even as to which leg was wooden, and for weeks after the fracas the lives of all men with wooden legs in the vicinity of Newport were placed in jeopardy.

When the din subsided and the smoke cleared it was found that the carnage was considerable. It was later testified that the troops fired no more than a hundred shots in all, but twenty-two Chartists were killed instantly and many others were severely wounded. Mayor Phillips was the only casualty on the side of law and order and he made a good recovery. While his arch enemy John Frost, along with Jones and Williams, would be sentenced to a traitor's death by hanging, beheading and quartering (mercifully commuted to transportation for life), Thomas Phillips received a knighthood and was invited to dine with Queen Victoria at Buckingham Palace.

At the first deadly volley from the Irish soldiers, the Chartists abandoned pikes, muskets, mandrils and other weapons and turned tail. Dodging through the withering fire of musketry Allan Pinkerton and his Glasgow comrades made for the Church road and never stopped running until they were back in Cefn. 'It was a bad day,' he later wrote of that fateful morning. 'We returned to Glasgow by the back streets and lanes, more like thieves than honest working men.'[7]

Sixty-two Chartists were convicted for their part in the Newport Rising and transported to Australia. John Frost was sent to hard labour in Tasmania, but in 1854 he was given a conditional pardon which meant he could leave the penal colony though he was not permitted to return to Britain. With his daughter Catherine (who had joined him at Hobart) he went to the United States and at the end of the Crimean War he was amnestied. After seventeen years in exile he came home, in July 1856. William Jones was issued a ticket of leave in 1846, having ingratiated himself as a police informer. Ironically, he informed on Zephaniah Williams, when the latter tried to escape to New Zealand. Jones eventually returned to Wales but died in great poverty in 1873. Williams fared best in the long run. After twelve months' hard labour in chains for his attempted escape he was released in November 1848. Subsequently he discovered a rich seam of high-grade coal in Tasmania and made a fortune. He died at Launceston in 1874, rich but alone, his wife (who kept the Boar's Head at Caerphilly) having refused to join him.

His gruelling experiences in South Wales changed Pinkerton. Gone was the impetuous hothead, and in his place was a hard man, tempered by a flinty resolve. The assault on Newport had been ill-timed and badly planned; never again would Allan become involved in any enterprise that did not have an almost hundred per cent chance of succeeding.

Back in Glasgow he found that the leadership of the movement had passed to James Moir, a prosperous tea-merchant. Despite a tendency to pomposity and the serious handicap of being a 'shopocrat', Moir was a populist leader with a fund of common sense and a reputation for kindliness and sincerity. In default of any outstanding personality in the movement, the mediocre Moir found himself as leader of the Glasgow Chartists and their delegate at the National Convention. In 1848 he even secured election to the town council and thereafter had a long but undistinguished career as a baillie and magistrate.

If Moir was the figurehead who gave the movement respectability, William Pattison was the ideas man. He was a steam-engine maker, a highly paid mechanic who kept his family in fine style and, exceptionally, had been enfranchised in 1832. As secretary of the Glasgow United Trades, he played the leading role in strengthening the organisation in Scotland. Pattison and the mainstream Chartists deplored violence and worked to achieve their aims through education and co-operative ventures. Inevitably, Pattison quarrelled with Thomas Gillespie, who opposed most of his projects. The final break came on 26 November 1839 when the two men squabbled at a public meeting over the vexed question of petitioning. Pattison saw petitions as a vital part of the Chartist campaign; but Gillespie and his followers were sick of this tactic which seemed to be leading nowhere.

That Tuesday evening the Universal Suffrage Hall in the High Street was full to overflowing, and men stood tightly packed in the ante-room as well as on the staircase, straining to hear the voices in the main chamber as they rose higher and higher in anger. Amid the babble could be heard the gruff, measured tones of Allan Pinkerton whose debating skills had not yet been developed to the point at which he could return like for like. Published reports on that stormy meeting show that he was taunted and baited by several of the Pattison faction, and there was some 'rather disagreeable talk' when Ross and Cumming tried to probe the young cooper 'about money matters'. As tempers rose, Pattison attempted to mediate, saying 'Mr Pinkerton, as a Director, is perfectly able to answer any liabilities that he may have incurred since his connection with the Association'. At that, however, Allan stalked out of the hall, mustering as much dignity as he could, holding his head erect and ignoring the jeers, hisses and catcalls. The most sympathetic report, in the *Scottish Patriot*, stated that Allan 'walked off, seemingly highly pleased with himself, and with the very able and gentlemanly way he had acted during the evening'.

Inwardly, Allan was seething. In the white heat of the moment he penned a 'scurrilous' letter to the Glasgow *Evening Post*, defending his actions and launching a virulent diatribe against his fellow directors in the Suffrage Association. Unfortunately there is a gap in the files of this newspaper for December 1839, but the letter was commented upon at great length in the *Scottish Patriot* of 7 December. Allan's response to this report came in a letter, published by the *Scottish Patriot* on 4 January 1840. The nub of his argument was that the Glasgow Universal Suffrage Association had failed to consult

England before taking action. Pattison retorted angrily that he saw no reason why Scotland should consult England; after all, the English never consulted the Scots before taking major policy decisions. In any case, who should they consult in England? Was there any Central Committee, or Convention, or any large, properly organised district with which they could communicate? [8]

The upshot was that Pinkerton resigned from the Universal Suffrage Association and formed the Northern Democratic Association. In an impassioned speech on 4 December, he said that his new association was not intended to divide, but to unite, Radicals and its motto would be 'We are determined to carry the People's Charter peaceably if we may, forcibly if we must'. In effect, the new association swiftly became a rallying ground for discontented Republicans and left-wing militants. Outside Glasgow, Pinkerton received enthusiastic support from the Renfrewshire Political Union and the Aberdeen Working Men's Association. From the outset it was Pinkerton, rather than Gillespie, who set the tone of the new club and its political direction. One of Allan's first acts was to extend an invitation to his old friend Harney to lecture to the working men of Glasgow.

Within weeks of the abortive Newport Rising, Harney travelled north and joined up with Dr John Taylor whom the Home Office labelled sourly 'as mischievous a man as any in the Kingdom'. An Ayrshireman, Dr Taylor was one of the more quixotic of the left-wing militants. A few years earlier he had squandered his inheritance by outfitting and commanding a warship in the Greek struggle for independence, and following the capture of Frost, Jones and Williams he had plans to outfit a ship to intercept the vessel transporting them to Australia. Taylor was actually free on bail under a charge of sedition when he and Harney managed to convert a sabbatarian meeting at Carlisle into a Chartist demonstration. During December, narrowly evading arrest, they stumped around Cumbria preaching revolution and armed insurrection if the government had the temerity to convict Frost, Jones and Williams. Shortly after Christmas Taylor and Harney parted company, and the latter, armed with letters of recommendation from Taylor, crossed the Solway and spent New Year's Eve at Dumfries in the congenial company of Andrew Wardrop and Robert Burns, eldest son of the Scottish poet, who regaled them by singing his father's songs. While the English Chartists were preparing a mass insurrection in support of Frost, Harney was travelling all over Dumfriesshire and Ayrshire, addressing meetings. By late January he was in the Gorbals, lodging with Allan Pinkerton. Later he would record his first impressions of the grimy Scottish city in the *Northern Star*:

Of all the wens of corruption and misery it has ever been my lot to visit, surely Glasgow is the worst. I have seen London, Manchester, Birmingham,

Leeds, and other great hives of human crime and human agony; but for undisguised profligacy, offensive brutality, squalid wretchedness, and unbearable filth, Glasgow, to my mind excels them all . . . I know of no remedies for the horrors of Glasgow but that of blocking it up at one extremity and setting fire to it at the other.[9]

Julian Harney's appearance in Glasgow got a very mixed reception. Moir and Pattison roundly condemned him, saying that the Scots did not welcome firebrands, and their organ, the *True Scotsman*, repeatedly told Harney to take himself back to England. Ridiculous rumours were even put about that Harney was a government agent, and the Universal Suffrage Association went so far as to place advertisements in the Glasgow newspapers disclaiming any connection with him and condemning his visit. Pinkerton, now acknowledged as the leader of the extreme militants, ignored these adverse comments and went ahead with his plans. Originally he hoped to hold the meeting in the Bazaar, one of the largest public halls in Glasgow, but the city magistrates refused permission; instead it took place in the Lyceum Theatre. On 27 January Allan's closest associate, John Govan, chaired the meeting, with secretary-treasurer Allan and the other committee members of the Democratic Association ranged on the platform behind him. Harney (whom Allan had appointed President of the Democratic Association) was the principal speaker. From the outset it was obvious that Allan's old comrades in the Glasgow Universal Suffrage Association, now his deadliest foes, were determined to disrupt the meeting and prevent the dapper little Londoner from speaking. There were angry shouts, demanding to know by what right Harney was speaking in Glasgow, and even why the meeting was necessary at all.

Allan jumped to his feet and shouted vehemently that it was by his invitation. If any hecklers tried to prevent Harney from speaking he, personally, would come down into the body of the hall and sort them out. There was a tense moment when the young cooper, his face livid with anger, stood eyeball to eyeball with his adversaries; but a brawl was only narrowly averted by the intervention of older and calmer men. The Universal Suffrage delegation eventually resumed their seats and the meeting continued. Harney, whom the *Scottish Patriot* described as 'a smart, good-looking little gentleman and rather showily dressed', spoke with great eloquence, beginning in quiet, reasonable tones but gradually building to an impassioned crescendo, and was cheered to the rafters for his impressive performance. He spoke for upwards of two and a half hours, ranged over many topics, cracked jokes and quoted Burns and Byron. The 'marks of disapprobation' which disrupted his address at the outset soon died down, and throughout his long peroration an increasingly appreciative audience hung on every word. Wisely he avoided contentiousness and immoderate language, and even Pattison was mollified by Harney's statesmanlike behaviour. After that evening the abuse moderated, though Pattison and Moir continued to treat Harney, and other English Chartists, with considerable reserve.

The youthful fervour with which Allan had embraced the cause a year earlier was characteristic of the working-class movement as a whole; but he echoed the sentiments in Harney's speech when the latter admitted to his Glasgow audience that he was 'much wiser in the year 1840 than I was at the commencement of 1839'. In the ensuing two years there would be precious little time for barrelmaking, as Allan devoted himself wholeheartedly to the cause. Sporadic outbreaks in England in sympathy with Frost, early in 1840, were swiftly crushed by the authorities and by March almost every Chartist leader of importance in that country was in prison. Scotland was quiescent, the well-organised moderates being then in the ascendant.

In April, however, Harney himself appeared for trial at Birmingham, but was discharged when the crown offered no evidence against him. Having narrowly escaped 'the fangs of the Whigs', he lost no time in returning to Scotland, where he remained for over a year. During this period he travelled more than two thousand miles on foot and addressed hundreds of meetings, from vast throngs in Glasgow to handfuls of crofters in the Highlands. For much of this time he was accompanied by Allan Pinkerton, the brawny barrelmaker acting as his guide and strong-arm man. They made an odd couple: Harney was small, slight and frail but always smartly dressed, while Pinkerton was thickset, muscular, taciturn and intense. Harney was animated and bird-like; Pinkerton the archetypal dour Scot. Harney could be vindictive, but was intensely loyal to his friends. Pinkerton was narrow-minded, doctrinaire, immensely opinionated and quick to anger. In the amazingly self-revealing letters written in old age to his son, Allan would recall with great relish the street battles with Tory bully-boys and his readiness to use his fists and his boots to combat the opposition. He had a rugged constitution but even he was hard put to keep up with his companion. On one occasion Harney walked eighteen miles in driving rain, immediately following a week's illness in Aberdeen, and then casually noted his method of self-medication: 'Drenched myself with physic . . . applied leeches to my throat, which did me some good'.[10]

Life was not all rigours and extreme discomforts by any means. Of all the parts of Scotland which Julian Harney visited, Ayrshire was his favourite. The banks of Doon, which had inspired Robert Burns to some of his finest lyrics half a century earlier, moved Harney to write 'A scene lovely as Eden and beautiful as Elysium . . . I gloated on its charms.' It was here that he met Mary Cameron, the daughter of Adam Cameron, a Mauchline weaver with a long record of Radicalism. Three months Julian's junior, Mary was described by a contemporary as a 'tall, beautiful woman of high spirit'.[11] It was love at first sight, and after a brief courtship the couple were wed at Mauchline on 14 September 1840. As his biographer put it perceptively: 'If Harney had been a lonely young man – and there is much in his behaviour and utterances to indicate this – then Mary Cameron more than filled the void, for their marriage was a rare compound of love and intellectual sympathy.'[12]

After Harney's return to England in April 1841, Allan Pinkerton worked assiduously to promote the views of the physical-force men. That very month William Pattison was ousted from his position as vice-president of the Universal Suffrage Association and other moderates soon followed. These upheavals were engineered on behalf of Feargus O'Connor, and in October the great leader of the left-wing element himself toured Scotland. There were monster meetings on Glasgow Green and several splendid soirées before O'Connor departed in triumph late in November. Two months later he was back in Glasgow to take his place, as the representative of Rutherglen and Elderslie, in the Scottish Convention which assembled in the city on 3 January 1842. O'Connor took little active part in the proceedings but in his reports, published in the *Chartist Circular* and the *Northern Star* (both dated 29 January), he confessed that he had been 'a most unhappy man', having to contend 'almost single-handedly' against the 'saints of the Glasgow Chartist Synod'. A great deal of politicking was going on behind the scenes. Allan Pinkerton was keeping a fairly low profile at this time, but he was working as intensively as ever, trying to unite the various physical-force groups. By now, he and his widowed mother were living in a flat at 176 Main Street, Gorbals,[13] and here he continued to plot with other eager, impetuous young men, increasingly impatient of the mainstream Chartists.

As part of their fund-raising efforts, the Democratic Association, like other Chartist bodies, organised concerts. Allan, writing forty years later, thought that, in the summer of 1841, he had been raising money during a cotton-spinners' strike, but this cannot be true; since the tragedy of 1837 the workers in that industry had been cowed into submission. On the other hand, Allan, as treasurer of the Democratic Association, was constantly involved in fund-raising activities. The story goes that one day he persuaded Dr Harris to let him hire the choir from the Unitarian Church in Union Street for a concert in the parlour of O'Neil's public house near Glasgow Cross. The concert was a sell-out and on that Thursday evening, Allan, dressed in his best suit, with his mother by his side, occupied seats in the middle of the front row. The star of the evening was a young soprano. Allan was transfixed: he could not take his eyes off the slender girl as she stood beside the piano while Dr Harris played. Afterwards Allan asked his friend Robbie Fergus who she was, and was told that her name was Joan Carfrae, and that she was a bookbinder's apprentice from Paisley.

She was, in fact, the fourth of five children born to John Carfrae and Jean or Joan Rodman in Neilston near Paisley. She was just past her fourteenth birthday when Allan first saw her,[14] but had an assurance and poise beyond her years. Joan and the other members of the Unitarian Choir were much in demand at Chartist concerts and thereafter Allan made a point of attending every one. Later he described this simply: 'I got to sort of hanging around her, clinging to her so to speak, and I knew I couldn't live without her.' By the autumn of 1841 the rising young politician and the little soprano were keeping company. Her greatest triumph came when she was chosen to sing before Feargus O'Connor himself at a soirée held in the Lyceum on 1 November.

Allan later claimed that Robbie Fergus was about to emigrate to the United States because he was a wanted man. There is now no evidence to support this, although weight is lent by Allan's own flight a few months later. It may be significant that whatever police records once existed from the Chartist period have long since been destroyed.

After a comparatively quiet period, Glasgow was once more in a ferment. Poor harvests followed by a hard winter had brought acute distress on the working classes, the numbers thrown out of work rose alarmingly and emigration was increasingly promoted as a solution to the problem. Indeed, something like an emigration fever gripped the country in the spring of 1842, moving the newspapers to comment anxiously about the drain of human resources to Canada and the United States. Much was made of the fact that the emigrants, by and large, were skilled artisans, taking pokes of gold sovereigns with them. Less prominence was given to the rising tide of immigration from Ireland. Those who could afford it went to America, but the poorest and most destitute took the short sea-crossing to Stranraer or Greenock, to swell the numbers of unskilled and unemployed in the Glasgow area.

The myth has grown over the years that Allan fled the country, a fugitive from justice, but the truth may have been less dramatic. Many of his closest friends, including Robbie Fergus, had already crossed the Atlantic. Allan's elder brother Robert may, in fact, have already gone, for there is no trace of him in local directories, parish registers or the 1841 Census returns, after his marriage to Elizabeth Barr in the Gorbals parish church on 5 June 1840. By 1842 Chartism was waning, not because it had achieved any of its aims but because of the general apathy of the working classes. Allan may simply have come to the grim conclusion, as so many others did, that there was no future in remaining in Scotland.

Pinkerton's letters to his son in 1879, however, paint a dramatic picture of being hounded, along with other militants, by the police. Several arrests were allegedly made by a police officer named Miller, and it was only as the result of a tip-off that Allan himself evaded capture. William Miller was, indeed, the sheriff officer for the Gorbals at this time and may well have been the 'former associate of my father' who gave him a whispered warning. 'I had become an outlaw with a price on my head,' Allan added theatrically. For months friends hid him in Glasgow. When Joan heard the news she went to the Coopers' union and begged some of his friends to take her to him. Forty years later Allan would recall:

> When I had the price set on my head, she found me where I was hiding, and when I told her I was all set up to making American barrels for the rest of my life and ventured it would be a pretty lonesome business without my bonnie singing bird around the shop, she just sang me a Scotch song that meant she'd go too, and God bless her she did.[15]

The pretty young soprano never warbled the Burns lyrics so joyfully as she did that early spring morning:

> O whistle, an I'll come to ye, my lad!
> O whistle, an I'll come to ye, my lad!
> Tho father an mither an a' should gae mad,
> O whistle, an I'll come to ye, my lad!

Allan whistled, and the pact was sealed. Lavine implies that it was Miller's secretly whispered warning that precipitated Pinkerton into marriage: 'Within a few hours he was both a married man and a wanted criminal fleeing to the New World.'[16] This was elaborated by Horan who stated that the young couple were secretly married in Glasgow on 13 March 1842, adding 'On the night of April 8th, after a hurried goodbye to his mother, Pinkerton and his bride were smuggled aboard a ship by Neil Murphy, his former patternmaker employer.'[17]

The marriage of Allan and Joan has been shrouded in mystery and befogged by family legend. Even the date on which the wedding took place has been disputed. For this, Allan himself must take much of the blame. On 28 March 1878 he wrote a long, rambling letter to his wife, recalling their courtship, marriage and subsequent journey from Scotland. The ambiguous wording of this letter led his biographers to suppose that he regarded that date as his wedding anniversary, although there is nothing actually in the letter itself linking the date to their wedding day. Horan, attempting to square this with the record, dismissed the latter with the comment: 'The only explanation for the difference in dates is the well-known laxity of early-nineteenth-century registers.' In fact, the marriage registers of the Glasgow parishes were meticulous, and there is absolutely no reason for supposing that the registrar of the City parish, in which Allan and Joan were married on 13 March, was at fault. In beautiful copperplate handwriting it was recorded that 'Allan Pinkerton, Cooper in Glasgow, and Joan Carfrae residing there' were wed on that date. Far from being a secret marriage, it was conducted in the High Church or Cathedral no less by the parish minister, the Revd Dr Duncan Macfarlan, after proclamation of banns on three successive Sundays from the pulpit. The Pinkertons were one of four couples married there on the same date.

The only irregular feature of the ceremony, in fact, was the bride's age. Joan, born on 7 January 1827, was just past her fifteenth birthday at the time and therefore under age, although she claimed to be eighteen. Were her parents, living in Neilston barely twelve miles from Glasgow, aware of their daughter's actions? The bare details of the marriage register indicate that both bride and groom were living across the river, in the city itself, at the time, which points to Neil Murphy having taken the young couple under his wing.

As to their departure from Glasgow, that too has been enveloped in a fog of contradictions. Lavine states that they were married the night before they sailed, without putting a specific date to either the wedding or the embarcation. Horan has Allan and Joan smuggled aboard ship by Neil Murphy 'after a hurried goodbye to his mother' adding that the ship 'sailed on the morning tide, April 9, 1842'. In a lengthy footnote, he added:

It has long been accepted by family legend, and has been included in the numerous error-ridden feature stories written about Pinkerton's life, that Pinkerton and his bride took the bark *Kent* from Glasgow to the United States and that the ship sank off Sable Island. The records of Lloyds of London do not list a ship sunk named the *Kent*.[18]

This is not the case. Lloyd's *Register of Shipping* for June 1842 shows the entry for the barque *Kent* with the laconic annotation 'Wrecked', though lacking details. Horan contended, instead, that the young couple had sailed aboard the barque *Isabella* and that it was this ship which came to grief off Sable Island, citing impressive sources in support of this contention. First of all, the date of departure, 9 April 1842, was derived from a letter written by Allan himself, but almost forty years after the event he could be forgiven if he got it wrong.

Lloyd's *Register of Shipping* for 1842–43 shows that there were, at that period, four ships named *Kent* but no fewer than fifty-six called *Isabella*. Of the first-named, there could be no doubt surrounding the 404-ton, copper-sheathed barque, commanded by Captain James Gardner of Glasgow, which had been built in New Brunswick the previous year for the Clyde-Montreal trade. The *Kent* arrived from Montreal on 28 February 1842 and berthed at the Broomielaw. She was still there a few weeks later when an advertisement in the *Glasgow Herald* announced that 'the fast-sailing, coppered Barque *Kent* will sail probably on 25th March. For freight or passage, having superior Cabin accommodation, apply to Sheppard & Co.' Departure, however, was delayed by several days and it was not until the evening of Sunday, 3 April, that she weighed anchor.[19]

Four of the ships named *Isabella* were Clyde-based. Of these, one plied the Mediterranean to Malta, another served the Jamaican trade and a third was employed on the direct route from Glasgow to Pictou, Nova Scotia. A fourth was a small collier that shuttled back and forward between Glasgow and Larne in northern Ireland and it was this vessel which Horan mistakenly identified as the emigrant ship, from a notice in the *Herald* of 25 March that she was off Cairnryan in Wigtownshire. Of these ships, the likeliest contender was therefore the 376-ton barque commanded by Captain A. Thomas. Like the *Kent*, she was built in New Brunswick but was a much older ship (1828). This *Isabella*, by coincidence, arrived from Pictou in the Clyde on 2 March 1842, only two days after the *Kent*, but departed from the Broomielaw on 30 March, bound for Pictou. Inexplicably, there is no further mention of this *Isabella* in Lloyd's records but it is evident, from other sources, that her voyage of 30 March was her last. On 27 April she was wrecked off Aspey Bay near Cape North, Cape Breton Island.[20] As she left Glasgow at the end of March, bound for Pictou, she could not have been the ship on which the Pinkertons travelled as Horan surmised. As the *Kent* was the only ship to leave Glasgow for Montreal in April 1842 there can be no doubt that, for once, family legend got it right.

• 3 •

Emigrant
1842–47

Go west, young man

JOHN BABSONE LANE SOULE, IN TERRE HAUTE, INDIANA *EXPRESS*

The Atlantic crossing in April 1842 was no honeymoon; it was the Pinkertons' misfortune to make the hazardous voyage during some of the worst storms on record. Allan had arranged that his young bride would share a cabin with some other women, while he lodged precariously in the fo'c'sle with the crew, cannily paying for their passage by signing on as ship's cooper. Due to the violent weather which blew up before the barque was even clear of the Hebrides, the hatches were battened down and the passengers were cooped up in their cramped quarters aft, where the stench of seasickness was indescribable. After three weeks out from the Clyde the weather abated and for the first time Allan and Joan were briefly reunited as they paced the after-deck and stared at the leaden ocean and the lowering skies. Joan, with an assurance born of total ignorance, even solemnly told Captain Gardner that the weather would improve, and that they would have smooth sailing for the rest of the trip to Montreal. Within hours they were being buffeted by a hurricane, and the wretched little vessel with shortened sail ran before the mountainous seas.

The exceptional run of foul weather which claimed the *Isabella* also brought the *Kent* to grief. On 19 April she was sighted by a passing vessel in mid-Atlantic 'listing badly with both pumps going'[1] but that problem was evidently put right and the voyage continued. In the hurricane that savaged the western Atlantic towards the end of the month, however, the *Kent* was blown very badly off course. Instead of entering the Gulf of St Lawrence for the passage to Montreal, she was actually two hundred and fifty miles farther south.[2] About 28 April the barque foundered on reefs off Sable Island, two hundred miles east-south-east of Halifax. The crew managed to get the lifeboats away without loss of life but the survivors of the wreck had no sooner scrambled ashore than they were set upon by a band of Indians and robbed of their few possessions. Although Allan himself never referred to this incident in his autobiographical letters, ninety years after the event his daughter Joan Pinkerton Chalmers, in the course of a newspaper interview, gave details of how the poor immigrants were robbed of their few trinkets:

> Father, in later years, told us how mother resolved to cling to her wedding ring, in spite of all the danger, and how he, feeling sure that the Indians would take it forcibly, said to her 'Oh, give it to them, Joan, and I will get you another ring'. She then surrendered it. But – though in later years she wore many rings – she would never wear another wedding ring. No other ring could take the place of that precious symbol of her marriage.[3]

After robbing the passengers, the marauding Indians disappeared into the woods. The following day, however, the crew managed to get out to the *Kent* before she sank, and retrieved some of the luggage from the hold. Fortunately Sable Island lay on the sea-lane between Halifax and Liverpool and a few days later the stranded crew and passengers were picked up by a west-bound ship. From Halifax they secured a berth on the coastal mail packet bound for Quebec, and from there they made their way up-river to Montreal where they finally arrived some time in May with what Allan ruefully called 'our health and a few pennies'.

They got a room in a lodging house and through the local coopers' union Allan obtained temporary employment making beef barrels. This job lasted several months, but with the onset of winter meat-packing ceased and Allan was laid off. According to Lavine, Allan had changed his mind about settling in Canada before he left the schooner taking them up the St Lawrence River, asserting that they immediately took a boat through the Great Lakes to Detroit and thence overland, 'in a ramshackle wagon drawn by an old spavined horse', to Chicago. This bears no resemblance to the truth, but is not untypical of the hoary myths that sprang up around Allan Pinkerton in later years. Allan himself recorded that when the Montreal job ended 'I all at once made up my mind to jump to that thriving little city of Chicago'.

Having made this decision he went off and purchased a couple of steamer tickets for Chicago, a voyage which would have taken them through Lakes Ontario, Erie, Huron and Michigan. Returning to their lodgings with the tickets and empty pockets, he sprang the news on Joan. Immediately the girl-bride began crying, not so much because he had taken this decision without consulting her, but because she had placed a deposit on 'a wee bonnet' and now had no chance of buying the hat. At the thought of the lost deposit, the canny lass begged Allan to go back to the ticket agent and get a refund, reasoning that they could go on the sailing the following week, and in the meantime he might get a few days' work, and she could get her bonnet after all.

At this Pinkerton 'roared like anything, but I finally let her have her way'. The tickets were taken back, Allan got a week's work, and Joan triumphantly purchased her bonnet. The night before they were due to set sail Joan wordlessly put the evening paper before her husband. On the first news page was a graphic account of the sinking of the steamer they had been scheduled to sail on the previous week. A boiler had exploded and the ship had sunk with all hands. 'I tell you, my wee wife has had her way about bonnets ever since,' Allan reminisced with a chuckle.

Apparently there was yet another change of plan. The Pinkertons probably went to Chicago as planned but for some reason were impelled to keep going farther west. Perhaps the legend of the ramshackle wagon and the old spavined horse has an element of truth in it after all, and Allan and Joan had decided to go west. Eventually they ended up in Warsaw, in the far west of Illinois, on the east bank of the Mississippi. This was not the likeliest jumping-off point for a journey into the wilderness of the Mid-West, especially with winter approaching; but ten miles upstream lay the city of Nauvoo which had been founded by Joseph Smith barely two years earlier. The Latter Day Saints had recently embarked on their great missionary enterprise which brought a flood of British migrants to this area from 1840 onwards. By the end of 1842 Nauvoo was a bustling city of over twenty thousand, by far the largest town in Illinois, and perhaps the prospects for barrelmaking there seemed excellent. Be that as it may, it was in the village of Warsaw that the Pinkertons met with disaster, for it was here that they were robbed of everything but the clothes they stood in.

Chicago, by contrast, was then a town of only twelve hundred inhabitants. The unpaved streets were deeply rutted and in hot summer weather permanently shrouded in thick clouds of dust thrown up by herds of bawling cattle driven in from the prairies on their way to the slaughterhouses. In bad weather these streets quickly became quagmires with dangerous sink holes, where the boatman's phrase 'no bottom' furnished the only description. An absence of civic pride made them the dumping ground of the community rubbish so that the gutters were filled with manure, discarded clothing and all kinds of trash, threatening the public health with their noxious effluvia. In Chicago, both then and for some years later, the drains in the streets, the alleys and the vacant lots were:

reeking with every description of filth; all the slops of the houses, and the filth of every kind whatsoever, incident to cities, are emptied in the gutters, and offend the nostrils of every traveler, either on the sidewalks or the streets.[4]

Cows roamed at will and often passed the night on the sidewalks. As in other parts of Illinois, hogs were employed as primitive scavengers and at one time almost outnumbered the human population, ending up a bigger nuisance than the mess they were supposed to consume. Even by the low standards of the Gorbals, Chicago in the 1840s was a disgusting place, far from the 'Garden City' which it later became; but meat-processing was its chief business and this promised good prospects for the Scottish cooper. Chicago had been founded less than a decade earlier and the raw frontier town had an aggressive vibrancy about it that appealed to Pinkerton. More importantly, it was where his Chartist friend Robbie Fergus had settled. With the last of his cash, a silver dollar wrapped in his handkerchief, Allan took a room and went out to look for 'auld Bobbie Fergus from the Gorbals'. Printers were thin on the ground in Chicago and it took no time at all to locate the twenty-one-year-old Glaswegian.

Fergus insisted that Allan and Joan should move in with him until they had got back on their feet. More importantly, Robbie knew the foreman at Lill's Brewery and the very same day Allan was taken on as a cooper, earning fifty cents a day for working from early morning till six at night making beer-barrels. Shortly afterwards Fergus and the Pinkertons attended a Scottish concert, and they wept together as they sang the familiar ballads of their homeland. This gave the resourceful Robbie the idea of collecting and printing the ballads of the old country. While Robbie set the type and ran off the sheets, Joan folded and collated them and Allan trimmed them with a shoemaker's knife and punched holes for the stitches with an awl. Joan's training as a bookbinder evidently came in handy in the production of *Old Country Ballads*, the first song-book published in Chicago.[5]

For several months Allan laboured at Lill's Brewery but in the spring of 1843 he gave notice to quit and told Joan that he had found the ideal spot to establish his own workshop. Some thirty-eight miles north-west of Chicago was a tiny Scottish settlement on the Fox River in Kane County. Here, in the heart of dairy country, the colonists had named their town Dundee. The nearby towns of Elgin, Inverness and Huntley also betrayed their Scottish origins. As Allan recalled, 'It was a fair and lovely spot, with its murmurous rivers, splendid farms, forests, noble hills, sunlit valleys and opulent herds in the district.' He proposed to go ahead, and would send for Joan when he had got a roof over his head. In the meantime, she would continue to lodge with Robbie Fergus.

Joan accompanied her husband to the end of the Tam o' Shanter trail which then marked the town boundary and took a lingering farewell by the little pontoon bridge across the East River. Nearby was the stockade of Fort Dearborn from which the city had sprung a decade previously. Across the river, the footpath disappeared into reeds and grasses taller than Allan himself, and beyond lay the endless prairie, silent but for the sough of the reeds in the light morning breeze. Neither of them ever forgot that poignant moment of parting. As he kissed her goodbye Joan had a terrible premonition that she would never see him again, but he kissed her and calmed her fears; then, shouldering his tool-bag he strode out across the rickety bridge. On the far side he turned and waved back, and to lift Joan's spirits he began whistling one of her favourite Burns songs. Joan's heart sank as she saw him swallowed up by the giant grass, but she knew, from the brave whistling she could hear long after he had disappeared from view, that 'there'd be a wee home soon for us'.[6]

Two days later Allan reached Dundee and began immediately making enquiries around the farms. What he heard was most encouraging; there was no cooper in the district and the farmers were only too ready to buy barrels and churns direct from him. On a grassy knoll only three hundred yards from the wooden bridge over the Fox River Allan with his own hands built a single-storey log cabin with a shack at the rear for a workshop. It was a prime site, and farmers, cattle-drovers, carters and merchants passing along the road to and from the bridge could see the freshly painted sign that proclaimed the premises of Allan Pinkerton, 'Only and Original Cooper of Dundee'. When the cabin was completed Allan went back to Chicago for his wife. Soon Joan was ensconced in the first home she could call her own, busying herself with keeping it clean and, as and when money permitted, attending to its furnishing. Outside, Joan cultivated her garden, grew fruit and vegetables and raised poultry. Many years later, from the comfort and security of a palatial mansion, she would look back nostalgically to the time when they had nothing but hard work and their dreams:

> In the little shop at Dundee, with the blue river purling down the valley, the auld Scotch farmers trundling past with the grist for the mill, or their loads for the market, and Allan, with his rat-tat-tat on the barrels whistling and keeping tune with my singing, were the bonniest days the good Father gave me in all my life.[7]

The political transformation of Allan Pinkerton came during this idyllic period. For the first time in his young life he was his own master. He was a fine craftsman, and proud of it. The word soon got around that he was honest and reliable, hard-working and energetic. He charged a fair price and gave value for money. He would rise at four-thirty, seven days a week, and labour till six in the evening. For fourteen hours a day his workshop rang with the sounds of sawing and the characteristic thump of the hammer on the iron hoops as they were driven into place. It was a hard life, well suited to the dour, serious temperament of Allan Pinkerton. There was no time for frivolity, though he always appreciated his wife's singing. Allan neither smoked nor drank; his only recreation was going for long solitary walks in the rolling countryside before turning in and going to bed around half past eight. The only indulgence he would permit himself was to read a chapter or two before the oil lamp was extinguished. Always a voracious reader, Allan was at this time addicted to the romantic novels of Bulwer-Lytton. In particular he loved *Eugene Aram*, based on the true story of the Knaresborough schoolmaster who had been tried and executed at York in 1759 for a murder he did not commit. Allan considered that this book, published in 1832, was the greatest novel ever written. As one acquaintance from the Dundee period later commented, 'He didn't think much of you if you disagreed with him on that.'

As the community expanded and farming developed, so the Dundee cooperage prospered. By 1846 Allan 'by industry and saving had gradually worked into a comfortable business at my cooper's trade and now employed eight men'. In three short, hectic years the tramp cooper, the erstwhile wage-slave, had become one of the bosses, an employer of labour. Only in America would hard work and frugality reap such satisfying dividends. Interestingly, Allan's employees were not fellow Scots but Germans from the other side of the river. Apparently there was a great deal of hostility in the older-established community of West Dundee against these newcomers from the Continent. In the fullness of time East Dundee would develop into a separate municipality, reflecting this ethnic tension. From the outset, however, Allan let it be clearly known that, in his eyes, all men were equal and the only sense in which he discriminated between them was whether they were prepared to give a good day's work for a fair day's pay.

In the meantime the Pinkertons rejoiced when Joan gave birth to a healthy boy on 7 April 1846. In the Scots custom he was automatically named William, after his paternal and maternal grandfathers, though Allan was added as a middle name. Willie grew into a sturdy boy and was always his father's favourite, though Joan later had five other children. The sole surviving daughter, Joan Pinkerton Chalmers, would recall that 'my dear little mother never had any choice in naming us – my father announced the name of the new arrival and that ended the matter'. In fairness to Allan, however, it should be noted that the choice of names was more or less dictated by Scottish custom anyway, and this would have been a matter with which his wife fully agreed.

Occasionally Robbie Fergus would drive out from Chicago and spend a

Sunday afternoon with the Pinkertons. His career reflected the meteoric rise of his adopted city. Three years after Allan first set foot in Chicago its population had risen ten-fold; a year later it stood at sixteen thousand and was growing by the day. There was an acute housing shortage and many of the dwellings were small and crude, often mere shacks known locally as 'balloons' for the speed with which they were erected. Rents for newcomers were uniformly high, often exorbitant. A substantial house in Chicago that cost $500 to build, might yield $400 a year in rent; this encouraged an orgy of jerrybuilding and there was no time to improve the infrastructure. Chicago was filthy, but it was booming, and the older-established settlers had boundless confidence that the boom would never end. Robbie now had his own printing works and was well on his way to becoming one of the largest publishers in the Mid-West. With the Illinois and Michigan Canal nearing completion, the task of joining Lake Michigan to the Mississippi would be accomplished. Then Chicago would be in the best position to become the transport centre of the United States. Already, half a million bushels of grain were passing through the city. By 1851, when the railroad was established, Chicago would be handling a hundred times as much, nearly twice as much as St Louis, its great rival on the Mississippi, and was soon to become the largest primary wheat depot in the world.

Fergus painted a glowing tale of this brash, precocious infant of a city and predicted that it had a bright future. Already those who had gambled a few dollars on waterfront sections were millionaires, and there was no telling where it might end. He suggested that Allan was wasting his talents in the backwoods of Kane County when fortunes were to be made in the booming metropolis.

For the moment, Allan was quite happy where he was, but soon afterwards there occurred an event that was to change his life utterly. In itself, this was a relatively minor incident, but it had long-term repercussions. One day in June 1846 Allan poled his raft up the Fox River to a little island a few miles above Dundee and close to the village of Algonquin. Here Allan had found a belt of trees which produced the right timber for barrel staves; why pay for costly imported lumber when the right stuff was on his own doorstep, just for the taking? All morning he worked hard, felling young trees, snedding branches and trimming the lumber, then moved on to explore a new copse. He was surprised when he stumbled across a blackened patch indicating that someone had been camping there. 'There was no picnicking in those days, people had more serious matters to attend to and it required no great keenness to conclude that no honest men were in the habit of occupying the place,' he wrote later.

Allan's curiosity was whetted by this. On several occasions he returned to the island, finding it deserted as usual but with further telltale signs of visitors.

What could it mean, he wondered. In the end his curiosity got the better of him and he returned to the island in the dead of night. Carefully he concealed his raft among the tall rushes and settled down to keep watch. An hour later his patience was rewarded. First he heard the sound of muffled oars, then caught sight of a boat in the moonlight. Presently the skiff ran aground and several men scrambled ashore. Allan crawled stealthily forward to where he could now make out the dim flicker of a camp-fire. What were these men doing there? Whatever it was, it had to be unlawful.

The following day Allan contacted Luther Dearborn, the sheriff of Kane County, and subsequently took the lawman to the island to see for himself. One night, 'in the right quarter of the moon', Pinkerton and Dearborn, together with a posse from Dundee, descended on the island and arrested a band of counterfeiters, together with 'a bag of bogus dimes and the tools used in their manufacture'. To this day the islet is known locally as Bogus Island. The arrest and subsequent conviction of the 'cony men' brought Allan a great deal of publicity; every farmer and trader who came to the shop for casks and kegs wanted to hear the story until Allan grew weary of telling it.

The affair had barely died down when Allan received a strange summons. One afternoon in July an errand-boy came into the cooperage and said that Henry Hunt, who ran a general store in Dundee, wanted to see him urgently. Barefoot and clad in a check shirt and denims, Allan followed the lad into town. At the store he met Hunt and another shopkeeper named Increase C. Bosworth who put a proposition to him. 'We want you to do a little job in the detective line.'

'Detective line!' chuckled Allan. 'My line is the cooper business. What do I know about that sort of thing?'

Hunt reminded Allan of his recent exploit. 'We're sure you can do work of this sort if you only will.' He then went on to say that they suspected that a counterfeiter was at work in the town, but admitted that they had very little to go on. Their suspicions had been aroused by a well-dressed stranger who had ridden into town and asked for directions to Old Man Crane's place. Allan knew Crane by reputation. He lived in Libertyville, in adjoining Lake County, some thirty miles distant. For some time Crane had been suspected of passing counterfeit money. This area, not far from the Canadian frontier, was plagued with worthless notes and dud coins, and several times Crane had been questioned by the county sheriff and even had his farmhouse searched on one occasion, without any positive result.

At this period there were numerous small banks, each issuing its own notes. Ohio 'red backs', Indiana 'shinplasters' and all sorts of 'rag money' of outside banks of unknown soundness plagued northern Illinois, but frequent failures and a flood of 'wildcat' notes made people distrustful of paper money unless it was issued by a bank known locally. In Kane County the only institution whose paper was trusted was the Wisconsin Marine and Fire Insurance Company of Chicago, controlled by George Smith, a native of Aberdeen who was noted for his toughness and integrity. Smith's money circulated readily, but the notes were typeset in a simple design which laid itself wide open to imitation. Now Hunt reported that at least two counterfeit ten-dollar bills had been passed in Dundee. Allan riposted that he had never seen a ten-dollar bill in his life and would not know whether it was a fake or not. Hunt pulled out one of the forgeries and handed it to the cooper, telling him that the person who had uttered the note was at that very moment down at Eaton Walker's harness shop having his saddle repaired.

Allan, barefoot and in his working clothes, sauntered across to Walker's saddlery. Eaton was seated at his workbench stitching the saddle and nodded imperceptibly to Allan, inclining his head towards the hitching rail outside where a sleek roan horse was tied. When the saddle was mended Walker sent his lad to the tavern to notify the customer. When he came back with the boy, Allan went outside and casually patted the horse. While appearing to admire the animal he was closely observing its owner and mentally recording his description: a grey-haired swarthy man with keen grey eyes, about sixty-five years old, with a plain gold ring on his left hand. As the stranger mounted, he asked Pinkerton for directions to Crane's house. Allan gave him detailed instructions, adding under his breath that Crane was certainly a man who could be relied upon – 'as good as cheese'. The stranger reacted to this with some guarded comments about a certain gunsmith in Elgin, a few miles to the south. When Allan nodded conspiratorially and said that he knew the smith, the stranger asked the younger man to meet him in a gully just outside the town.

That afternoon Allan met the stranger again. The latter questioned the cooper closely and Allan answered him straight. There was no point in lying, for the stranger could easily check his story with any lounger in the town. He said he had been working at the cooperage for several years but that he was looking for 'a good scheme' that might bring him some hard cash. The stranger now identified himself as John Craig, a farmer from Fairfield, Vermont, and confided that he and Crane 'had done a great deal of business together'. After a good amount of quizzing and probing, Craig came to the conclusion that Pinkerton was not averse to making a few bucks on the side. In the end he agreed to let Allan have fifty $10 bills for twenty-five per cent – $125 – in silver. They agreed to meet later to conclude the deal, the venue being the unfinished building of Elgin Academy on a hill overlooking East Elgin. Allan walked the five miles back to Dundee, where Hunt and Bosworth got together the cash to pay for the counterfeit notes. Late that afternoon, in the rough, incomplete basement of the academy, Allan, still barefoot, handed over the coins. Craig, ever-suspicious, asked Pinkerton to leave the basement for a few minutes, and when he returned the cooper found the forged notes under a rock.

Knowing that an arrest would only stick if Craig were caught with counterfeit notes on him, Allan made an appointment to make a bigger purchase in Chicago. On that occasion, as the deal worth $4,000 was about to be done in the lobby of the Sauganash Hotel, Allan gave a pre-arranged signal and a deputy-sheriff of Cook County burst in, caught Craig red-handed, and arrested him. Craig was handed over to the Kane County authorities for trial and indicted on Pinkerton's deposition before a grand jury, but he escaped from the local gaol soon afterwards, 'leaving behind a certain law officer much richer than he had been', as Allan noted wryly. It was his first experience of police corruption, but by no means his last.

Having been put to a great deal of time and trouble which he might have used more profitably in his cooperage, Allan sought reimbursement for the expenses he had incurred. Hunt and Bosworth blandly told him that he should go to Chicago and claim expenses from George Smith. Allan, wearing a smart suit and polished boots, returned to the city and after waiting for some time in an ante-chamber, was ushered into Smith's office. The canny Scots banker listened attentively to Allan's story then leaned forward in his chair.

'Have ye nae mair to say?'

'No. Not anything,' said Allan.

'Then I've juist this tae speak: ye werena authorised tae do this wark, and ye hae nae right tae a cent. I'll pay this, I'll pay this; but mind ye nou,' and he shook his finger unpleasantly at the cooper, 'if ye ever dae wark for me again that ye hae nae authorisation for, ye'll get ne'er a penny, ne'er a penny!'

Smith paid Allan's expenses on that occasion, but also taught him a valuable lesson: never undertake an assignment without a written contract.[8] It was a lesson Allan never forgot. Later he would write of this momentous period: 'The country being new and great sensations scarce, the affair was in everybody's mouth, and I suddenly found myself called up from every quarter to undertake matters requiring detective skill.' Soon afterwards Luther Dearborn offered Allan the post of deputy sheriff of Kane County. Pinkerton needed no second thought; he accepted on the spot and told Joan afterwards. The appointment was a part-time one, and he continued to spend most of his working day at the cooperage, downing tools only when Sheriff Dearborn required him to apprehend a thief, serve court processes or settle minor disputes in the community.

About this time, however, Allan was feeling the old stirrings of politics again. Back home, Chartism seemed all but dead (although there was a remarkable but short-lived resurgence in 1848, when the whole of Europe was engulfed by revolution) and Allan was still finding his feet in his new country, bewildered by unfamiliar party tags such as Democrat, Free Soil and Know-Nothing. But there was one subject on which he retained strong feelings and firm convictions, and that was slavery. By the 1840s the issues that polarised North and South had not clearly emerged, but there was much to divide opinion right across the United States. Allan devoured the remarkable writings of Frederick Douglass, a runaway slave from Maryland who had settled in Massachusetts and made his mark as an eloquent public speaker. Fearing his recapture, his friends persuaded him to go to Britain in 1845. He lectured widely in England, Scotland and Ireland where his admirers raised the money to purchase his freedom. Allan's pulse quickened when he read the speeches of the black orator, widely reported on both sides of the Atlantic.

In Illinois a sturdy band of idealists stood out uncompromisingly in utter disregard of the scorn and hostility of those who upheld the traditions of conservatism and respectability. In and around Chicago the leading abolitionists were Ichabod Codding, Zebina Eastman, Philo Carpenter and Charles V. Dyer, with whom Allan Pinkerton made contact, and for whom he acted in a number of 'commissions', Allan's codeword for the clothing, feeding and care of runaway slaves. The network of escape routes was known popularly as the Underground Railroad, from its adoption of railway jargon. Levi Coffin and Robert Purvis, the chief organisers, were known as the 'presidents of the road', the various routes were 'lines', the stopping places were 'stations', the runaways were 'packages, commissions or freight', those who acted as guides were 'conductors' and those who gave them shelter were 'foremen'. Allan Pinkerton's cooperage in Dundee was, for several years, a station on the line running north from Missouri and Kentucky to Wisconsin and the Canadian border. Some of the runaways stayed with the Pinkertons long enough for Allan to give them rudimentary instruction in carpentry and barrelmaking, in the hope that a useful trade would enable them to earn their living as free men.

This clandestine activity soon brought Allan into conflict with the religious establishment in Dundee. The pillar of conservatism in Dundee was M.L. Wisner, pastor of the Dundee Baptist Church whose congregation was largely composed of pioneers from New England and the Scots who, in default of a Presbyterian church of their own, threw in their lot with the Baptists. The church was a potent force in the community – just as it was back in Scotland – and it exercised a strict control over its members and adherents through the system of a church court, analogous to the Kirk Session in Scotland. The records preserved in the old 'Church Book' of Dundee reveal frequent cases of members being put on 'trial' for a wide variety of moral offences, breaches of church discipline and the like. Sooner or later, an independent spirit like the new deputy sheriff would fall foul of Pastor Wisner and his band of zealots.

There had apparently been some rumblings about Allan, who regularly drove to Sunday services with Joan in a farm-wagon, and had his son baptised in the church, but nothing came out into the open until the spring of 1847 when local elections were imminent, and Allan stood as candidate for the office of county sheriff, on the Abolitionist ticket. Soon after he declared his candidature, the county was scandalised by a letter in the *Western Citizen* questioning Pinkerton's fitness for public office. The letter was signed by Wisner. The following week the newspaper contained a 'collective protest' against the pastor's strictures, signed by a number of young Scots. Wisner retaliated by formally filing charges against Allan and demanded that he be put on trial in the Dundee Baptist Church.

The resultant storm shook northern Illinois, reverberating from Chicago to Wisconsin. Solidly backing Pinkerton was the younger element in the Scottish community, whereas the older, more conservative and predominantly New England community stood by Wisner who charged Pinkerton with atheism. There may have been some grounds for this; on his own admission Allan had not a great deal of time for organised religion. But Wisner overstepped the mark when he accused Allan of 'selling ardent spirits'. This was the last straw to a man who never allowed alcohol in his own home. Barely curbing his wrath, Allan swiftly organised a committee in time-honoured Chartist fashion and sent messengers to the Scots in Elgin, Chicago and Crystal Lake to gather statements from witnesses averring that he had never tasted strong drink and had never even smoked.

As Allan entered the fray with fists flailing, scattering his enemies like skittles, Wisner and his battered deacons struck back with ever more ludicrous charges. One heated session of the church court was wholly occupied that summer debating the charge that Allan had circulated a book which stated that Jesus Christ was a bastard. A church jury packed with Wisner's cronies found Pinkerton guilty, but the net result was to split the congregation down the middle. Allan and most of the Scots left the Baptist Church and established their own independent congregation. This was by no means an isolated incident; the charges brought by Wisner barely concealed the real issue of slavery which, within a decade, would divide families and lead to armed insurrection throughout the frontier states.

In the end the American Baptist Church itself was rent asunder, and polarised between its Northern and Southern wings. In a small community like Dundee, however, the bitter dispute left a legacy of hatred in what had hitherto been a peaceful settlement. Old friends crossed the street to avoid Allan, and women hurried past Joan with averted gaze. Farmers and cattle dealers still came to the cooperage for their barrels, but there was a stiffness in their business transactions. The pettiness of it all rankled with the aggressive, ambitious Scotsman. Suddenly the cooperage, which ought to have been his life's work, palled. He was restless and felt stifled by the smallmindedness of Wisner and his elders. His regular contacts with Carpenter and Dyer gave him a heady vision of Chicago, still rough and untamed but exciting. Later Joan would put the situation in a nutshell; recalling their time in Dundee she said wistfully, 'They were bonnie days, but Allan was a restless one.'

Having failed in his bid for the sheriff's office, Allan was more unsettled than ever. Consequently, when he received an invitation from William L. Church, Sheriff of Cook County, to move to Chicago as his deputy, Allan accepted with alacrity. He had no second thoughts about selling the cooperage for an excellent price, loaded up the wagon with furniture and household goods, and took his seat on the buckboard beside Joan and baby Willie. They left Dundee for good and, if Joan had regrets, Allan never looked back. There was little room in his life for sentimentality.

◆ 4 ◆

Chicago
1847–59

And westward ho! on either side,
See towns as if by magic rise;
What Genii then the wonder works?
Why, none – but Yankee enterprise.

ANONYMOUS, 'WESTWARD THE STAR OF EMPIRE TAKES ITS COURSE', 1849

The Chicago that the Pinkertons returned to in the autumn of 1847 was vastly different from the small town Joan remembered. The streets were still unpaved and in an even more ruinous state than ever, but the city had spread out in all directions. Allan, of course, had been to the city a number of times in the past year, but Joan had not seen it since she moved to Dundee. What impressed her most of all was the range of shops. There was still a raw, crude, frontier atmosphere about this noisy town, where the rasping of saws and the clangour of hammers almost drowned out the lowing of cattle and the shouts of the people. Farmers still drove into town to barter nuts, butter and eggs for buttons, beads, powder and shot.

Despite the deafening noise, the choking dust and the awful smell, Chicago was an exhilarating city. Here a man with fifty dollars in his pocket might hope to start a business. Half that sum would purchase sufficient lumber, doors, windows and nails to erect a tiny clapboard house (with the free labour of friendly neighbours thrown in) and the rest would purchase the materials of trade. It mattered not that the city was a mess, if business was brisk.

Michigan Avenue, one of the principal thoroughfares, was decorated with manure heaps while the contents of stables and pigsties were deposited on the lake shore, giving rise to a horrible stench that covered the city like a miasma. The rain washed this filth into the lake, to be mixed with the drinking water supply of Chicago; frogs and fishes frequently blocked the supply pipes. Of public utilities there was none, but Chicago laid claim to having more free public schools than any city of its size in the world.[1] It was called 'the city of churches' from the astonishing number of magnificent buildings whose tall spires were in sharp contrast with the meanness of the houses, workshops and factories. Already one or two impressive warehouses and stores, five or six storeys high, were being erected on the lakeshore, but these splendid structures, in brick and dressed stone, were surrounded by wooden huts and crude shanties. The streets, though filthy in the extreme, were generally broad and already there was a commendable zeal for planting rows of trees that would, within a few years, provide much-needed shade and contribute to the beautification of Chicago.

On the lakeshore, the huge grain elevators and vast abbatoirs of the stockyards showed what lay ahead. As the prairies were opened up, colonised and cultivated, so Chicago mushroomed. By 1850 the city was shipping over twenty million bushels of wheat to the eastern states and exporting meat and grain as far as Britain and Europe. The railway came in 1851 and within three years seventy-four trains every day would pass through Chicago's bustling station, tapping the upper Mississippi and the whole north-west. In 1851 the total value of the trade of the lake port was almost $30 million. By 1850 Chicago had a population of 29,963 – an increase of thirteen thousand in three years alone. Five years later it had risen to 80,028 and by 1860 stood at 109,260. These bald statistics take no account of the many thousands who passed through Chicago in that decade. The city itself lost about ten thousand in 1848–49 when California gold fever was at its height, but it quickly recovered.

Allan and his family lodged with Robbie Fergus on Lake Street for a week or two until their own two-room clapboard house on Adams Street was ready. This unpretentious single-storey house was to be home to the Pinkertons for several years, and it was here that Joan gave birth to twins on 2 December 1848, named Joan and Robert. The family seemed to be completed by Mary, born on 13 April 1852, but she died two years later, shortly before Allan's mother whom he had brought out to the States the previous year. Then, in her seventh year, little Joan succumbed to a fever. Allan's long-suffering wife became pregnant again soon after these triple tragedies and in due course gave birth to another daughter on 22 July 1855. The ghoulish Scottish custom of naming a child after a recently deceased brother or sister was observed and the baby was duly christened Joan. This girl, however, was destined to live to a ripe old age. The family was completed by another daughter in 1857, named after her paternal grandmother but always known as Belle; she was a sickly child and required careful nursing all of her life. A few years before he died, Allan wrote a reflective letter to his wife, calling over the hard times of their early life, and extolling her great courage and enormous devotion to her family.

Little is known about Allan's work as a deputy sheriff of Cook County, an area that extended west almost as far as Dundee and Elgin and eastwards to the lake and the border with Indiana. This relatively small area, however, contained about half the population of the entire state of Illinois and most of the industry. Peter Schuttler's wagon manufactory, established in 1843, was known from Texas to Oregon, while Cyrus Hall McCormick relocated his reaper factory in Chicago in 1847 to supply the demand of the prairie farmers. By contrast, Springfield, the state capital, was a city of only 4,500 in 1850 and 9,320 in 1860 and was a place of few attractions. It had little civic beauty, was notorious for the wretched condition of its streets, and for a long time lacked a single decent hotel. Chicago, whatever its faults and failings, was an exciting and lively place. Not far from the Pinkerton home was the lakeshore, an area which as yet had escaped the commercial exploitation farther north (and which eventually would be laid out as Grant Park). This section of the city, at mid-century, was still semi-rural.

William Church was evidently well pleased with Allan for when he retired in 1848 he recommended to his successor, C.P. Bradley, that the young Scotsman be retained. Pinkerton was highly regarded as an honest, tough and fearless lawman; his duties at this time were largely taken up with routine police work, but late in 1849 the newly elected mayor, Levi D. Boon, reorganised the city police and appointed Allan as its first detective. In fact, for some time, he was the only detective on the force. The responsibility for solving crime in a rumbustious city of thirty thousand, with many transients and a high proportion of undesirables fleeing from eastern justice, must have been a daunting prospect, but Allan, ambitious, aggressive and self-driven, was just the man for the job. Still in his twenties, he stood about five foot eight but had a broad, muscular frame and a penetrating gaze which made wrong-doers flinch. Never afraid to tackle criminals on his own, he soon acquired a formidable reputation for rough justice. The man who had advocated physical force was always ready to use his fists or his boots when confronting young thugs on the violent streets, and on several occasions he disarmed robbers to their severe injury.

There is some confusion over the manner in which Pinkerton left the Chicago police. Allan himself stated many years later that he resigned late in 1850 'because of political interference'. There may be some truth in this for Mayor Boon, a Democrat, took a very dim view of Abolitionism and it was not long before he learned of the detective's connection with this movement. Assuming that pressure from City Hall was put on Boon to distance himself from the Chicago abolitionists, it is hardly likely that a man of such firmly held principles as Allan would knuckle under. Ironically, Boon, along with other Copperheads, would be subjected to arbitrary arrest a few years later and suffered close confinement for 'disloyalty' during the Civil War.[2]

Allan was not long out of work, for he was eagerly snapped up by the United States Post Office which appointed him Special United States Mail Agent, charged with the task of solving a series of thefts which had been plaguing the commercial community of Chicago. Cheques, bank drafts and money orders had been disappearing from the mail for some time, causing considerable embarrassment to the Postmaster General in Washington. It seemed that the thefts were taking place in the sorting section of the Chicago Post Office, so Allan went to work there as a sorter. For several weeks he sorted letters and packets, sealed mailbags and loaded mail-cars while keeping his workmates under discreet surveillance. Eventually he discovered that one of the sorters, Theodore Dennison, had a brother named Perry who had once been arrested for pilfering mail in another town. Allan, in his guise as a recently arrived Scottish immigrant, befriended the Dennisons and learned that they were, in fact, nephews of the Chicago postmaster. When Allan divulged this to Washington, his report was greeted with intense embarrassment. Meanwhile, Allan flattered Dennison by saying how nimble he was at sorting the mail, and Theodore boasted that his fingers were 'so sensitive he knew when a letter contained a penny or a dollar'. Allan maintained covert surveillance and on several occasions observed the light-fingered sorter slip envelopes into his pocket.

One Saturday morning, as Theodore Dennison was leaving the sorting office, he was arrested by Allan, accompanied by a Cook County deputy. The sorter tried to run away but was felled by a flying tackle from Pinkerton. When Dennison was formally charged, and his family connections made known, the Chicago postmaster grimly told the detective that he had better substantiate his charges with hard evidence. Allan and two deputies then searched Dennison's room in a boarding house. Hours were spent meticulously examining the room and its contents; even the carpet was lifted and the floorboards raised, but to no avail. In the words of the local newspaper:

> The search was nearly concluded without finding any trace of Dennison's crimes when Officer Pinkerton decided to continue the search and took the pictures from the walls. On removal of the backs, several bank bills, to the amount of $3,738, were found concealed, many of them of large denominations.[3]

The report mentioned that the picture of the Virgin Mary concealed the largest amount, $1,503.

The case caused quite a sensation, owing to the scandal involving the postmaster himself. Belatedly, the United States Post Office in Washington responded by sending to Chicago W.J. Brown, the General Agent of the Postal Service, who was to interrogate young Dennison and obtain a statement of guilt from him; but by the time Brown arrived Pinkerton already had a full written confession in his hand. As the newspaper jubilantly concluded:

> For three weeks Mr Pinkerton scarcely has had repose in the devotion with which he has followed up the criminals. Complaint after complaint poured into the department and call after call came from Washington to Pinkerton to redouble his efforts, until body and brain were nearly exhausted. As a detective, Mr Pinkerton has no superior, and we doubt if he has any equal in this country.

Some time after this incident Allan decided to form his own detective agency. Like so much else in his life and career, the circumstances are shrouded in mystery and confusion. To this day, Pinkerton's dates its foundation to 1850, the year in which Allan is supposed to have entered into partnership with Edward A. Rucker, a rising young Chicago lawyer. This date has been generally accepted, although Horan,[4] on no good ground, was sceptical of this and suggested 1852 as a more probable date. Unfortunately, no commercial directories for Chicago covering the period 1850–52 exist, so the matter cannot be verified. Horan supposed that because Allan continued to work for the United States Post Office after 1850 this would have precluded him from embarking on any private venture, but this cannot be said with any certainty. It is even possible that the detective agency was started while Pinkerton was still with the Chicago police force, and 'moonlighting' rather than 'political interference' may have been the reason for his resignation.

At any rate, the partners in the North-Western Detective Agency rented a tiny office on the second floor of 89 Washington Street, on the corner of Dearborn, right in the heart of the city. Within a short time branch offices were established in the neighbouring states. A lithographed heading of a letter dated 1856 proclaimed:

> Allan Pinkerton and Edward A. Rucker, under the style of Pinkerton & Co., have established an agency at Chicago, Illinois for the purpose of transacting a General Detective Police Business in Illinois, Wisconsin, Michigan and Indiana; and will attend to the investigation and depredation (*sic*), frauds and criminal offenses; the detection of offenders, procuring arrests and convictions, apprehension or return of fugitives from justice, or bail; recovering lost or stolen property, obtaining information, etc.[5]

In this enterprise Allan was clearly the dominant partner. Indeed, little is known of Rucker and legend has it that 'he withdrew within a year, and Pinkerton resigned his city connections to give full time to his venture'.[6] Rucker's name continued to appear on Pinkerton's letterhead but this, in itself, proves nothing. The idea of forming the agency may have originated with the young attorney, conscious of the inadequacy of the Chicago police force in the burgeoning commercial metropolis, and perhaps his connections with the legal and business community were useful at the outset. Perhaps he and Pinkerton fell out – someone as ruthlessly egocentric as Allan would not have been easy to work with – but this is mere speculation.

It has often been claimed that Allan Pinkerton invented the private detective, a myth reinforced by the bold emblem of the company, a wideawake human eye, with the slogan 'We Never Sleep', which, in due course, gave rise to the expression 'private eye' as a nickname for private investigators. In fact, credit must go to the Parisian detective Eugène François Vidocq who established his Bureau des Renseignements (information office) in 1832. Fourteen years later Messrs McDonough and Breuil, previously the captain and lieutenant of the St Louis police, had left the force to set up their own independent police. That this was no innovation was borne out by the press report that 'This kind of police has been tried in nearly all the Eastern cities and has been found to be much more efficient than the regularly appointed police.'[7]

It is significant, however, that this newspaper referred to McDonough's enterprise as an 'independent police'. There was no hint in the report that this venture was engaged in detective work, and this is confirmed by the reference to Eastern cities. A careful examination of the newspapers of New York, Philadelphia and Boston has failed to turn up a single advertisement for anything approximating to the Pinkerton agency. On the other hand, it is clear that privately run security guards were operating in the East. For example, after a spate of burglaries in Boston in 1821 a private guard service was formed when the official city watchmen had been shown up as corrupt and inefficient, and this concept soon spread to other cities. But these guards, popularly known as 'specials', were not detectives in any sense.[8]

It is not improbable that Pinkerton got the idea from Vidocq who had progressed from a state informer during the Revolution to found the Sûreté in 1811. In 1828 he published his memoirs, which were subsequently translated and ran to many editions on both sides of the Atlantic. Vidocq, born at Arras in 1773, joined the French Army and rose to the rank of lieutenant before falling foul of the Revolution. At Lille he was sentenced to eight years' hard labour and sent to the galleys at Brest, whence he escaped twice but was recaptured. It was a case of third time lucky, and for some years he lived in the company of thieves and criminals in Paris, making a careful study of their methods. In 1809 he offered his services as a spy to the Paris police and was so successful that he was commissioned two years later to reorganise the detective department. It was he who coined the phrase 'set a thief to catch a thief' for his Sûreté was composed of ex-convicts under his personal command. In 1827 he retired and started a paper-mill, staffed by ex-cons, but the venture failed and it was then, in 1832, that he tried to get his old job back. To further his chances he even organised a daring theft but when his complicity became known he was dismissed from the service. He then turned to private work, but the fact that he died in 1857 in poverty, despite his best-selling book, seems to indicate that his detective agency was none too successful.[9]

From the outset, however, the Pinkerton agency differed from Vidocq's organisation and McDonough's police in several fundamental respects. While the Frenchman was primarily concerned with crime in Paris and McDonough preoccupied with guarding warehouses on the Mississippi waterfront, Allan had an infinitely broader vision, as his letterhead implied. Policing in the United States was organised on a county basis, while the writ of law did not extend beyond the frontiers of each individual state. Time and time again, deputy sheriffs in pursuit of criminals were forced to turn back at the county line. The states, jealous of their rights and ever watchful against Federal encroachment (a matter which would be at the heart of the dispute that caused the Civil War), did not co-operate in such matters as law enforcement, yet the rapid development of the railroads meant that criminals could roam over vast areas, perpetrating crimes far apart. Robbery, assault, rape, murder, arson and other violent crimes were commonplace in all large urban areas as well as along the Mississippi, the wild frontier to the west; New Orleans, in particular, being notorious as the crime capital of the United States. What urban police forces existed were, even by 1850, notoriously corrupt, while rural areas were sparsely populated and had very poor communications. In the boom atmosphere of the mid-nineteenth century, organised crime and general lawlessness thrived as never before, and were without parallel anywhere else in the world.

While other countries had federal or centralised systems of law and order, the United States lagged far behind. It would not be until 1908 that the Federal Bureau of Investigation was established, and then its remit was confined to the investigation of offences against the United States – interstate transportation of kidnapped persons and stolen automobiles, bank robbery, espionage and sending letters of extortion. By organising an agency whose detectives could work unhampered by county or state boundaries in pursuit of criminals, Allan Pinkerton filled a very large gap. The wonder is that it took the Federal government so long to emulate him.

Those who had known Allan in the heady days of Chartist agitation in Glasgow appreciated his genius for organisation and his attention to detail. This experience now stood him in good stead. He started off on his own but within three years he had eight employees – five detectives, a secretary and two clerks. The first man he hired was George Henry Bangs and he could not have made a better choice. Bangs was tall, handsome, elegantly dressed and patrician, proud of his descent from *Mayflower* pilgrims, 'with the cold aloof air of a successful city banker considering the loan application of an unsuccessful businessman'. Bangs was that rare combination, the extremely efficient business manager and the natural-born detective, with an uncanny intuitive flair, a diabolical memory for minute detail and a lightning mind which could make connections and unravel a complicated mystery in no time at all. Like his boss, he had a passion for order, neatness and courtesy, although he never let his old-fashioned New England manners get in the way of business efficiency. Within a year he had become Allan's right-hand man and long-time general superintendent.

In the summer of 1853 Pinkerton paid his first visit to New York City, where the Crystal Palace was a major attraction. What impressed Allan most about this exhibition was not the industrial and artistic displays but the sergeant in charge of the police patrol. Through the good offices of Captain James Leonard of the New York Police Department with whom he had business dealings, Allan was introduced to the young man with the English accent and smart bearing. Timothy Webster had been born at Newhaven, Sussex, in 1821 and had emigrated at the age of twelve, settling with his parents in Princeton, New Jersey. It had been his ambition to join the New York police but he soon discovered that for such a plum job one needed good political connections. Fortunately he had caught the eye of Leonard, a maverick who had nothing but contempt for the corrupt politicians of Tammany Hall, and against all the odds Webster had been taken on as a patrolman for the Crystal Palace, earning rapid promotion.

Allan offered him a position with the agency and Webster, realising that his prospects in New York were limited, accepted. Allan promptly gave him the money for his rail fare to Chicago and told him to report to Bangs. Two more Englishmen were recruited shortly afterwards. Pryce Lewis was in his mid-twenties, always well dressed, handsome, intelligent and possessed of great Old World charm, not unlike Bangs himself. John Scully, on the other hand, would prove to be an unwise choice; with a fondness for the bottle, his actions a decade later would have tragic consequences for both Webster and Lewis. The other early recruit was John H. White who, Allan would joke, looked more like a con-man than a detective. None of these men had had any previous experience in law enforcement, far less criminal detection. Allan's own experiences provided the basis of what training they would receive, but Chicago in the roaring Fifties was a wild place where you learned quickly on the job or you did not survive, as Allan himself soon found out.

Inevitably his robust approach made him hated and feared among the criminal fraternity and on several occasions attempts were made on his life. One September evening in 1853, as he was walking up Clark Street on his way home, a gunman drew a revolver and shot him twice from behind at point-blank range. Luckily Allan had a habit of walking with his left hand behind him under his coat and it was this that saved his life:

> The pistol was of large calibre, heavily loaded and discharged so near that Mr Pinkerton's coat was put on fire. Two slugs shattered the bone five inches from the wrist and passed along the bone to the elbow where they were cut out by a surgeon together with pieces of his coat . . . Mr Pinkerton is Chicago's most efficient and courageous law officer, one who has done a great deal in keeping the community free of thugs and killers who are on the run.[10]

By 1856 Allan had enrolled three other detectives, a cheery talkative New Englander named John Fox, an athletic young man named Rivers who, on one occasion, jogged twelve miles after a suspect's carriage rather than lose sight of him, and Adam Roche, a stolid, pipe-smoking German. Later the same year, however, Allan hired America's first female detective. Kate Warne was a comely young widow of twenty-three, described as 'a slender, brown-haired woman, graceful in her movements and self-possessed. Her features, although not what could be called handsome, were decidedly of an intellectual cast . . . her face was honest, which would cause one in distress instinctly (*sic*) to select her as a confidante . . .'[11] She walked into Allan's office one day and said that she wanted to be a detective. Momentarily nonplussed, he asked her why she thought she would make a good detective. Kate replied that she could 'worm out secrets in many places to which it was impossible for male detectives to gain access'. The canny Scot would not give an immediate answer but asked her to call back the following day. He was up half the night weighing up the pros and cons of the idea, but the more he considered it the more he liked it. The following day he took her on, and after a few days' training he gave her an assignment in which, as Allan stated later, 'she succeeded far beyond my utmost expectations'. Kate proved to be an extraordinarily gifted and resourceful woman, courageous and tenacious. She could have had no better commendation than Allan's comment that 'Mrs Warne never let me down'. By 1860 Allan had several women on the payroll, referring to them as 'my Female Detective Bureau', with Kate at their head.

Just how revolutionary this was may be seen in comparison with the official police departments who lagged fifty years behind Pinkerton. Women were first employed in 1891, but only as matrons in charge of female prisoners in police detention. They were first employed as investigators, in New York City, in 1903, and not officially known as policewomen until 1920. Allan's views on female detectives were not shared by his sons, who got rid of the female force after Allan's death. Over the years the myth has grown that Allan's relationship with Kate Warne was not wholly professional. The many references to her in his letters indicate the affection which he felt for her, but this sprang from admiration of her skill and dedication rather than from any sexual feelings.

Even by the 1850s the corrupt practices of the official police had given detectives an unenviable reputation for venality. For this reason Allan preferred to refer to his staff as 'operatives' (perhaps a subconscious borrowing from his Chartist days, when the word was widely used to describe manual workers). The agency was extremely strict about the business it would take on, and all prospective clients were thoroughly vetted before a case was accepted. Credentials, identification and just cause were the watchwords of the organisation. At the outset Allan drafted a code of conduct under the title of *General Principles* which, in essence, serves the company just as well today. The parameters which Allan set on his agency's operations shed an interesting light on the times, as well as on the high moral character of the man himself:

The Agency will not represent a defendant in a criminal case except with the knowledge and consent of the prosecutor; they will not shadow jurors or investigate public officials in the performance of their duties, or trade-union officers or members in their lawful union activities; they will not accept employment from one political party against another; they will not report union meetings unless the meetings are open to the public without restriction; they will not work for vice crusaders; they will not accept contingent fees, gratuities or rewards. The Agency will never investigate the morals of a woman unless in connection with another crime, nor will it handle cases of divorce or of a scandalous nature.

The role of detective is a high and honorable calling . . . Criminals are powerful of mind and strong of will, who if they had devoted themselves to honest pursuits would undoubtedly have become members of honorable society . . . The detectives who have to gather the evidence and arrest these criminals must be men of high order of mind and must possess clean, honest, comprehensive understanding, force of will and vigor of body . . . Criminals must eventually reveal their secrets and a detective must have the necessary experience and judgment of human nature to know the criminal in his weakest moment and force from him, through sympathy and confidence, the secret which devours him.

Allan placed great emphasis on his view that a detective with 'considerable intellectual power and knowledge of human nature as will give him a quick insight into character' would crack even the most hardened or cunning criminal. Significantly, the same document showed Allan's kinship with Machiavelli: 'The end justifies the means, if the ends are for the accomplishment of Justice.' Nevertheless, he was at pains to warn his operatives against obtaining confessions in such a manner as to undermine the case when it came to court. In particular, he adjured them not to obtain statements from witnesses or defendants who were drunk at the time. 'Such statements, when brought into court, tend to shake the strength of evidence, and it is not considered that such statements are as much entitled to reliance as those drawn from sober moments!'

There was also something of the old Radical liberalism in this remarkable document. While Allan had only contempt for crime and its perpetrators, he never lost sight of the fact that they were human beings. Consequently he urged his staff, when they had brought the criminal to justice:

to do all in their power to elevate and enable him, because sometime in the future he most probably will again come out into the world and take the chances of life. If criminals are treated as men, capable of moral reform and elevation, if they were instructed in their duties and responsibilities – as good citizens – and better still, perhaps, if they could be taught some useful handicraft, whereby they might secure an honest livelihood when they return to society and maintain an honest and reputable character; no one can calculate the great service that would thereby be rendered to them and to humanity. Unfortunately, under our present system, this is too little thought of.

Allan's Machiavellian streak also showed in his philosophy about befriending suspects as a means of incriminating them. Many years later, in his *Reminiscences*, he wrote:

Such a technique was distasteful to me but the course pursued was the only one which afforded the slightest promise of success, hence its adoption. Severe moralists may question whether this course is a legitimate or defensible one . . . but the office of the detective is to secure the ends of justice; to purge society of the degrading influences of crime; and to protect the lives, property and honor of the community at large; and in this righteous work the end will unquestionably justify the means adopted to secure the desired result.

Oliver Wendell Holmes[12] suggested that the foundation of the Agency was 'in response to suggestions from several railroad presidents, following a series of robberies'. While this is extremely unlikely to have been the case in 1850–51 when the railroads were in their infancy, it was certainly true that, by 1854, the Pinkerton agency derived a not inconsiderable portion of its income from railroad protection. This is indicated by the contract between Pinkerton and the Illinois Central Railroad which was signed on 1 February 1855. Although the preamble to the contract began 'Whereas the said Pinkerton and Company propose to establish a Police Agency, the office of which is to be at Chicago' it is clear that this was already well established, for later on the document mentions the sterling service given to the railroad companies over the preceding months, the agency receiving in 1854 alone retainers of $2,000 from each of four railroad companies – the Michigan Central, the Michigan Southern and Northern Indiana, the Chicago and Galena Union, and the Illinois Central. The Chicago and Rock Island line and the Chicago, Burlington and Quincy Railroad each contributed a further $1,000. A regular income of $10,000 per annum from railroad security work alone shows how lucrative private detective work in and around Chicago had become in a very short space of time, and this of course took no account of the other private and commercial cases which the agency investigated at the same time. Under the new contract Allan promised to have in readiness:

> a sufficient number of reliable, active and experienced assistants, to enable them to respond to the call of any; or either of the said companies, without delay; and in case the business of either of them shall be of an unusually urgent character, and needing either more assistants or those having different qualifications than those then in their employ, they shall procure as soon as practical as many as may be needed . . . they are to give their personal attention to the investigation of the preliminary facts and maturing and adopting the plan of action.

Significantly, his contract did not preclude Pinkerton from conducting other business. In particular, his work for the United States Post Office in investigating breaches of security and theft from mail-cars and sorting offices throughout the Mid-West was highlighted, with the concession that the exigencies of the USPO 'are to stand of the same class and priority or preference as those of said companies'. The contract went on to specify the type of work undertaken and the charges laid down for the three classes of work, ranged in order of priority:

> according to their skills and abilities, having in view also the personal risk of the employment, and the charges for the first class, besides necessary expenses and disbursements shall not exceed ten dollars a day; the second class not to exceed seven dollars per day; and the third not over three and a half dollars per day. For such special assistants or special and sudden exigencies may render necessary, there shall be charged what they have to pay therefore, and a reasonable sum for their personal supervision of them when necessary.

The contract also took note of the fact that express cars were about to be introduced on the railroads, the American Express Company having entered into agreements with the Illinois Central and Chicago and Galena railroads to rent a portion of their baggage cars for the shipment of express packets. American Express paid $180 a month to the Illinois Central and $324 a month to the Chicago and Galena for this facility. Interestingly, the express company assumed all responsibility for 'risks of injury and danger of any kind arising from any cause to their messengers or agents, and also all losses of bank bills, gold and silver coins and jewelry and valuable papers in said trains'. Eventually, however, responsibility for security in the American Express compartments would also devolve on the Agency.

As the railroads pushed farther and farther west, they came under increasing attack from organised bands of robbers and ruthless desperadoes. Trains were stopped or even derailed, express cars smashed open and strong-boxes rifled. Any attempt by railroad employees to resist was invariably met with murderous force. In 1854 a gang attacked a railroad construction camp near La Salle, Illinois, killed or drove off most of the workers, and besieged the superintendent and his assistant in a wooden shack. Eventually the gang rammed open the door with a telegraph pole, but the railroad men managed to shoot their way out. The assistant, though badly wounded, escaped; but the superintendent mounted his horse and rode off, with the villains in hot pursuit. He hid in a barn but was dragged out, beaten to death and his mutilated corpse dragged around the yard. With great difficulty the railroad company browbeat the local sheriff into mustering a posse to go after the murderers, and it appears that this incident impelled the Illinois Central to employ Pinkerton.

As the incidence of railroad crime escalated, so the business of the Agency mushroomed. At the same time, however, Allan was engrossed in fighting crime in general. An echo of his earliest feat of detection came in the summer of 1857 when he and Bangs apprehended Jules Imbert, a notorious French counterfeiter whose forgeries of bank bills and other securities had been causing severe damage to the New York financial sector. This was a major coup for Allan, and brought him for the first time to the serious attention of the powerful and influential bankers of the north-east.

In the same year Allan had his first meeting with a man who was to play a very important part in his life. George Brinton McClellan, seven years Allan's junior, was of Scottish descent, his ancestors having been sheriffs of Galloway and barons of Kirkcudbright from the thirteenth century onwards.[13] On his mother's side, McClellan was descended from William Bradford, a passenger on the *Mayflower* who became Governor of Massachusetts Bay Colony. Born at Philadelphia in 1826, McClellan graduated second in his class from West Point in 1846 and was commissioned as an engineer second-lieutenant, just in time to take part in the Mexican War (1846–48) where he was breveted for gallantry. At the end of that campaign he was assigned to West Point as an instructor in practical engineering and in 1851 he supervised the construction of Fort Delaware. The following year he served with distinction in the Red River expedition and in 1853–54 was engineer officer in Washington Territory and Oregon. Early in 1855 he was sent to Europe to study military methods and organisation, and witnessed action from both sides of the Crimean War as well as visiting military bases all over Europe. Before returning to the United States he took time off for a sentimental journey to Scotland.

The outcome of this European sojourn was a detailed report which formed the basis of his book *Armies of Europe* (1862), and the adoption of an improved saddle by the army, ever afterwards known as the McClellan. In December 1856 the dashing young captain resigned his commission to embark on a career in civil engineering. A few weeks later he arrived in Chicago as chief engineer of the Illinois Central Railroad, at a salary of $3,000 a year. Although he had an office in Chicago and a room at the St Nicholas Hotel, the thirty-year-old engineer, still unmarried, preferred the nomadic life, exploring the wilds of Illinois from the comparative comfort of his personal sleeping-car as he roved up and down the 704 miles of track.

McClellan had more than his share of thrills and spills, the one provided by the inevitable brush with railroad bandits, the other the frequent derailments and breakdowns to which this line was prone before his appointment. It was not long before he encountered the Scottish detective who not only had a free pass on the railroad but the privilege of stopping express and freight trains at any point and at his own discretion. From the outset Allan was deeply impressed by 'Little Mac' (though, in fact, they were the same height). Both had a single-minded dedication to work, and took immense pride in their highly professional approach. Both were obsessive, with a passion for order and a mania for preserving even the most trivial scraps of paper.[14] Both were driven by a sense of destiny, egotistical and disinclined to suffer fools lightly. Supremely confident in their own abilities, they were impatient of shortcomings in others. But in each other Pinkerton and McClellan recognised themselves, especially the attitudes and characteristics which they admired the most.

McClellan's progress up the ladder was meteoric; within a year he was vice-president of the Illinois Central, and in September 1860 he left to take up his appointment as president of the Ohio and Mississippi Railroad's Eastern Division, at a salary of $10,000 a year. Even after McClellan and his new wife Ellen moved to Cincinnati, close contact with Allan Pinkerton was maintained. Indeed, the latter benefited from his friend's transfer for soon the security business of that railway company landed in his lap as well.

There was one other contact that came Allan's way in the 1850s which would have important repercussions on his career. The lawyer who drafted the contract of February 1855 was the leading partner in the Springfield firm of Lincoln and Herndon. Abraham Lincoln had been retained by the Illinois Central as its legal consultant and in this capacity frequently came in contact with the company's security chief. Although by this time Lincoln was already being drawn inexorably into the political arena – nailing his colours to the mast by his great speech at Peoria in October 1854, when he spoke out against the Kansas-Nebraska Act that opened these north-west territories to slavery – he continued to be actively embroiled in the affairs of the railroad until 1858 when he accepted the Republican nomination for the Senate. On that occasion he uttered the most telling sentences of all his speeches: 'A house divided against itself cannot stand. I believe this Government cannot endure permanently, half slave and half free.' These ringing words were intoxicating to Allan who, at this time, was performing a dangerous balancing act between his official duties and his private anti-slavery inclinations, now coming out into the open more and more.

Both McClellan and Lincoln were powerful personalities, and both left their indelible stamp on Allan Pinkerton, in different ways and for different reasons. The influence of the middle-aged lawyer is probably the more understandable. He had been born in a log cabin in the backwoods of Kentucky and had had even less in the way of a formal education than Pinkerton. Like the detective, he was totally self-made with the same innate hunger for self-education and, like Allan, he would succeed against all the odds entirely by his own efforts. McClellan had a rather patronising view of the company lawyer and the detective at this time; they were typical of 'the good people who were rather primitive in their appearance and habits' that he worked with in Illinois. It is probable that the aristocratic young McClellan formed mistaken ideas of the socially crude Lincoln, underestimating his intellectual powers and brilliance of mind, with disastrous results only five years later.

The close friendship which developed between Pinkerton and McClellan, on the face of it, is hard to understand, and even harder to explain. What could have drawn the handsome, elegant West Pointer, the brilliant engineer, so closely connected with the affluent and the influential to the quondam revolutionary from the slums of the Gorbals? Where McClellan was witty and urbane, with the polish borne of centuries of good breeding, a man who was perfectly at home with European royalty, Pinkerton was dour, humourless, socially awkward and blunt-spoken with a raw Glasgow accent which he never shook off. The motivation for Pinkerton's enduring loyalty and affection for the younger man has been dismissed as very simple: McClellan represented everything Pinkerton ever wanted.[15] There is no evidence, however, in the voluminous correspondence and reports from Pinkerton to McClellan in support of this contention. Allan was always his own man but he admired the cool professionalism of McClellan and doubtless learned a great deal from him in this respect.

This is undoubtedly the key to their relationship, both in the railroad period and later, during the Civil War. Previous biographers of Pinkerton have dwelt on what appeared to them to be an inconsistency in Allan's character: 'There were times when Pinkerton seemed two men, each with his own belief and philosophy. One could embrace the ideas of the most violent of the abolitionists, while the other could admire and form intimate friendships with financiers and railroad executives who were certainly never the champions of the slaves.'[16] Horan adds that McClellan's political beliefs were poles apart from Pinkerton's. By this he meant their attitude towards abolitionism, an issue that was, by 1859, fiercely dividing the country – almost as much as the issue of slavery itself.

For Allan the matter was clear-cut: slavery was an abomination that had to be rooted out by whatever means possible, although he stopped short of the armed rebellion advocated by John Brown. Allan's interest in the emancipation of slaves had been kindled in the 1830s and was entirely consonant with his left-wing sentiments. In Chicago his clandestine activity in the Underground Railroad increased over the years, notwithstanding the passage in 1850 of the Fugitive Slave Act which made it a Federal offence to assist runaway slaves. A fervent admirer of John Jones and Frederick Douglass, the free Negro leaders, Allan frequently put his career in jeopardy by giving temporary sanctuary to runaways, coming up the Mississippi and Ohio rivers from the South to Chicago which was, by the mid-1850s, the preferred point of embarcation for Canada. Inevitably much of the inconvenience, to say nothing of the danger, fell on Joan's uncomplaining shoulders, as Allan was often absent from home on railway work. By 1858 the Pinkerton's new house between Fifth and Franklin Streets was bursting at the seams; the attic, cellar and kitchen often crowded with runaways. John Jones was a frequent visitor, bringing parties of slaves for Allan and his friends to load on board lake steamers.

As one writer observed succinctly: 'While Pinkerton's right hand caught lawbreakers, his left hand broke the law. But his conscience was, of course, clear as that of any Quaker patriot out on the long Underground route.'[17] Allan himself was emphatic in his detestation of slavery: 'This institution of human bondage always reclined (*sic*) my earnest opposition.'[18] Incidentally, in this regard Allan was not 'poles apart' from McClellan who, on one occasion, wrote to his wife saying that when he thought of some of the features of slavery he could not help shuddering. 'Just think for one moment, and try to realize that at the will of some brutal master you and I might be separated forever! When the day of adjustment comes I will, if successful, throw my sword into the scale to force an improvement in the condition of these poor blacks.' In the next breath, however, McClellan added hastily, 'I will never be an abolitionist . . . I will not fight for the abolitionists.'[19] To what extent Pinkerton differed in his thinking from McClellan over this matter is open to speculation. Allan *was* a committed abolitionist, but it is doubtful whether he was prepared to take up arms for the cause, as he had done, in somewhat similar circumstances, all those years before. This was the overriding factor which explained the lawman's ambivalent attitude. Almost twenty years had elapsed since Allan had been an ardent advocate of physical force, and had risked his life for his principles in the Newport Rising, but something of the old, grim fanaticism is evident in his overt support for John Brown.

On 25 January 1859 some three thousand men and women congregated in Chicago's Metropolitan Hall after parading through the city. As the din of a hundred-gun salute on the lakeshore died away the Scots took their seats to listen to Mayor Haines, ex-Governor McComas and others extoll the virtues of Robert Burns whose birth centenary they were celebrating. Seated in the audience were Allan Pinkerton and his two young boys, William and Robert. When Joan, then aged thirty-one and at the height of her powers, walked out on stage to sing some of the auld sangs of the Auld Country and lead the Highland Guard of Chicago in the spirited rendition of 'A Man's a Man', the stern, unbending father astonished his sons by weeping uncontrollably.

Apart from Jones and Douglass, whose views seem to have been closest to Pinkerton's, the militant figures of the movement were no strangers to the detective's home. John Henry Kagi, described by Artemus Ward as 'a melancholy brigand', was a frequent caller, as was Aaron Dwight Stevens, in many ways the most interesting and attractive of the personalities gathered round John Brown. Kagi, born at Bristolville, Ohio, in 1835, was the son of a Swiss emigrant blacksmith. Like Allan he had little formal schooling but the range and depth of his self-education was formidable and he was an able businessman as well as an excellent speaker and persuasive writer. In 1855 he had gone to Nebraska, one of the frontier states where the slavery issue was fiercely fought over by armed bands. For his part in these skirmishes he was sent to prison, but on release was assaulted by the pro-slavery Judge Elmore, who shot him three times. Eventually he recovered from his wounds, more fiercely opposed to the pro-slavery faction than ever.

Stevens, born in 1831, ran away from home to fight in the Mexican War, transferred to the regular army but was convicted of mutiny at Taos, New Mexico, in 1855 and sentenced to death, later commuted to three years' hard labour at Fort Leavenworth from which he escaped and joined the Free State forces, becoming colonel of the Second Kansas Militia. Of Puritan New England descent, he was proud of his great-grandfather who had fought as a captain in the War of Independence. Well over six feet tall, he had a commanding presence and a noble bearing, with black, penetrating eyes that transfixed everyone.

These were not untypical of the fanatics John Brown gathered around himself, earning notoriety from such incidents as the Pottawatomie Massacre (the cold-blooded killing of five pro-slavery settlers in revenge for the deaths of five Free State men) in May 1856. In the ensuing years Captain John Brown and his supporters left a trail of havoc throughout the frontier states. He was in Chicago in August 1855, late October and much of December 1856, April and June 1858 and the spring of 1859. On 20 January that year he set out from Garnett, Kansas, with Kagi and Stevens and a party of eleven runaway slaves, bound for Canada where he had established a 'provisional government' with eleven whites and thirty-five blacks. There was a bloody skirmish on the last day of that month, the Battle of the Spurs, before they reached Sabetha and crossed the Nemeha River from Kansas into Nebraska. During February and early March the party made a slow and painful progress across Nebraska and Iowa before resting for several days at Springdale, a Quaker community which had often helped Brown in the past. On 9 March Brown, Kagi and Stevens loaded the runaways in a boxcar which had been booked for them by William Penn Clarke, who apparently bluffed the agent at West Liberty that this had the blessing of the railroad officials. During the night one of the female slaves gave birth to a boy who was promptly named John Brown after his liberator. The train rolled into Chicago in the early hours of 11 March and by 4.30 a.m. the strange party of three white men and a dozen runaways trudged up Adams Street to knock on Pinkerton's door.

Allan, a loaded revolver in his hand, silently let them into his kitchen where Joan gave them breakfast. In short order Allan had organised the party, sending John Brown to the home of his close friend, the free Negro John Jones, and hiding some of the others in his own house. Later that morning he hurried over to see Brown who was in dire straits: his clothing and especially his boots were in very poor condition and the temperature outside was well below freezing, and he had little money left. Allan promised to get fresh clothing for the party, and raise some cash. Later, Jones's wife would recall how Pinkerton and Brown had embraced warmly, like brothers. Allan explained that there was a lawyers' meeting in town that day and he would try to get some money there. The meeting was, in fact, a session of the Chicago Judiciary Convention, the main item on the agenda being the selection of a candidate for Cook County circuit judge. Allan drew up a subscription list and delegated this matter to two friends, 'because I was too well known as being an anti-slavery man and I thought my absence from the meeting would be the best thing'. When the friends returned empty-handed, saying that the lawyers had refused assistance, Allan was not the man to be put off so easily. Taking the list himself he strode into the meeting 'while there was a great deal of caucusing going on about the time'. The babble of voices ceased abruptly as he jumped on to the platform:

Gentlemen, I have one thing to do and I intend to do it in a hurry. John Brown is in this city at the present time with a number of men, women and children. I require aid, and substantial aid I must have. I am ready and willing to leave this meeting if I get this money; if not, I have to say this. I will bring John Brown to this meeting and if any United States Marshal dare lay a hand on him he must take the consequence. I am determined to do this or have the money.[20]

There was a deathly silence, as the Scotsman, his face flushed, glowered down at the audience. Then John Wilson, a rising politician and later a judge, rose slowly and walked up to the platform, and handed over a fifty-dollar bill. Allan took off his hat and held it out as other delegates silently shuffled forward with banknotes. Within a few minutes he had collected almost $600.

Allan thanked them politely, and left the hall as quickly as he had entered. Then he called on Colonel C.G. Hammond, the general superintendent of the Michigan Central Railroad, who personally saw to it that a boxcar was stocked with water and provisions. At four o'clock Allan left home with his thirteen-year-old son Willie and Kagi, loaded the slaves hidden in the house into a wagon and then drove around the neighbourhood collecting the others from the homes of sympathisers. Then he drove to the station and saw Kagi and Stevens off with the runaway slaves who had journeyed eleven hundred miles in eighty-two days, much of it on foot in the rigours of a harsh Mid-Western winter.

Around three o'clock that afternoon John Brown had gone ahead by an earlier train to Detroit to liaise with Frederick Douglass and supervise the arrangements for getting the blacks aboard the ferry-boat for Windsor. Allan and Willie, along with John Jones, had accompanied the abolitionist to the station and there exchanged farewells. Old Brown's steel-blue eyes blazed as he gripped the detective's hand warmly and delivered his parting shot: 'Friends, lay in your tobacco, cotton and sugar because I intend to raise the prices.' It was his cryptic way of warning them that the insurrection he had been planning for months was imminent. As the great bearded figure disappeared from view Allan turned to his son. 'Look well upon that man,' he said. 'He is greater than Napoleon and just as great as George Washington.'[21]

On Sunday, 16 October 1859, John Brown led his band of twenty-one men (sixteen whites and five blacks) in the assault on the Federal arsenal at Harper's Ferry. The insurrection was brief and bloody and at daybreak on 18 October Brown and the survivors were taken prisoner. The following day they were transported to Charlestown, Virginia, and incarcerated there. Their trial began on 25 October and by the end of the month it was all over; a jury had found Brown and his co-conspirators guilty of treason and first-degree murder. On 2 November Judge Richard Parker pronounced the death sentence, execution to take place thirty days later.

There was a great deal of wild talk, all over the Yankee states, of some kind of armed intervention to liberate Brown and save him from the gallows, and inevitably the myth grew up over the years that Allan Pinkerton himself had planned some kind of gaol delivery after the old man's arrest.[22] It has even been alleged that Allan went to Harper's Ferry and Charlestown in the aftermath of the trial, but of this there is absolutely no proof. What is incontrovertible, on the other hand, is that in the thirty days between sentence and execution, Allan moved heaven and earth on behalf of his friend. In Chicago he raised money for the defence fund, persuaded George McClellan to use his considerable influence, through his Southern Democratic connections, on Brown's behalf to win a stay of execution if not a reprieve, and assiduously wrote letters and sent telegrams to many of the nation's leading political figures urging clemency for the Middle Border fanatic whom he regarded with the reverence due to a biblical prophet. Almost a quarter of a century later Allan would comment elliptically, 'Had it not been for the excessive watchfulness of those having him in charge, the pages of American history would never have been stained with the record of his execution.'

But it was all to no avail. On the morning of 2 December fifteen hundred soldiers were on parade in Charlestown to see justice done, and to prevent any last-minute attempt to save Brown's life. Among those on parade that fateful morning was Professor T.J. Jackson, soon to acquire fame as one of the greatest generals of the Confederacy; and in the ranks of a Richmond rifle company stood the sinister figure of John Wilkes Booth.

The despised and execrated abolitionist clambered down from the prison wagon and ascended the scaffold to take one last look at the Blue Ridge Mountains before the hood was drawn over his leonine head. The noose was adjusted, and a single blow of the hatchet in the sheriff's hand severed the cord on the trapdoor. As John Brown swung between heaven and earth, Colonel J.T.L. Preston, in command of the parade, solemnly cried out, 'So perish all such enemies of Virginia!' adding, almost as an afterthought, 'All such foes of the Union! All such foes of the human race!'

Allan Pinkerton, around the age of sixty

The house in the Gorbals where Allan Pinkerton was born

Allan with his wife, Joan

Extract from the Glasgow parish register, showing the marriage of Allan Pinkerton, cooper in Glasgow, to Joan Carfrae

THE SCOTTISH PATRIOT.

SPIRIT OF THE MOVEMENT.

GLASGOW UNIVERSAL SUFFRAGE ASSOCIATION.

On Tuesday evening, the weekly meeting of the Directors, along with Delegates from Trades, Shops, and Factories, was held in the Hall, College Open. Mr Allan Pinkerton rose and said—Previous to withdrawing from the Association, he would trouble them with a few remarks as to the late proceedings in the Lyceum, on the subject of petitioning. These proceedings, he was sorry to say, had led to very unpleasant results. An Association had been formed in Glasgow, under the title of the "Northern Democratic Association." (Hear) Mr P. here proceeded, at some length, to refer to the proceedings in the Lyceum, when himself and a few others had endeavoured to carry an amendment to the motion almost unanimously come to by the meeting, in favour of petitioning. That amendment, he remarked, only asked the Association to wait until England had been consulted. It was not against petitioning. He then alluded to the recommendation of the Central Committee, and proceeded to stigmatize that body for giving out any such recommendation before testing the country. The Democratic Association coming into the field was not intended to divide, but to unite Radicals, and its motto would be, "We are determined to carry the People's Charter peaceably if we may, forcibly if we must." (Hear, hear, and a hiss.)

servations
Mr Pattis
Mr Pr
Committe
to such a
had a muc
of opinio
tion. Su
majority o
vour of pe
appear, if
up an Ant
most ridi
holding th
work, ther
for the Ch
show a b
country (
anxious fo
were not t
do? The
their prin
tives for se
part, what
solved to
onet, he w
blind his
He would
pared to
take their
cloak his

John Brown, the leader of the militant Abolitionists, who was
executed on 2 December 1859

OPPOSITE
(top) Julian Harney, Allan's political mentor,
from an engraving of c.1850
(bottom) Extract from the *Scottish Patriot*,
reporting a meeting of the Glasgow
Universal Suffrage Association

Robert Pinkerton

William Pinkerton

Kid Curry and
the Soiled Dove

The Sundance Kid
and Ella Platt

• 5 •

The Road to War
1859–61

A wild and confused tale of lofty idealism smothered by lust for wealth.

ARTHUR CHARLES COLE, 'THE COMING OF THE RAILROADS',
IN VOLUME III OF *THE CENTENNIAL HISTORY OF ILLINOIS*, 1919

In 1839 Frederick Harnden, a conductor on the Boston and Worcester Railway, undertook on his own account to carry small packages between these towns. When this came to the railway's notice he was ordered to desist forthwith or leave the company. Harnden chose the latter and branched out on his own, developing a business of executing commissions for clients and carrying parcels between Boston and New York. The initial success of this enterprise, the world's first express service, encouraged Alvin Adams to emulate it the following year with his own service linking New York and Boston. An attempt to extend these express services to letters was promptly suppressed by the US Postmaster General, but there was plenty of business to be picked up in the rapid transportation of parcels and valuable packets, a service not provided by the US Post Office until 1912. Soon express companies were springing up all over the eastern states, often confined to two or three towns; but gradually Adams absorbed them into his own rapidly expanding network and in 1854 amalgamated with Harnden to form the Adams Express Company.

When Alvin Adams took over the express route between New York and Philadelphia in 1843 he also acquired Edward S. Sanford, who became a vice-president of the enlarged company. Seven years later, Sanford negotiated a contract with the New York and New Haven Railroad for the conveyance of express packets. A measure of the importance of this business was the fact that Sanford was prepared to pay the railroad $1,000 a month for space in their baggage cars. When the line was extended shortly afterwards, Sanford readily agreed to pay an additional $700 a month. Within four years Adams Express had carved a vast fief for itself, covering southern New England, New Jersey, Pennsylvania, Ohio and the south-eastern states, with general headquarters in New York and branch offices in Augusta, Georgia, and Montgomery, Alabama.

In the same period another giant express company was developing along similar lines, but concentrating on northern New England (with headquarters at Buffalo, New York). William George Fargo, born at Pompey, New York, in 1818, started his career as a freight agent for the Auburn and Syracuse Railway in 1841 and became express messenger between Albany and Buffalo a year later. In 1844 he left the railway company to form a partnership with Henry Wells (1805–78) and Daniel Dunning which offered an express service west of Buffalo. This expanded rapidly as the railroad network spread to Chicago, St Louis and other western cities. In March 1850 the partners formed the American Express Company. A separate company, named Wells, Fargo and Company, was formed a year later to conduct operations between New York and San Francisco via the isthmus of Panama. Although he eventually controlled a nationwide express company, Fargo continued to reside in Buffalo till his death in 1881, and was mayor of the city in 1862–66.

We have already seen how American Express had contracts with the railroad companies operating in and out of Chicago by 1854. Eventually responsibility for security would pass to the Pinkerton Agency, but at the outset American Express preferred to handle this themselves. Allan's first direct contract for overseeing the safety of valuable express parcels in transit, however, came later that same year when he was approached by Sanford of Adams Express, who wrote to him saying that the sum of $40,000 had been stolen from a locked pouch somewhere between their Montgomery and Augusta offices. Frustrated by the ineptitude of the Alabama and Georgia lawmen to pinpoint this crime, Sanford had asked contacts in the New York police if they could recommend someone to investigate the matter. Robert Boyer, a New York detective who had worked with Allan on the Imbert case, recommended the Chicago agency.[1]

At first Allan was nonplussed by Sanford's simplistic approach to the crime and, particularly, his blunt question 'Can you identify the thief?' purely on the basis of Sanford's letter. He was inclined to turn down the case, especially as he was at that time extremely busy organising the squad of uniformed security men recruited to guard railroad depots and factory installations. But he was touched by Boyer's 'unselfish recommendation' so he spent the weekend in his office, weighing up every aspect of Sanford's letter. He carefully drafted a detailed reply, running to nine pages, which was dutifully copied out by his secretary on Monday morning and posted off to Sanford in New York. Based solely on the information conveyed in Sanford's letter Allan had come to the conclusion that Nathan Maroney, the manager of the Montgomery office, was the guilty man. Allan pithily concluded his report with the advice to keep Maroney 'under strict surveillance before he bites you twice'.

This report was never acknowledged and Allan soon forgot all about it, until one Saturday evening when he received a telegram: 'Can you send a man, half horse, half alligator? I got bit once more. When can you send him? Edward S. Sanford.' Allan was intrigued, and though he now had more work than he could really cope with, he decided to follow up the enquiry personally. Besides, the prospect of adding the prestigious Adams Express to the Agency's growing list of clients was very tempting. Telling Bangs that he was taking the case, Allan cabled Sanford to meet him in Montgomery. Remarkably, Allan later claimed that he 'knew very little about the Adams Company at this time, as they had no office in the West', but he sensed that this could be the sort of case that would help his business to expand in the densely populated north-eastern states.

In Montgomery Allan discovered that Sanford had taken his advice. Maroney had been arrested and charged with the theft. Because of the large amount stolen, and Maroney's social standing, the affair caused a major sensation. Maroney was released on $40,000 bail, raised by the most prominent citizens of Montgomery, who felt that the elegant young man was being unfairly victimised by the express company. At the preliminary hearing, moreover, Adams Express could only produce the flimsiest of circumstantial evidence, with the result that Maroney's bail was slashed to $4,000 and his trial was set for the following September. Adams suffered a great deal of unfavourable publicity in the Alabama newspapers, and as it now seemed likely that no jury would convict the defendant, Sanford had decided to call in Pinkerton.

Realising the crucial importance of this case, Allan quickly organised a high-powered team, led by himself and George Bangs, to investigate the matter thoroughly. Exceptionally for the period, Allan moved the team, lock, stock and barrel, to Philadelphia. Here he and Bangs, assisted by Kate Warne, Adam Roche, John Fox and John White, formed their plans. Roche, disguised as 'a dull-witted Dutchman' in an old cap and baggy pants, was assigned to shadow Mrs Maroney. Even more elaborate was John Fox's cover. Allan supplied the former watchmaker with a box of watch parts so that he could set up shop in the Pennsylvania village of Jenkintown – Mrs Maroney had been seen in Philadelphia posting a letter to an address there. It was not long before Fox was reporting back to Allan that Maroney had relatives in that village. When Mrs Maroney arrived there, Kate Warne checked in at the village boarding house, posing as the wife of a wealthy businessman. With her sumptuous wardrobe and elegant manners, Kate looked the part. Soon she had engineered an introduction to Mrs Maroney and began to cultivate her friendship. In due course she let slip the fact that her supposed husband had made his money from forging bank bills.

At first it looked as if these elaborate schemes would not produce the desired results, but the first big break came when Bangs copied the address of a letter Maroney sent to New York City. This proved to be the shop of a locksmith who was copying a key for Maroney. When Bangs examined this key he found that it belonged to Adams Express. Reporting this development to Sanford, Allan suspected that it would be a vital part of Maroney's defence that employees other than office managers had keys to the mailbags. By midsummer, however, the Adams lawyer was advising Sanford that the case was very weak and there was every likelihood of an acquittal. In desperation Allan suggested that Maroney should be re-arrested on the vague charge of conspiracy. He was counting on the fact that Maroney, unable to get at the money he had stashed away, was now flat broke and would not be in a position to renew bail. In due course, therefore, he was re-arrested and remanded in custody at the Eldridge Street Prison in New York.

Allan now arranged for John White to share Maroney's cell, posing as a big city forger, with Bangs pretending to be his attorney. To pile on the pressure, Allan now began sending anonymous letters to Maroney saying that his wife was being courted by a handsome stranger (another Pinkerton man) in Jenkintown. Confronted by these accusations on her next visit to the prison, Maroney's wife at first refuted the gossip, but eventually admitted that she was seeing someone. White pretended to sympathise with poor Maroney over his wife's infidelity and won his confidence. When Bangs visited his 'client' he made no secret of his contempt for the corrupt legal system which could be bent if you had the right kind of money. One day Bangs turned up with a release order for his client, implying that justice had been bought. At this Maroney broke down. Worried at the prospect of his faithless wife spending his loot with her new boyfriend, he pleaded with White to help him.

White said that this would cost real money, but Maroney arranged for word to be sent to his wife, ordering her to turn over the stolen cash to White who would arrive in Jenkintown shortly. Mrs Maroney was unsure whether this was the right course of action. At this point she confided her dilemma to her new friend Kate, who told her that it was the only way. Once the bearer bonds had been cashed, she said, 'they could go down to Texas and live high'. Mrs Maroney then dug up the Adams pouch and handed it over to White as arranged. Within a matter of hours Allan, Bangs, White, Kate Warne and Sanford were in a room at the Astor House in New York City, counting the money. Amazingly, it was all there, but for $400.

This was not the end of the story by any means. To ensure a watertight case and a sure conviction against the Maroneys, Allan had to keep up the masquerade. Bangs and White continued to string along the worried Maroney, while Kate returned to Jenkintown to console the wife, and keep a close watch on her. In September 1855 Maroney appeared for trial at Montgomery on the original charge. His self-confidence was greatly bolstered by the appearance in court not only of his beautiful young wife but also of a large contingent of well-heeled supporters there to denounce the Yankee express company. This feeling was reinforced by the rather feeble circumstantial evidence set out by the prosecutor on the opening day.

On the second morning, however, Maroney's arrogance vanished in an instant when the day's first witness was called. 'John H. White' meant nothing to Maroney until he saw his former cell-mate take the stand; the colour drained from his handsome features as he slumped in his chair. Before White could give evidence, Maroney had a hurried consultation with his lawyer who interrupted proceedings to say that his client wished to change his plea to guilty. He was duly sentenced to ten years' hard labour in the state penitentiary, while his hysterical wife received a suspended sentence. Throughout the case Sanford had been impressed with the skill, integrity and professionalism of the Pinkerton team, and particularly the amount of time personally devoted to the investigation by the Agency's principal. Shortly after the Maroney trial he persuaded the Adams board to emulate the railroads and put Pinkerton on an annual retainer.

When Sanford went on to greater things, becoming the president of the American Telegraph Company, he made sure that Allan was entrusted with its security work. By 1860, therefore the Agency was handling security for the US Post Office, the two major express companies and a growing number of railroads. Spectacular results spoke volumes: the Agency not only secured convictions, it also had an excellent record for the recovery of stolen property. In this crucial first decade of the company Allan, he of the stern, unflinching eye, evolved the symbol which is used to this day. To the criminal fraternity Pinkerton did, indeed, become 'the Eye that never sleeps'. Just as the Mounted Police across the border in Canada were then winning their reputation for always getting their man, so too the Pinkerton reputation for tenacity was being established. The choice of the open Eye was singularly apt; in time it would become Allan's nickname in underworld circles, and the almost supernatural notion of the Eye that somehow saw everything became a powerful deterrent to wrong-doers. It was uncanny how Pinkertons, as the Agency's operatives soon came to be known, seemed to be everywhere and to know everything almost before it happened. There is no doubt that Allan's meticulous approach to intelligence-gathering stood him in good stead, not only in the 1850s but a few short years later when America itself was convulsed by the war between the states.

Allan, however, suffered one defect which is often characteristic of the self-made businessman: he never quite knew when to delegate matters to his subordinates. It was a matter of pride that he never gave his operatives assignments that he could not handle himself; but all too often in this early period he interfered in cases, even taking over the investigation himself if he thought the man on the job was not making satisfactory progress. Allan ran his business like he ran his family – with a rod of iron. It says much for the tact and forbearance of George Bangs that he put up with his egocentric, often irascible employer; the strange thing is that, for all his domineering ways, Allan inspired an almost fanatical loyalty in his staff. One old colleague would later say that Allan 'would storm the gates of hell for you – but cross him and he'd leave you to burn in there'.

Pinkerton was a driven man. To some extent the stern Calvinist background of his youth was a factor, but he seemed possessed of boundless energy. He was a man who could get by on two or three hours' sleep at most, a tireless worker with reckless courage and a formidable grasp of detail. These characteristics were a powerful combination; they were recognised and admired by others cast in the same mould – men like George McClellan of the Ohio and Mississippi Railroad, Samuel Felton of the Philadelphia, Wilmington and Baltimore Railroad, George Smith of Wisconsin Fire and Marine Insurance, as well as Edward Sanford and William George Fargo. Pinkerton was, in some ways, greater than them for he was not only an astute businessman and a shrewd administrator as they were, but he was also nothing less than a genius in his own chosen field. The science of criminology simply did not exist in the mid-nineteenth century; crime was combated on the street or in the field by force meeting force, and detection was at its most basic, relying almost entirely on betrayal by informers. Vidocq had pointed the way, thanks to his instinctive use of ex-criminals who understood the workings of the devious criminal mind; but Allan eschewed such crude techniques.

For him detection was all about deduction, as his penetrating analysis of the Maroney case from a distance of hundreds of miles proves. The scientific approach to the merest shreds and scraps of evidence, which fellow Scot Sir Arthur Conan Doyle would one day popularise through his creation Sherlock Holmes, and the uncanny ability to build up the profile of a crime and the person committing it, was due to Allan Pinkerton. Such methods as observing the addresses on letters, used so effectively in the Maroney case, would later be refined. The use of disguises may seem theatrical, but in this manner Allan pioneered the undercover techniques which would later be used so devastatingly in combating industrial terrorism and organised crime. For someone who had been born when the Industrial Revolution was in its infancy, and who had had little formal education, Allan was quick to embrace the latest technology as it developed, and adapt it to the task of detecting or preventing crime. His work for the railroads gave him unlimited free travel and consequently a mobility that matched the most ingenious criminal, but he was also an enthusiast of the telegraph system even in the early years when transmissions were uncertain and expensive. The process of fixing pictures by sunlight, patented by Niepce and Daguerre in 1840, had come to America soon afterwards. Soon every town of any size had its 'daguerrian artist' and Americans were early devotees of daguerrotype portraits; but none was ever more enthusiastic for this medium than Allan Pinkerton. Within a few years he had built up an impressive Rogues Gallery of mugshots and circulated copies of photographs of wanted criminals to lawmen all over the country, together with detailed descriptions of physical features, dress, habits, mental characteristics, criminal specialities and mode of operation. When it is remembered that Pinkerton kept efficient criminal records long before the Federal Bureau of Investigation was even dreamed of, this organisational feat is all the more remarkable.

While embracing the railroad, the telegram and the photograph in the unending war against crime, Allan never lost sight of traditional methods. Like Vidocq, he also relied heavily on tip-offs from criminals and took great pains to protect the identity of his informants, devising elaborate codes which were used in letters, telegrams and reports. Although much of the Agency's records prior to 1871 were destroyed in the great fire that devastated Chicago on 8 October that year, sufficient material has survived, especially in the archives of other law enforcement institutions and the railroad companies, to give a flavour of Pinkerton's manic attention to detail.

From its inception, Allan had been adamant that the Agency would never accept rewards. This proved to be a very wise policy for it ensured the co-operation, rather than the antagonism, of the official police forces who were quite happy for the Pinkertons to do the detective work so long as they 'made the collar' and got any rewards on offer. By 1860, therefore, Allan had established a good working relationship with the police forces throughout the north-eastern states as well as the Mid-West.

In the same year Allan diversified from detection to protection by organising a guard service for the Chicago meat-packers and other commercial installations along the lakeshore. This has often been claimed as the first of its kind, although, as previously noted, something of the sort was in existence at Boston as early as 1821 and by the middle of the century was well established in the eastern cities. In 1860, however, there is no doubt that Captain Paul Dennis and his six smartly uniformed private policemen, guarding Chicago factory premises, were something of a novelty, a significant departure from the plain-clothes detectives who rode the express cars to monitor railroad crime. It will be recalled that Allan's *General Principles* expressly excluded his operatives from interfering in the lawful business of trade unions, a hangover from his Chartist days; this is a policy which has been rigorously enforced for many years now, but there would be a period, around the turn of the century, when it was breached – with tragic results for American labour relations and dire consequences for the Agency.

All that, however, was a long way in the future. Other matters were much more pressing in 1860. This was an election year and Illinois was, for once, in the very thick of it. Hitherto the eastern states had dominated the four-yearly presidential contests, the great southern state of Virginia in particular; but the country was changing and the old Southern aristocratic predominance was waning. Two years after he drafted the railroad contract with the Pinkerton Agency, Abraham Lincoln joined the newly created Republican Party and within two years secured his party's nomination for the Senate. His Democratic rival was an old opponent, Stephen Douglas, the epitome of everything Lincoln was not: old money, landed interests and slave-owning connections. Both men were eloquent orators and the Illinois senatorial contest was transformed into a national gladiatorial arena when the political duel between those giants culminated in the series of well-publicised Lincoln-Douglas Debates. In the end Douglas won the election to the senate, but was outmanoeuvred by his wily opponent who succeeded in splitting the Democrats in two over the slavery issue. This remarkable feat brought Lincoln into the national limelight and the following year, 1859, he was asked to let his name go forward when the Republican Convention met to nominate their candidate for the presidency. At the Cooper Union Institute, New York, on 27 February 1860, Lincoln delivered a masterly speech dissociating the Republican cause from John Brown's recent attempt to foment a slave uprising, and thus gave the Republican Party a sober, responsible and conservative cast. One wonders whether the former cooper of Glasgow and Dundee, Illinois, was present on that momentous occasion.

Propitiously, the Republican National Convention was held on 16 May 1860 in Chicago. Although Lincoln was by no means the first choice of the delegates from the eastern states, and the matter was deadlocked, many of them combined with the western supporters of Lincoln and nominated him uproariously on the third ballot. In the subsequent presidential election in November, Lincoln polled only two million votes, out of four and a half million cast, and all but 24,000 of these were in the so-called Free States. Because of dissensions in the Democratic camp (which fielded two candidates, Douglas and Breckinridge) this minority of the popular vote was so distributed that it gave Lincoln the electoral college which put him into the White House.

On 13 February 1861 Congress met to ratify him formally, his term to commence on 4 March that year.

It may be supposed that Allan was one of those who voted for Lincoln. The Republican Party in its early days was the new broom in American politics, opposed to slavery even if not openly committed to abolitionism, and containing many radical elements whose left-wing views were pretty much in line with Allan's own outlook. Not until very much later did it become a more right-wing party, with a strong reactionary fringe.

A few weeks after the election, the crisis over slavery came to a head when Republican leaders travelled to Springfield to ask the President-elect if he was prepared to work out a compromise on the issue. In a speech on 20 December, however, Lincoln effectively closed the door. While he was prepared to uphold slavery in those states where it already existed, even to the extent of strenuously enforcing the law for the return of fugitive slaves to the South, he resolutely excluded the extension of slavery to those territories which had not yet attained statehood.[2] This was immediately greeted with anger and dismay in the South; on the very same day, therefore, South Carolina formally seceded from the Union.

Secession from the United States was nothing new; there had been talk of it, off and on, virtually since the United States emerged at the end of the War of Independence in the 1780s. Indeed, the Constitution which established the United States was only carried by a hair's breadth and the struggle between the centralising Federal government and the individual states had been long and, at times, bitter. On a previous occasion (1832) South Carolina had threatened to secede, and as recently as October 1860, fully a month before Lincoln was elected, Governor William H. Gist had sent out a secret circular to members of the state legislature hinting at possible action 'for the safety and protection of the State'. There were many anti-slavery leaders in the North who, in December 1860, would have been quite happy to cut the slave-owning states adrift. Conversely, many of Lincoln's fiercest opponents, including Stephen Douglas himself, put country before party and swung public opinion behind the Union. Illinois was a Free State but its southern counties were strongly sympathetic to the South and at the turn of the year there was much talk of armed rebellion. Lincoln's departure for Washington was delayed by the crisis in Illinois; he took up quarters in the Governor's office at Springfield and worked round the clock to find some way of averting the rebellion.

South Carolina's act of secession was soon emulated by the other southern states; from Mississippi on 9 January to Texas on 1 February, the state legislatures formally renounced membership of the United States. Three days later delegates of the first six states met at Montgomery, Alabama, and on 8 February produced a draft Constitution for the provisional government of the

Confederate States of America. The following day the provisional Congress elected as president Jefferson Davis of Mississippi, who was, up to that time, Secretary of War in the Federal government. Events moved on swiftly. Virtually all Federal arsenals and coastal fortifications on Confederate territory were seized and their garrisons disarmed. The Confederate Congress authorised the mobilisation of an army of 100,000 men and raised $15 million by means of an export tax on cotton. Eleven southern states, with a free population of five and a half million (and three and a half million slaves), were now ranged against the remaining twenty-three states with a population of twenty-three million.

Meanwhile, there was a strange lull in the North and something of a vacuum between the outgoing administration of James Buchanan and the arrival of the new President. As the date of the inauguration approached, Lincoln received invitations from the legislatures of Indiana, Ohio, Pennsylvania, New York, New Jersey and Massachusetts to visit them on his way to Washington. Many towns made similar invitations and the railroad companies offered to put executive cars at his disposal. Lincoln's staff arranged an itinerary that would take the President-elect through Indianapolis, Columbus, Cincinnati, Cleveland, Pittsburgh, Buffalo, Albany, New York, Trenton, Philadelphia and Harrisburg. Monday, 11 February, was fixed as the date of his departure from Springfield and a programme of special trains from point to point was arranged, extending to Saturday, 23 February, when he was scheduled to arrive in Washington.

Early on the Monday morning the presidential entourage gathered in the rather dingy little station at Springfield. A crowd numbering more than a thousand had gathered outside in the sleety drizzle to say farewell to Honest Abe. A strong wind was blowing, and the cold wet weather added to the gloom and depression of the event. In the spartan waiting-room, the great man took leave of his closest supporters before boarding the special train. He was accompanied by his wife Mary and three of their four sons, but there was also a considerable number of personal friends and local dignitaries. There was no presidential bodyguard, but Lincoln was surrounded by several military men, including Major David Hunter. The Hon. Norman Buel Judd was also in attendance, as the President's personal aide. As Lincoln made his slow, circuitous journey towards the nation's capital, other people joined the entourage for various sections while others left.

On 22 February, which happened to be Washington's Birthday and a public holiday, Lincoln was in Philadelphia where he made a rousing and highly emotional patriotic speech at Independence Hall. Later that day he delivered a speech before the legislature of Pennsylvania at Harrisburg. Touched by the impressive parade of Pennsylvania militia volunteers, Lincoln said, 'I do most sincerely hope that we shall have no use for them.' It was with the sombre thought of 'the shedding of fraternal blood' that he reboarded his train for the last leg of the journey. It had been planned that the President-elect would make a grand arrival in Washington the following afternoon, after spending the night in Baltimore.

On Saturday morning, however, the citizens of Washington awoke to the telegraphic announcement that Lincoln, after his long and triumphal journey, had suddenly abandoned his programme and made a rapid and secret night journey through Baltimore to the Federal capital. Public opinion at the time, and for many years afterwards, was puzzled by the event. Reaction ranged from the highest praise to the severest detraction, ridicule and denunciation. The true story only began to emerge two years after Lincoln's death. From the outset, rumours of an assassination plot in Baltimore (a city riddled with Southern sympathisers) were rife, but Lincoln himself, long after the event, merely stated, 'I did not then, nor do I now, believe I should have been assassinated, had I gone through Baltimore as first contemplated, but I thought it wise to run no risk, where no risk was necessary.'[3] The first person to reveal the plot was Samuel Morse Felton, the President of the Pennsylvania Central Railroad (as the Philadelphia, Wilmington and Baltimore Railroad was renamed). He had arranged the last stage of the presidential journey and was one of only four people privy to the sudden change of plans. Felton's revelation was confirmed by Norman Judd[4] and described at some length by Allan Pinkerton in his own book *The Spy of the Rebellion*, published in 1883. This book, written long after the event, was intended as a corrective to Ward Lamon's biography of Lincoln, published in 1872, which stoutly denied that a Confederate plot had existed and implied that Allan Pinkerton was a liar.[5] Remarkably, charge and counter-charge have continued to this day, part of the politically inspired detraction both of Lincoln and Pinkerton.

This extraordinary chain of events began several weeks before Lincoln's departure from Springfield. On 19 January Samuel Felton sent a brief note to Allan in Chicago, asking him to come as soon as possible to New York City on a matter of the greatest importance. Two days later Allan heard from the railroad president that he had received numerous threats from secessionists in and around Baltimore; they would blow up the line and destroy locomotives, bridges and tunnels if the North made any hostile moves against the South. As the line connected New York and Washington, it was of the greatest strategic importance to the Union. On the very day of this meeting, the Maryland legislature was hotly debating whether to follow the lead of South Carolina and secede. In the end this drastic step was only narrowly averted and the Federal government took immediate steps to strengthen its garrisons along the approach to Washington.

Allan returned to Chicago to mull over Felton's worrying predictions. On 27 January he replied at great length, outlining his plans to maintain security on the railroad. 'Should the suspicion of danger still exist' he himself would come to Baltimore with half a dozen of his top operatives, and do his best to infiltrate the secessionist organisations in order to monitor their plans and movements closely. In this seven-page document he stressed 'the tedious and very frequently slow operations' used by the Agency 'to attain a controlling power over the mind of the suspected parties'. Above all, he stressed to Felton the need for total secrecy. 'I would not consider it safe for myself or my operatives were the facts of my operating known to any politician, no matter of what school or of what position.' Far from seeking this business, Allan was reluctantly drawn into it, his letter ending brusquely, 'I have other matters pressing on me.'[6]

Felton agreed this course of action, and responded by immediately selecting two hundred of his most trusted railroad workers to guard the line between Susquehanna and Baltimore. These men were drilled secretly by night, but by day they were apparently employed in whitewashing the bridges, some of which acquired as many as eight coats, saturated with salt and alum to render then as fireproof as possible. On Pinkerton's advice, Felton also managed to infiltrate the three Maryland militia units to ascertain who were loyal to the Union and who were in league with the Confederacy.

As January drew to a wintry close, Allan and several of his best detectives set out for Baltimore. Timothy Webster and Hattie Lawton were sent to Perryville, in the northern part of Maryland, where Webster had heard rumours of a rebel organisation. Allan himself, under the alias of J.H. Hutcheson of Charleston, rented accommodation in an office building, immediately across the hallway from a leading secessionist named Luckett. With his assistant, Harry Davies, Allan merged into the local business community. The normally teetotal Pinkerton, in line with his assumed persona of the bluff, jovial Scotsman, began frequenting the pubs and taverns of Baltimore, identifying the Copperheads who made no secret of their hatred of Lincoln and the Union. Soon he was ingratiating himself with Luckett over a dram. Luckett introduced Allan to Cypriano Ferrandini, a wild-eyed fanatic who bluntly told him that 'murder of any kind is justifiable and right to save the rights of the Southern people'. Ferrandini had only recently come to America from Europe, but three years earlier he had been implicated in the Orsini plot to assassinate Napoleon III and had narrowly escaped the guillotine. Allan, as usual, began keeping company with the Italian revolutionary who was then working as a barber at Barnum's Hotel. Allan noted, on the evening of 5 February, that Ferrandini was 'a man well calculated for controlling and directing the ardent-minded. Even I, myself, felt the influence of this man's strange power, and wrong though I knew him to be, I felt strangely unable to keep my mind balanced against him.' Ferrandini had, by this time, become captain of one of the Maryland militia companies whose loyalty was decidedly suspect. In addition, he was drilling a sinister fifteen-man body called the Constitutional Guards and also involved with a shadowy formation known as the National Volunteers who were implicated, two months later, in a wave of rioting, murder, sabotage and bridge-burning throughout the state.[7]

Meanwhile, Davies had established a rapport with a Southern dandy of good family named Hillard, who was boasting openly that he was 'ready and willing to die to rid his country of a tyrant such as he considered Lincoln to be'. Davies accompanied Hillard on a late-night binge, which took in the bar of the Fountain Hotel and the Pagoda Concert Saloon before ending up at 'Anne Travise's house of prostitution, No. 70 Davis Street'. There Davies had to sit around while the gallant 'Hillard and his woman hugged and kissed each other for about an hour'. Afterwards, however, they talked secession till one in the morning, and Hillard boasted that he was working with Ferrandini 'to kill the President-elect as he walked through a narrow tunnel to the waiting Washington express' and agreed to take Davies to meet the Italian at Barnum's Hotel the following day.[8]

Webster went so far as to enlist in the Confederate militia cavalry and gleaned from some of its officers that as soon as news of the assassination reached them they would cut the telegraph lines and blow up the railway bridges to prevent Federal troops getting to Baltimore. These and similar reports from other Pinkerton operatives were wild and reckless in the extreme, but Allan could not afford to ignore or dismiss them. He deduced that the assassination would be carried out by a determined band, numbering 'not over fifteen or twenty men'. The whole of Baltimore was in a volatile condition; even the police chief, Marshal George P. Kane, was a notorious secessionist and the city was a hotbed of Southern agitators and spies. On 11 February, the very day that Lincoln set out, Allan sent a laconic telegram to Norman Judd, a prominent Chicago businessman, for many years a close friend of both Lincoln and Pinkerton, who was in charge of the presidential entourage: 'I have a message of importance for you – where can it reach you by special messenger?' Judd cabled back that he would be in Columbus on 13 February and Pittsburgh the day after, but before the message reached Allan he had already sent one of his most trusted operatives, named Scott, to Cincinnati where Judd received word of the plot to murder Lincoln as he passed through Baltimore. In Buffalo, where an over-enthusiastic mob of supporters had burst into Lincoln's hotel bedroom, severely injuring Major Hunter and dislocating his shoulder, Norman Judd received further details of the plot. The attempt on Lincoln would take place 'at the Calvert Street Station [Baltimore] until he can pass to the depot of the Washington branch Railroad. The danger will come from a small body of men, armed, prepared to give a life for a life.'

At four o'clock on 19 February Lincoln and his party checked in at the Astor House in New York. The previous evening Kate Warne had arrived from Baltimore and immediately sought out Judd with further information. She witnessed Lincoln's arrival and noted apprehensively that the President-elect was 'very pale and fatigued'. Judd had missed the presidential train at Albany and arrived more than two hours later. Kate had left a note in his pigeonhole and presently he visited her room where she handed over a sealed envelope from Allan. The contents alarmed Judd to the extent that he wanted to show the letter to Vice-President Hannibal Hamlin, but Kate emphasised that no one could be trusted, and that the only man who should be told was Lincoln himself – and then only if he considered it absolutely necessary.

Judd agreed to this and arranged for Allan to meet Lincoln in his room at the Continental Hotel in Philadelphia at six o'clock on the evening of 21 February. Judd, a florid-faced little man (whom one contemporary Washington newspaper described as 'a character of much more tact than talent, who is fully impressed with the onus of the mysterious position he occupies in relation to the President-elect'), fussed round Lincoln, strenuously urging him to take Allan's advice and proceed straight to Washington on the eleven o'clock train that night. 'If you follow the course suggested,' said Judd pompously, 'you will necessarily be subjected to the scoffs and sneers of your enemies, and the disapproval of your friends, who cannot be made to believe in the existence of so desperate a plot.' This passage, published a few years later, smacks of hindsight.[9]

Lincoln replied that he appreciated these suggestions, though he could stand anything that was necessary. But, he added, 'I cannot go tonight; I've promised to raise the flag over Independence Hall tomorrow morning, and then to visit the legislature at Harrisburg. Beyond that I have no engagements.'

The significance of this was that the territory of Kansas, which had been rent by civil war since 1854, was about to be admitted to the Union as a Free State, Washington's Birthday being deliberately chosen for this historic event. This meant the addition of a star to the national flag, and Lincoln would signal the entry of Kansas by ceremonially hoisting it for the first time. To duck out of these engagements in a loyal state such as Pennsylvania would have been politically disastrous. Hitherto, all Lincoln's movements had been made under the invitation and organisation of committees of legislatures, state governor and municipal authorities. No such invitation, however, had come from Maryland, where the only gesture of friendship had come from two private citizens; Mr Gittings, president of the Northern Central Railroad, who invited Lincoln and his family to dinner, and Mr Coleman of the Eutaw House who extended a similar invitation to Lincoln and his suite. While Lincoln appreciated these acts of personal courtesy he felt that, so far, there seemed little prospect of an official welcome from Maryland. Consequently he agreed to consider the matter carefully. Lincoln was not entirely convinced that there was a deliberate plot to murder him, but in the end he compromised; he would carry on with the engagements at Philadelphia and Harrisburg. If a delegation from Baltimore should meet him at Harrisburg, he would go on with them. If not, he would return to Philadelphia and review the situation.

Judd and Pinkerton devoted the rest of 21 February and nearly the whole of the night to a discussion of alternative arrangements. This meeting was attended by only two other men – Mr Franciscus, general manager of the Pennsylvania Railroad, and Henry Sanford, the son of Edward S. Sanford of the American Telegraph Company. At four in the morning they separated, having formulated a plan. Two hours later, in the cold light of dawn, Lincoln performed the flag-raising ceremony and was bundled aboard the Harrisburg train soon afterwards. Around midday the train rolled into the state capital and Lincoln was officially received by Governor Andrew Curtin of Pennsylvania. There was a reception at the State House, but that afternoon Lincoln and Judd divulged the change of plans to other members of the suite. There was a diversity of opinion and heated discussion before Judge David Davis turned to Lincoln and asked him what his judgement was in the matter. Lincoln replied, 'I've thought over this matter considerably, since I went over the ground with Pinkerton last night.'

Then he revealed that a warning had reached him just before leaving Philadelphia that morning. The messenger was Frederick W. Seward, son of William Seward, the Secretary of State who had received a tip from Lieutenant-General Winfield Scott, head of the United States Army. Scott had been informed by Colonel Stone (commanding the Washington District Militia) of an assassination plot which had been communicated to him by John A. Kennedy, Superintendent of Police of New York City, who had despatched one of his best detectives, David Bookstaver, to Washington with the message.

What Kennedy's detectives had uncovered was substantially the plot alleged by the Pinkertons. Lincoln questioned Fred Seward closely: 'Did you hear any names mentioned? Did you, for instance, ever hear anything said about such a name as Pinkerton?' This was the first time Seward had heard that name, though later he and Allan would become very close friends. This confirmation from an independent source finally decided Lincoln. Allan had told Lincoln that there was every likelihood that Marshal Kane, the chief of police, would not attempt to prevent the unruly elements in Baltimore disrupting the presidential progress. He had also pointed out that, in changing trains at Baltimore, the President-elect would have to travel from the Calvert

Street depot of the Northern Central Railroad to the Pennsylvania station more than a mile away. Making this short trip in an open carriage, as occasion demanded, would be tempting fate, and the point at which the carriageway ran through an underpass would be completely exposed to sniper fire.

After the State House reception in Harrisburg, the party broke up around four o'clock. The presidential suite returned to the Jones House, where they dined at five. Judd and Pinkerton in the meantime had been at the station finalising arrangements for the train. At 5.45 p.m. Judd returned to the hotel to collect Lincoln who got up from the dinner table, went to his room to change from evening dress to a travelling suit, and reappeared fifteen minutes later disguised in a long, threadbare military cloak and with a Tam o' Shanter woollen cap on his head.[10] As the group crossed the hotel lobby Judd told Ward Lamon in a low tone, 'Go ahead. As soon as Mr Lincoln is in the carriage, drive off; the crowd must not be allowed to identify him.' Lamon led the way to the carriage waiting at the side door and got in, followed by the strange figure in the shabby cloak and Scotch bonnet. Colonel Sumner was close behind, but Judd put his hand on his shoulder, and while Sumner was momentarily distracted the carriage sped off, much to Sumner's perplexed annoyance.

Lincoln and Lamon travelled alone on a special train laid on by the Pennsylvania Central Railroad from Harrisburg back to Philadelphia where they were met at the station by Allan Pinkerton. As soon as this train left Harrisburg a linesman of the American Telegraph Company was deputed to climb the poles at the station and cut all the wires in and out of Harrisburg, a drastic measure recommended by Edward Sanford to prevent Copperheads passing word of the President's departure to their friends along the line. Just before the wires were cut, Judd telegraphed Philadelphia to let 'Plums' (Allan's codename) know that 'Nuts' (Lincoln) had departed safely.

Meanwhile, Kate Warne hired the two rear sleeping-cabins of the Washington train 'for herself and an invalid brother' while Allan assigned every available operative to strategic positions along the route. Each one was told to flash a lantern as the train passed, as a signal to Allan (standing on guard on the rear platform of the train) that the tracks were clear. At 9.45 p.m. Allan silently greeted Lincoln and Lamon as the Harrisburg special came to a halt in the West Philadelphia depot. In the cold, draughty shed with its acrid reek of smoke, the tall figure, the collar of his cloak turned up against the freezing temperature as much as to disguise his craggy features, met the stocky, bearded detective. Here Lincoln and Lamon shook hands and parted company, the latter proffering the President a Derringer pocket pistol and a Bowie knife for his personal protection. Lincoln smiled as he declined the offer, but Pinkerton scowled. Later he would describe this incident, saying, 'I would not for the world have it said that Mr Lincoln had to enter the national Capitol armed. If fighting had to be done it must be done by others than Mr Lincoln.' Probably Allan said something to this effect at the time, but his tactlessness unnecessarily made him an enemy. Lamon never forgot the insult, and got his revenge eleven years later when he published his biography of Lincoln, in which he categorically declared that there had never been a plot. The whole conspiracy, he averred, was 'a mare's nest gotten up by the vainglorious detective [Pinkerton]'.

The party crossed to the Washington train. Samuel Felton himself led the way, followed by Allan and then Lincoln. Kate Warne was already on board and showed the President to his sleeping-cabin. When the conductor appeared it was Allan who gave him Lincoln's ticket. Three minutes later, the train set off dead on time. Allan went over the latest reports from his operatives, written and verbal, relayed by Kate, and then left her compartment to take up his vigil at the rear of the carriage. The trip to Washington went without incident, although there were some nervous moments. At 3.30 a.m. the train pulled into Baltimore and seemed to stop for an inordinate time at the platform. Later Allan described the tense situation:

> An officer of the road entered the car and whispered in my ear the welcome words 'All's well' . . . An hour and more the train waited for a connecting train from the west. A drunken traveler on the train platform sang 'Dixie', sang over and again how he would live and die in dear old Dixie. Lincoln murmured sleepily, 'No doubt there will be a great time in Dixie by and by'.

At six o'clock the following morning the train pulled into Washington and Allan helped the President down from the carriage. The two men were met at that ungodly hour by William Seward and E.B. Washburne and whisked off to Willard's Hotel on Pennsylvania Avenue. From here Allan sent a telegram to Judd, still in Harrisburg, 'Plums arrived with Nuts this morning'. Identical telegrams were transmitted to Felton and Sanford as well as to George Bangs in Chicago.

Ironically, in light of subsequent events, Lamon later wanted to telegraph the whole story to the *Chicago Journal* but Allan dissuaded him. In his biography of Lincoln (1872) Lamon, dismissing the plot as a nonsense, would write that afterwards Lincoln 'was convinced that he had committed a grave mistake in listening to the solicitations of a professional spy and of friends too easily alarmed'. When the Presidential Special from Harrisburg did arrive at Baltimore as scheduled, with Mary Todd Lincoln, her sons and the rest of the presidential entourage aboard, more than ten thousand people crowded the Calvert station. As the train halted, Lincoln being supposedly on board, the crowd gave three terrific cheers for the Confederacy, three more for Jeff Davis and three loud and prolonged groans for Lincoln. Had the President-elect been present, there is no doubt that his life would have been in jeopardy, plot or no plot.

After he had had a hot bath and a hearty breakfast, Allan went up to Lincoln's suite where he was formally thanked for his services, in front of Seward and a congressional delegation. Allan then caught the 3.10 p.m. train for Baltimore. At Annapolis Junction he caught up with the rest of Lincoln's entourage and was wryly amused by 'some very tall swearing'. At Baltimore station he bumped into Luckett, who 'was very excited and swore against those damned spies who had betrayed them'.

Colonel E.E. Ellsworth, who had been Lincoln's military aide at Philadelphia, was not so fortunate. A few weeks later, on 16 April, his regiment, the 6th Massachusetts Infantry, while marching through Baltimore, was attacked by a Copperhead mob; their commanding officer was shot dead.

In light of the 'mare's nest' started by Lamon in 1872, and which bobs up periodically to the present day, it is worth noting that although the Pinkerton archives covering this crucial period were destroyed in the Chicago fire of 1871, some five years previously William H. Herndon, Lincoln's erstwhile law partner, began collecting papers and memorabilia of the President shortly after his assassination. In August 1866 he wrote to Allan asking for copies of the Agency's reports on the Baltimore plot. In response Allan sent Herndon copies of all the relevant files. About 1870 Herndon sold his collection of Lincolniana to Lamon, then preparing his biography. Lamon appears not to have examined this collection carefully, else he might have taken care to destroy the three bulky files of Pinkerton papers. When his estate sold his papers to the Huntington Library in 1914 the papers were discovered and subsequently published. There is a curious tail-piece to this strange story. In November 1913 Mr and Mrs Archer Huntington were passengers aboard the SS *Olympic*, along with William A. Pinkerton, Allan's elder son. It is tempting to speculate that the idea of purchasing the Lamon Collection was put to Huntington by Willie on that occasion.

The collection was also found to contain a letter from Allan to Herndon, dated August 1866, requesting that:

All matters confidential about the Philadelphia, Wilmington & Baltimore R.R., also the name of the broker [Luckett] who occupied rooms adjoining me in Baltimore should be omitted as although he was undoubtedly a rebel at heart, yet he is a man of not much means; he has lost considerably during the war and the publication of his name might tend to serious injury in business. I deprecate this in any publication coming from my records.

Allan Pinkerton may have presented a flinty exterior, especially to the criminals he fought against so long and hard, but deep within the granite was a golden lode of generosity and kindliness. It is to his everlasting credit that he never lost sight of that feeling for his fellow man, especially for people who were down on their luck.[11]

• 6 •

Setting Up the Secret Service
1861

For secrets are edged tools,
And must be kept from children and from fools.

JOHN DRYDEN, *MARRIAGE À LA MODE*

Even if those in the highest circles had dismissed Allan Pinkerton as an alarmist, as Ward Lamon later implied, the detective was very soon proved right. The morning after his inauguration, Lincoln received the disquieting news that the Federal garrison at Fort Sumter, under virtual siege by the Confederate forces around Charleston harbour, was desperately short of provisions. So far, the rebels had made no move to eject Major Robert Anderson and his men, but sooner or later they would be starved into submission. As hinted in his inaugural speech, Lincoln hoped that the crisis would blow over and that a policy of conciliation and diplomacy would bring the rebel states back into the Union before long. Lincoln's Cabinet (9 March), facing the hopeless task of mounting a full-scale land and sea expedition involving an estimated 20,000 men (rather more than the total strength of the US armed forces at that time), were for the immediate evacuation of the fort. The sole dissent came from Postmaster General Montgomery Blair (a Maryland Democrat!) who all along favoured prompt and vigorous measures against the insurrection. By way of a compromise, Captain Gustavus Vasa Fox of the US Navy was sent to Charleston where a close friend, now a Confederate officer, introduced him to Governor Pickens and General Beauregard. Under Confederate escort, he was allowed to go out to the fort on 21 March under cover of darkness. His two-hour meeting with Major Anderson convinced him that the fort would not be able to hold out after 15 April.

Subsequently, Stephen A. Hurlbut, a prominent Chicago businessman and lawyer who had been born in Charleston, was sent south, accompanied by none

other than Ward Lamon. While Lamon was hobnobbing with the young secessionists at the Charleston Hotel, Hurlbut was quietly visiting family and friends
and assessing the situation. In light of Hurlbut's report, Lincoln, advised by
General Scott, told his Cabinet on 28 March that Sumter was to be evacuated.
Nevertheless, a few days later he was giving orders to Captain Fox to prepare an
expedition to relieve the forts. This was a period of indecision; the danger of
letting the Confederates get away with it was recognised, but the desire for peace
was strong and the initial anger against the seceding states had given way to
lethargy. It is probable that the crisis would have run out of momentum if left to
its own devices, but the Confederacy committed an act of the most extreme folly.
On 12 April, with no sign of a relieving force, Major Anderson was on the point
of surrender, when suddenly the guns of Fort Moultrie opened fire. The
bombardment of Fort Sumter, a totally unnecessary act, changed the situation
utterly. Immediately the North was galvanised into action and America
embarked on a deadly conflict that would last for four years.

Anderson surrendered on 14 April. Eight days later, Lincoln received two
letters. The first was from Norman Judd, the second from Allan Pinkerton.
Judd, addressing the President familiarly as 'Dear Lincoln', reminded him that
the Pinkerton Agency had a well-trained force of detectives, prepared to go
anywhere:

> I believe that no force can be used to so good advantage in obtaining
> information. His men can live in Richmond and elsewhere with perfect
> safety. Of course profound secrecy is the keynote to success. If you approve,
> Pinkerton can come to Washington and arrange the details. I have no doubt
> the importance of this, surrounded as you are by traitors . . . our people
> expect you will call out immediately 300,000 men and that they will not
> remain cooped up in Washington waiting for events but that your active
> military will be in Virginia with Richmond as its seat. Aggression is the only
> policy now . . . our people are crazy with excitement and furor.[1]

Allan's letter, addressed to 'His Excellency A. Lincoln, Prest. of the U.S.',
was less emotional, more carefully considered:

> When I saw you last I said that if the time should ever come that I could be
> of service to you I was ready. If that time has come I am on hand.
>
> I have in my Force from Sixteen to Eighteen persons on whose Courage,
> Skill and Devotion to their country I can rely. If they with myself at the head
> can be of service in the way of obtaining information of the movements of
> Traitors, or Safely conveying your letters or dispatches, on that class of
> Secret Service which is the most dangerous, I am at your command.

In the present disturbed state of affairs I dare not trust this to the mail, so send by one of My Force who was with me at Baltimore. You may safely trust him with any Message for me – written or verbal. I fully guarantee his fidelity. He will act as you direct and return here with your answer.

Secrecy is the great lever I propose to operate with. Hence the necessity of this movement (if you contemplate it) being kept *Strictly Private*, and that should you desire another interview with the Bearer that you should so arrange it as that he will not be noticed.

The bearer will hand you a copy of a Telegraph Cipher which you may use if you desire to telegraph me.

My Force comprises both Sexes – all of good character and well skilled in their business.

The bearer of these letters was Timothy Webster, the English-born operative who had been with the Agency since 1853. Lincoln immediately gave him a brief written reply, asking Allan to come to Washington as soon as possible 'for your services are greatly for the government'. Webster screwed up the flimsy paper into a tiny ball and concealed it in the head of his walking-cane. Back in Chicago, Allan delegated the day-to-day business to George Bangs and set off at once for the national capital. In Washington on 3 May he had a meeting with Lincoln and his Cabinet, at which he was asked how he would go about keeping the vast number of Southern sympathisers under surveillance. Later he would recall that 'I stated to them my ideas which I had entertained upon the subject . . . and after I concluded I took my departure, with the understanding that I would receive further communications from them in a few days'.[2]

Allan hung around Washington, kicking his heels for several days, but when the expected message from the executive mansion never came, he set off for Chicago in high dudgeon. Years later he commented ruefully that he had 'seen all along that the confusion in government had been too great for anything systematic to be done'. This was true enough; there was a long-established tradition of muddling through and no one could comprehend the magnitude of the crisis, but Allan was mortified at the President's seeming neglect. 'I felt confident that I would be required to wait a longer time than I could conveniently spare from my business.'

At Philadelphia on 6 May he called at the post office for mail forwarded from Chicago, and there found a letter from his old friend of the Illinois Central Railroad, George McClellan. On the very day that Allan's letter reached the President, McClellan, now General Superintendent of the Eastern and Western Divisions of the Ohio and Mississippi Railroad, had been approached by several of his political contacts, as well as old comrades in the army, and offered a variety of senior military commands. In the end, however,

McClellan chose the job of raising a division of militiamen from Ohio, with the rank of major-general. This was an immense task, for the state arsenal at Columbus had little equipment, and much of that dated from the War of Independence. He had no money, few officers and men, no orders and no supplies. To make matters worse, Ohio was cut off from Washington by the riots in Baltimore, and the neighbouring state of Kentucky was unstable, with Confederate sentiment growing stronger by the day. The tireless energy and organisational genius that had taken the young engineer to the head of one of the country's largest railroads was soon harnessed to the war effort. Within days the militia general was submitting a report to the General-in-Chief, Lieutenant-General Scott, in Washington suggesting a unified command structure to face the menace on the western frontier. On 3 May McClellan was placed in command of the Department of the Ohio, which included the states of Indiana and Illinois as well as Ohio. A few days later western Pennsylvania and part of West Virginia were added. On 14 May he was appointed a major-general in the regular army. McClellan was then aged thirty-four and his appointment effectively made him the highest-ranking officer of the army, after General Scott himself.

McClellan's most pressing problem, on assuming command of the Department of the Ohio, was a complete lack of a staff. He promptly commissioned his father-in-law Randolph B. Marcy as a major and chief-of-staff, and his old friend Seth Williams as major and adjutant-general. Both men later became brigadier-generals as the work expanded. Without a trained staff and efficient administration, an army is incapable of movement. This was a lesson McClellan had learned during his time in the Crimea, but it was a lesson which the Union army as a whole was slow to grasp. Military intelligence was another matter which was then barely understood and certainly undervalued. This appears to be borne out by the Cabinet's seeming indifference when Allan put his ideas to Lincoln on 3 May; but it was fortunate that, more or less simultaneously, George McClellan had come up with the same idea. The letter which caught up with Allan on 6 May asked him to come at once to McClellan's headquarters in Cincinnati. Interestingly, McClellan told him to come secretly, using his Christian name as an alias. Allan had previously done this at Washington when escorting Lincoln from Baltimore. From Philadelphia Allan wrote back to McClellan immediately:

Confidential. From what I learned from the President on the 3rd inst. – I believe your appointment as Commander in Chief of the forces in the West is secure – I learned that General Scott had told the President that he considered you an abler officer than Beauregard, etc., etc. – I could only say to the President what I knew of you. Governor Dennison's [of Ohio] letter to the President calling attention to your plan had a marked effect. I do not know as you are aware that the Plot to assassinate the President was discovered by me – and that it was with me he made the passage through Baltimore. Please to destroy this when read. Respectfully yours, A.P.[3]

Fortunately for posterity, McClellan did not destroy this letter, but carefully filed it. Pausing briefly in Chicago to deal with only the most pressing matters, Allan set out for Cincinnati. On the way, however, he stopped off at Pittsburgh where his most valued operative, Timothy Webster, was languishing in gaol, having narrowly escaped a lynching as a suspected Confederate spy. Fortunately Allan knew the police chief well and immediately secured Webster's release. Together they travelled on to Cincinnati and the following day were ensconced in the parlour of McClellan's mansion on Ludlow Street. Originally McClellan had intended to establish his headquarters at Camp Dennison, sixteen miles north-west of the city where thousands of raw recruits were even then being turned into fighting soldiers, but the press of official business kept him in town. Thus his home was turned into general headquarters, reflecting the makeshift nature of the way the Union went to war.

McClellan asked Allan to organise a Secret Service Department for his army. Allan was embarrassed at first, saying that Lincoln had proposed something similar for the US Army as a whole, but he admitted that he had left Washington 'without arriving at any definite understanding with the President'. McClellan persuaded Allan to give the Agency's services to the Department of the Ohio, and Allan eventually agreed, subject to approval from General Scott. A telegram was sent to Washington the same day, and Scott cabled his endorsement. Within a couple of days Allan and Webster organised McClellan's Secret Service, establishing its headquarters in an office block in the centre of Cincinnati. Thither came Allan's most experienced operatives, including Sam Bridgeman, a Virginian who had seen active service in the Mexican War before becoming a detective with the New York and Chicago police; John C. Babcock, a crack shot with the Sturgis Rifle Corps in Chicago; Gustav H. Thiel, who would later set up a rival detective agency and become a bitter rival; Seth Paine, resourceful and intrepid to the point of recklessness, who became one of Allan's best agents behind enemy lines; and the English-born John Scully. Kate Warne and Hattie Lawton were the female agents, proving their value many times over. The urbane Englishman, Pryce Lewis, joined the team later; at this crucial period he was actually in Mississippi investigating a murder. In charge of the field agents was Timothy Webster.

By 13 May the secret service swung into operation. On that day Allan himself travelled, under the alias of E.J. Allen, to Louisville, Kentucky, and witnessed his first slave auction, an incident that caused such utter revulsion that he hardened his resolve to do everything in his power, regardless of personal cost, to bring this vile trade to an end. Webster moved southwards to Memphis, Tennessee, and thence to Bowling Green and Clarksville, while Allan himself moved slowly through Kentucky into eastern Tennessee. By all accounts Webster's dangerous journey was a great success. Cultivating the persona of a Maryland Copperhead (which had almost brought him to a rope's end in Pittsburgh), the quiet-spoken Englishman easily made friends in the towns and villages of Tennessee and had no difficulty in inspecting the Confederate military preparations.

The extremely detailed reports compiled by Allan and his agents in the field gave McClellan a very accurate picture of Confederate forces in Tennessee and Kentucky, but they also got wind of the ordinance of secession passed by the Virginia convention (a breakaway element of the state legislature which met in secret) on 17 April, and the covert alliance with the Confederacy concluded a week later. Pinkerton agents learned that the Governor of Virginia had called out ten thousand troops, under the command of Colonel Robert E. Lee, at that time one of the most senior and experienced officers of the US Army. Acting on Allan's reports from Kentucky, McClellan was keen to send troops into that state but decided to hold back until after imminent elections there had been held.

On 8 June 1861 Sam Gill, a classmate of McClellan at West Point who was now superintendent of the Louisville and Lexington Railroad in Kentucky, telegraphed McClellan saying that Simon Bolivar Buckner wished to see him and enquired whether he would be at home. Captain Buckner was a close friend of Gill and likewise a West Pointer with whom McClellan had served in the Mexican War and later on the staff at the Military Academy. McClellan telegraphed in return that he would be glad to see his two old friends that night, and accordingly they came to the general's home about ten o'clock. Kentucky at this point was still neutral, hence the smooth operation of railway and telegraphic communications with Ohio. McClellan received his friends alone and they spent the night discussing the condition of affairs in Kentucky. Buckner brought no credentials from Governor McGoffin, and McClellan did not assume that Buckner was empowered to make any arrangements in his name. At that time Buckner was the commander of a small but élite force, the Kentucky State Guards, and was military adviser to the Governor, but Kentucky had not mobilised troops. The purpose of the meeting was to compare views and see if anything could be done to reduce the tension along the border.

In particular, Buckner wished to know what McClellan, as commander of the Union forces, would do in the event that Kentucky was occupied by Confederate forces under General Pillow, then massed in Tennessee near the

Kentucky border. Buckner was anxious to maintain Kentucky's neutrality and promised to drive Pillow's men out of the state should they cross the line. McClellan agreed to this, so long as Buckner's forces acted promptly, but added, 'You'd better be quick about it, Simon, for if I learn that the rebels are in Kentucky I will, with or without orders, drive them out without delay.'

Five days later McClellan was in Cairo, Illinois, on a tour of inspection when he bumped into Buckner who had come, with a three-man delegation from Kentucky, to protest at the cutting down of a secessionist banner at Columbus, Kentucky, by a Union gunboat, and also about the incursion into his state a few days later by Union troops under General Prentiss. A conversation took place, in the presence of John M. Douglass, a friend of Lincoln. McClellan bluntly told Buckner that if secession flags were hoisted on the Kentucky riverbank, Union forces would continue to cut them down. Furthermore, if the secessionists in Kentucky continued to harass and intimidate people who were loyal to the Union he could not restrain his subordinates from aiding these loyalists.

McClellan thus made his position quite clear, but Buckner shortly afterwards sent a letter to Governor McGoffin saying that McClellan had agreed to respect the neutrality of Kentucky. This letter was subsequently published and did McClellan considerable damage. The Yankee press seized on it and inflated a chance meeting into an official treaty. The incident caused a furore, not only along the Ohio River but in Washington itself. Allan Pinkerton himself became embroiled in the affair. Sadly, McClellan has suffered at the hands of posterity, and in spite of the scholarly reassessment of his career in recent years, there is still a general belief that he was timid and indecisive at a critical point in the war.[4] The reversal of this verdict began with the detailed biography by Myers in 1934 and was confirmed by Eckenrode and Conrad in 1941. The latter were purely military historians who made a detailed study of all McClellan's campaigns and battles and came to the conclusion that McClellan was a great general who had been underestimated. They concluded that it was McClellan who prevented the defeat of the North in 1861–62 when the Confederacy was relatively stronger than in the latter stages of the war. Ironically, both men were Southerners, working for the Virginia Historical Commission, but they were solely concerned to set the record straight. As there seemed to be no military reasons for the animadversions cast on McClellan, they concluded that the hostile feeling towards him was politically motivated.[5]

Unfortunately, the simplistic popular view seems to have been shared by Horan, and this also coloured his judgement of Allan Pinkerton:

The detective idolized McClellan so completely and unquestioningly, his usual good common sense always appeared to be badly tilted. He soon took on the role of McClellan's protector, with no protest from the general. In June, 1861, for the first time Pinkerton came to his general's defense against the Washington 'cabal' as he called it.[6]

Horan swallowed the tale of McClellan entering into a secret agreement with 'General' Simon Buckner of Kentucky (in fact, Buckner's commission as a brigadier-general only came in October, after the Union invasion of Kentucky propelled that state into the war on the Confederate side). Horan, in fact, reproduced Allan's telegram to the President, sent from Cincinnati on 26 June:

> The report of compact having been made with Buckner of Kentucky by Genl. McClellan stipulating not to occupy or enter that state is completely untrue. Buckner has been profuse in offers to keep secession troops out of Ky. but Genl McClellan has offered him no consideration in return. I have personal knowledge of this.[7]

Horan went so far as to say that Pinkerton was even prepared to lie to his President to protect his idol, implying that the detective had no first-hand knowledge of the encounter. Allan, in fact, had been with McClellan that fateful day in Cairo when they ran into Buckner. Allan also wrote to McClellan the same day:

> The statement of Buckner in regard to the arrangement made with you is creating great excitement. You should take immediate steps to rebut it as evil disposed persons are using this to your injury at Washington and I fear may produce some effect. I have telegraphed the President a denial of Buckner's statements as published.[8]

Allan also sent substantially the same telegrams to Thomas A. Scott (Assistant Secretary of War) and Simon Cameron (Secretary of War). As a result, McClellan wired Douglass and he telegraphed back at considerable length giving his version. Independently, Sam Gill wrote to McClellan from Louisville saying that he had questioned Buckner who denied authorship of the report, with the explanation that Governor McGoffin had published his own version of it solely with the good intention of quelling agitation in Kentucky. This controversy was a hint to McClellan that there would always be people of partisan or jealous disposition only too ready to attack him or make capital out of any seeming mistake on his part, in order to belittle or supplant him. Sadly, it also showed how two honourable and well-intentioned men, as McClellan and Buckner, could be led to take such opposite views of the same matter, and subject to such different interpretations.[9]

Pinkerton's spirited intercession with the President on McClellan's behalf had the desired effect. Far from the incident destroying the general's career, he was soon to be called to greater things. In the meantime, he sought a detailed survey of the districts south of the Ohio River, in the states of Kentucky, North Carolina, Mississippi and Louisiana. This was a task which Allan undertook with relish. Pretending to be a 'gentleman from Georgia', he purchased 'a splendid bay' and embarked on the most hazardous adventure of his career so far. He had some narrow escapes from Southern justice, and on one occasion was recognised by a German barber he had known in Chicago and almost betrayed inadvertently. By 18 July, the day of the Union disaster at Bull Run when Washington itself was almost overrun by Confederate forces, Allan was back in Cincinnati filing a lengthy report on his trip behind the lines. This was written in his own neat handwriting and ran to many pages, with precise, detailed information, of which this gives the flavour:

> The Rebels have sunk two boats loaded with stone at the mouth of the Kanawha River near the Red House Shoals twenty or thirty miles from Charleston [West Virginia], and they are now erecting a battery of two six pounders concealed by bushes . . . there are fifteen hundred troops in the Kanawha Valley, about one thousand near Charleston, say about one mile below on the level ground by the river and about five hundred at the mouth of the Cold near Charleston . . . there are only fifty soldiers at the Red House . . . they had little ammunition at either of the above places . . . the soldiers are equipped with muskets and poor rifles and with the exception of the Kanawha Rangers (100 strong) were very poor specimens of mortality, many not exceeding fifteen years of age . . .[10]

Meticulous attention to detail, long the hallmark of Allan's work, was evident in this report. Describing Confederate breastworks, for example, he gave exact specifications of thickness, height, type of timber used, the precise location of batteries and the calibre of guns. An invaluable aspect of the report consisted of names and descriptions of Union sympathisers who could be expected to 'furnish experienced help'.

Almost as soon as this report was completed, Allan was off again. Out of this trip came a second report, concentrating on the roads that intersected the strategically important Kanawha Turnpike, with a wealth of detail concerning the number and type of bridges, and the depth, width and quality of streams and rivers. He also sought out loyalists, an extremely dangerous procedure in unfamiliar territory even for an experienced spy, which Allan, at this time, was not. Whether by luck or good judgement, however, he returned unscathed to report to McClellan on armed mountain men 'ready to act at a moment's notice for the government'. There were excellent pen portraits of Colonel Tompkins, commander of the Confederate forces in the Kanawha Valley, and Colonel Dickerson, 'one of the wealthiest men in the district who is a strong Union man', whose son was a staunch loyalist and would make an excellent scout. On the strength of these reports, McClellan launched an attack on West Virginia, though his troops were still only half-trained.

It will be remembered that Virginia had formed a secret alliance with the Confederacy and seceded from the Union on 17 April. Beyond the Allegheny mountain ranges, however, the western part of the state was believed to be generally well disposed to the Union. The state government at Richmond (soon to become the Confederate capital) countered this by sending a regiment of raw troops under Colonel G.A. Porterfield, who cut the Baltimore and Ohio Railroad near Grafton and disrupted communications between Washington and the West. In May McClellan had immediately sent a small force which surprised and routed Porterfield's troops at Philippi on 3 June. The Confederates then sent four thousand men to reinforce Porterfield, fearing that McClellan might advance from the west to the Shenandoah Valley and outflank the armies of Beauregard and Joseph Johnston, then located in northern Virginia and threatening Washington. While the main Union army was in complete disorder after Bull Run and Manassas, McClellan's Army of the Ohio was enjoying spectacular success in the Kanawha Valley, thanks in no small measure to his superior staff work and excellent field intelligence.

In addition to Allan's first-hand reports, McClellan had the despatches of Allan's operative, Pryce Lewis. It will be recalled that Lewis was busy on a murder enquiry in Mississippi when the war erupted in April. Apart from ruling out the chief suspect, Lewis's investigations were inconclusive, but he used his time well to observe the preparations for war which were going on all around him. On his return to Chicago on 11 June he went on to Cincinnati for a thorough debriefing. From this came a detailed memorandum which McClellan, in due course, forwarded to Simon Cameron in Washington.

McClellan's letters to his wife are very revealing in this period. 'Everything here needs the hand of the master and is getting it fast,' he wrote on 23 June. In a letter of 7 July he confessed, 'I have been obliged to inflict some severe punishments, and I presume the papers of the Western Reserve will be hard down on me for disgracing some of their friends guilty of the small crime of burglary.' This alluded to a criminal matter which Allan, in addition to his espionage, was asked to investigate. In no time Allan had uncovered a network of thieves who were looting military stores in the vicinity of Parkersburg. The culprits were arrested and sentenced to hard labour at the Federal fortress in the Dry Tortugas, an isolated island group beyond the Florida Keys which was used as a penal settlement and remained in Union hands throughout the war.

In connection with McClellan's campaign in West Virginia, Allan sent Pryce Lewis behind the lines, posing as Lord Tracy, an English aristocrat on a cotton-buying trip. Allan went so far as to purchase a gleaming carriage and 'a team of the finest bay horses' so that Lewis could play the part in style. The coach boot was stocked with several cases of imported champagne, a case of port and a box of the best Cuban cigars. Sam Bridgeman was given the role of footman and, according to Lewis, 'handled the reins in a style worthy of a turnout in Pall Mall or Piccadilly'. Allan even lent Lewis his gold half-hunter watch and diamond ring, charging him to take good care of them. Lewis, tall, elegant and well groomed, certainly looked the part. He was dressed in the finest broadcloth of the latest English style and a shiny new top hat, while his purse 'bulged with an abundance of English sovereigns' and in his coat pocket was 'a handsome cigar case with the British lion in ivory conspicuously embossed on it'. At this time British sympathies were mainly with the Confederacy, so Lewis had no difficulty in travelling freely around Virginia, being warmly welcomed and entertained wherever he went.

The details of the exploits of 'the Spy in the Top Hat' need not concern us; Lewis himself produced a racy account of his adventures which was published many years later.[11] There was a hair-raising encounter with a fire-eating young colonel by the name of George S. Patton (grandfather of 'Old Blood and Guts') whom Lewis utterly charmed, cracking a bottle of his vintage champagne with him. But the chief significance of Lewis's reports are that they give the lie to a canard which grew later and endures to this day. Even Horan was taken in by this myth and wrote: 'Relying on what he saw or heard, Pinkerton was an excellent spy behind the lines, but as a front-line analyzer of the reports of other agents, he would prove to be totally incompetent.'[12]

It has frequently been alleged that Allan Pinkerton's agents were unskilled in military matters and therefore unable to assess the strength and disposition of the enemy; that he was given to exaggerating numbers, and that this, in turn, made McClellan over-cautious, with disastrous results on the course of the war. If this were true, then Allan should be blamed that the war did not end in 1862, but dragged on, with immense loss of life on both sides, until 1865. As this grave imputation rests on Allan's faulty or inaccurate assessment of his agents' field reports, it is necessary to examine them. Nowhere in the voluminous reports or in Pinkerton's correspondence, either with McClellan or with the President himself, is there a shred of evidence to support these suppositions. Once more, one can only assume that this slur on Allan's competence was part of the political campaign in Washington that engineered McClellan's downfall in 1862.

For example, it has often been alleged that Pinkerton agents relied too heavily on second-hand information and were only too ready to accept what they were told without checking it out. As an example to the contrary, however, one may cite the incident when Lewis and Bridgeman returned to Union field headquarters at the Red House. The Union commander, Brigadier-General Jacob D. Cox, told Lewis that he had been informed by Colonel Guthrie, encamped several miles away, that 'two good Union men, Virginians' had come into his camp to report that General Henry A. Wise had 60,000 Confederate troops deployed on the road to Charleston, West Virginia. As a result, the Union advance through the Kanawha Valley had come to a halt, with Cox wiring to McClellan for urgent reinforcements which were just not available.

Lewis, on the other hand, reported that Wise's army numbered 5,500 at most, and denounced the report of the 'two good Union men' as a piece of Confederate disinformation. Lewis was so convincing that Cox acted resolutely and advanced on Charleston, defeating Wise and scattering his forces. While the North was reeling under the massive defeat at Bull Run there was some crumb of comfort to be had from McClellan's successes in the same crucial period. The West Virginia campaign may have been nothing more than a side show and its battles comparatively insignificant, but the newspapers of the North and West eagerly seized on them and magnified McClellan's victories. He was hyped as a great conqueror and the epithet the 'Young Napoleon' was freely used. To be sure, McClellan played this up for all it was worth, with speeches to his men and orders of the day couched in Napoleonic language.

Allan now wished to send Lewis and Bridgeman to Baltimore where the situation was rapidly deteriorating in the aftermath of the débâcle at Bull Run, but on the day they were due to set out Bridgeman went on a drinking spree. Allan was beside himself with rage and sacked the drunken detective on the spot. Bridgeman, coming to his senses, pleaded with Lewis to intercede on his behalf. Later Lewis recalled Bridgeman 'shaking from the whiskey, swearing he would never let liquor again touch his lips'. Allan relented, but not before he gave the hungover recalcitrant the rough edge of his tongue.

Pinkerton agents were already under cover in Baltimore, for it was there that they gained an extremely valuable piece of information concerning William Lowndes Yancey, one of the Confederacy's chief agents, which Allan conveyed to Lincoln on 19 July:

I have positive information from a reliable source of T. Butler King of Georgia, now in England, being on his return home – W.L. Yancey is expected to be with him. They are to pass through the Northern States in disguise. Should you desire it, I can arrange to have them arrested at some convenient point in the Loyal States. It occurred to me that it might be advisable to have a few such hostages should the Rebels undertake to carry out their threats of retaliating on loyal men now their prisoners.

It is essential to success in this matter that I should have a reply at as early a moment as possible as I have much Mental machinery to move before my plans are perfected. And the traitors are expected soon.

The source of my information is such that if you can consistently keep this matter to yourself you would oblige me.

Read in modern terms, this seems an extraordinary letter from Allan to be writing to his President, and indeed it led some previous writers to criticise Allan for his lack of trust, and for his arrogant presumption. But in the context of 1861 the insistence on secrecy was only too necessary. Allan was acutely aware of flagrant breaches of security in the White House and the need to be on a constant guard against Copperheads – Northerners who secretly sympathised with the South.

On the day after the battle of Bull Run, the Adjutant General, Lorenzo Thomas, sent a despatch to McClellan ordering him to Washington forthwith. McClellan, then at Wheeling, West Virginia, handed over command of the Department of the Ohio to General W.S. Rosecrans. Early on the morning of 23 July McClellan, accompanied by his chief of staff, Seth Williams, rode forty-eight miles to the nearest railhead and caught a train for the capital. The day before, he received a note from Allan saying, 'The hopes of the nation now are upon you. – All, All say McClellan is the man. He can and will carry our Flag to victory.' McClellan replied, saying, 'Keep me fully posted and be prepared to hear from me that I need your services elsewhere. I do not know what exactly the position is that I am to occupy in Washington. Thank you for your good wishes.' With this letter McClellan enclosed a draft authorising payment of $1,000 to Allan for his secret service work to date. When Allan submitted the draft to the paymaster general at Washington it was accepted, but months passed before the money was paid over, the government accountants being unsure what it was to be charged to.

McClellan reached Washington late in the afternoon of Friday, 26 July, and reported to General Scott that evening. The following day he had an audience with the President, who told him that he was now in command of the Army of the Potomac, responsible for the defence of Washington against imminent attack. He had not been in the capital more than twenty-four hours when he fell foul of the crusty general-in-chief, piqued because Lincoln had asked the young general to attend a Cabinet meeting. Winfield Scott, angered that he himself was excluded, sent McClellan off on a wild-goose chase – rounding up stragglers from Bull Run who were believed to be skulking in the suburbs. This footling exercise taught him not only about the touchiness of his commander but introduced him to the utter chaos then prevailing in Washington.

One of McClellan's first acts, therefore, was to write to Pinkerton, saying that he needed him to set up a secret service for the Army of the Potomac. Later Allan recalled:

> I was to have as much strength of force as I required. It was arranged I was to go whenever the army moved. I was to go forward with the General, so that I might always be in communication with him. My corps was to be continually occupied in procuring, from all possible sources, information regarding the strength, position and movements of the enemy. All spies, counter brands, deserters, refugees and prisoners of war coming into our lines from the front were to be carefully examined by me, and their statements taken in writing.

Under the name of Major E.J. Allen, Pinkerton was assigned to the Provost Marshal, Colonel Andrew Porter, formerly of the 16th United States Infantry, but later he would report directly to the Assistant Secretary of War, Thomas A. Scott. Born in Pennsylvania in 1823, Scott had been orphaned at ten and forced to go to work to help support his widowed mother and ten siblings. By 1840 he was a clerk in the office of state tolls and a decade later had become a station agent for the Pennsylvania Railroad at Duncansville, then the western terminal. When the line to Pittsburgh was opened in 1852 Scott was made third assistant superintendent of the Western Division with his office in Pittsburgh. Handsome, charming and tactful, he proved to be an outstanding administrator and a born leader who inspired his employees. One of these was a young telegraph operator named Andrew Carnegie, whose Chartist family had migrated from Dunfermline in 1848. The pint-sized telegraphist caught Scott's eye by his bustling efficiency and chirpy outlook, and from the outset Scott took an avuncular interest in the lad, referring to him as 'my boy, Andy'. Soon the term was being adapted by other railroad staff; in 1853, at the age of seventeen, 'Mr Scott's Andy' was selected by the superintendent as his personal telegraphist. Thereafter, as Scott moved up the corporate ladder, young Andy followed in his wake. The personal telegraphist became private secretary and then office administrator, rising to each new challenge with flair and immense self-confidence. Ten days after the fall of Fort Sumter, Scott (then vice-president of the Pennsylvania Railroad) was summoned by Simon Cameron to become his right-hand man, his immediate task being to restore communications between Washington and the North.

In the nation's capital, Scott found utter chaos; the vital rail link with the North had been destroyed by the Maryland Secessionists. Instinctively he, in turn, summoned Carnegie who arrived in Philadelphia on 20 April with a band of hand-picked railmen. Under Andy's supervision, the railroad crew, backed by the 800 troops of General Ben Butler's Eighth Massachusetts Infantry, repaired the line, rebuilt the bridges and restored the telegraph wires. Carnegie was on the footplate of the first train to enter Washington, his face streaming with blood from a whiplash telegraph wire that gashed his cheek and forehead. Later in life, Carnegie would boast that he had been the first man wounded in the defence of the capital.

At the War Department, Carnegie organised the rail communications and the Military Telegraphers Corps. He worked twenty hours a day, suffered severe sunstroke that summer and in his weakened state feared that he would contract typhoid which was endemic in the crowded military camps ringing the capital. By September 1861, therefore, he was back in his prewar job as supervisor of the Western Division in Pennsylvania, but his six months at the War Department had been crucial. In that period he worked closely with Allan Pinkerton who, like many others, tended to adopt a paternal attitude to the tiny Scotsman. Allan, who stood only five-foot eight himself, positively towered over Andy whose height was a mere five-foot three, but he very soon discovered the fire and mettle in the little fellow, and that same single-minded ruthlessness that eternally drove himself. After his return to Pittsburgh, Carnegie continued to work closely with Allan in security aspects of the military telegraphs and railroad services.[13] Their collaboration in 1861 laid the foundations of a lifelong friendship, but eight years after Allan's death the names of Pinkerton and Carnegie would be linked in the blackest episode in the history of American labour, the tragic Homestead strike.

Before closing down his Cincinnati headquarters, Allan sent Timothy Webster back into Tennessee. Over the ensuing weeks the good-looking and affable Webster engaged in casual conversation with countless Confederate officers, soldiers and civilians and by piecing together a snatch here, a snippet there, compiled massively detailed reports, with exact numbers and precise troop movements. Once more, these meticulous reports give the lie to the notion that Pinkerton agents were incompetent. Webster's reports are extremely illuminating on all manner of subjects: of how the rebels had seized 3,000 pairs of Yankee handcuffs at Bull Run, or how farmers along the border were openly trading with the enemy, and how beans and bacon packed in Cincinnati were finding their way to the Confederate armies. At the end of his assignment Webster coolly obtained a pass signed by none other than Judah P. Benjamin, the Confederate Secretary of War, and crossed the lines at New Albany, Kentucky, to report to Pinkerton in Washington.

In Washington, Allan was soon bogged down in a sea of paper. His immediate concern was to root out corruption in the commissary department. His reports on the fiddles then going on make fascinating reading. In colourful language Allan commented on one Chicago abattoir butchering cows that were 'almost skeletons, and steers with thirteen wrinkles on their horns'.

Soon, however, he had an infinitely more serious matter on his hands.

·7·

The Wild Rose of the Confederacy
1861–62

When shall the stars be blown about the sky,
Like the sparks blown out of a smithy, and die?
Surely thine hour has come, thy great wind blows,
Far-off, most secret, and inviolate Rose?

WILLIAM BUTLER YEATS, *THE SECRET ROSE*

Washington in 1861 was a fascinating place but, after only six decades as the national capital, it still had a half-made air about it. It was no longer a sleepy little Southern town; even before Lincoln's inauguration it had begun to swell like one of General McClellan's new-fangled observation balloons. Twelve months later it had become the desperately overcrowded general headquarters of a nation at war. Considering the vast size of the country, it was remarkable that barely eighty miles separated the capitals of the opposing sides. After the first Bull Run, when Confederate cavalry penetrated almost to its suburbs, Washington was virtually in the front line for most of the war. The forty-mile railway line from Baltimore to the capital, which before the war had been picturesque in its rustic squalor, was rapidly transformed; all along the route it seemed to have become one vast army camp.

The decent citizenry feared pay-day, when Washington would swarm with blue-coated soldiers on a drunken rampage which the Provost Guard could not control. Soon after McClellan took command he tried to introduce some slight military discipline in the capital, placing the city out of bounds to all officers and men except on public duty. The mayor, James G. Berret, co-operated by bringing forward closing time in the saloons, from midnight to four o'clock, but overlooked hotel bars and restaurants. Congress passed an Act prohibiting the sale of liquor to any soldier, but this was a dead letter from the beginning. In a survey of pubs, taverns, saloons and drinking dens, which Allan Pinkerton carried out for McClellan, it was estimated that there were no fewer than 3,700 'fountains of ruin', and 'the lowest places of intoxication' occupied two sides of the market square. In many low dives the stock might consist of little more than a cask of beer and a keg of villainous rot-gut Bourbon, dispensed in rusty iron cups for ten cents a drink. Next, as a hotbed of moral depravity, were the canterburies – music halls where, nightly, men were drugged, robbed and sometimes murdered.

Wartime Washington was a honeypot which swiftly attracted girls, characterised by Allan as 'either young or in the prime of life, and frequently beautiful and accomplished' from New York, Boston, Philadelphia and Chicago. Originally this was a seasonal business, at its peak when Congress was in session. Then the high-class whorehouses along Pennsylvania Avenue between the White House and the Capitol were regularly frequented by Senators, Congressmen, lawyers and government executives. The war changed all that and soon prostitution and gambling were going on round the clock, even in the oppressive heat of the summer.

In this riotously amoral atmosphere, Confederate agents moved and mingled easily. Ardent female patriots of Dixie flocked to Washington to trade their virtue for the secrets of the patrons of bordellos and casinos, and their male counterparts were all too ready to supply funds to officials in distress because of gambling losses. The lolling tongues of the saloons and canterburies disclosed many secrets, great and small. Pitted against Southern exploitation of Northern vice was Allan Pinkerton and his handful of operatives. Although initially serving the Army of the Potomac, Allan was soon inundated with the security problems of the various government departments, notably the Department of State whose head, William Seward, had an unquenchable zeal for dabbling in everybody else's business. Seward, fanatical in his devotion to the Union, was hell-bent on rooting out Southern sympathisers at all levels. The Chief Justice was described as disloyal, 'his heart sweltering with treason', and Seward prevailed on Congress to scrap the existing judicial system, and replace suspect judges by Republican stalwarts. Arbitrary arrest on the merest suspicion of disloyalty became commonplace; yet, paradoxically, many Southern sympathisers, confident that the Confederates would soon overrun the capital, openly flaunted their views.

By September 1861 something of Allan's enormous workload was lessened when Seward, suspicious of Pinkerton's close connections with the President, set up his own Secret Service under Lafayette C. Baker. His grandfather, christened Remember Baker, had been a captain under Ethan Allen in the War of Independence; his father, christened Green Mountain Boy Baker, alluded to the family's impeccable Revolutionary credentials. Born at Stafford, New York, in 1826, Lafe Baker had been raised in Lansing, Michigan, and had a swashbuckling career as one of California's leading vigilantes in the 1850s. In many respects he was remarkably like Pinkerton, both physically and mentally. Short but heavily built, he was lithe and sinewy, his forehead was 'of intelligent outline', he wore a beard, and his grey eye, 'cold in repose, was sharply piercing when he interviewed a victim of his vigilance'. He was a fine horseman and reputedly the best shot in the country. He had few vices; 'he did not curse, and had not tasted liquor for twenty years. To those less fortunate than himself, and to his family, his fidelity and kindness of heart were well known.'[1] At the outset of the war Baker had gone hot foot to Richmond and came back with a colourful tale of having been arrested, thrown into prison, and there having three interviews with Jefferson Davis during his enforced three-week stay. How much of this is true is debatable. Gideon Welles summed him up as 'wholly unreliable, regardless of character and the rights of persons, incapable of discrimination, and zealous to do something sensational'. Lucius Chittenden, Register of the Treasury, depicted Baker as 'cruel and rapacious', his detectives behaving in the most corrupt and arbitrary manner.

In June 1861, however, Washington was a hotbed of unrest. Most of the long-time residents of the District of Columbia were Tory in the extreme, and had no sympathy with the new administration. The city seethed with Southern sympathisers among whom Confederate agents moved freely and had access to the highest levels of Federal government. The loyalty of many Senators and Congressmen was in question; for Lincoln, the task of holding the Union together and defending the national capital seemed overwhelming. On the very day that Fort Sumter capitulated, Lincoln sent an urgent summons to Stephen Douglas to a private meeting at the White House. At this time 'the Little Giant' (barely five feet tall, but with a massive head and barrel chest) was a far better known figure than the prairie politician who had narrowly beaten him to the presidency. At Lincoln's inauguration, however, Douglas had held the President's hat, a symbol that whatever happened, he would support the Union and the Constitution. At the meeting on 15 April the leader of the North's Free Democrats pledged his solidarity and endorsed Lincoln's call to arms. Without Douglas's staunch support it is doubtful whether Lincoln could have kept the country from disintegrating into total chaos. At Lincoln's request he undertook a mission to the Border States and the North-West to rouse the spirit of Unionism. Though in poor health at the time, he did not spare himself as he toured West Virginia, Ohio and Illinois, and he was in Chicago on 3 June when he suddenly took ill and died.

While the unswerving loyalty of Stephen Douglas was not in doubt, the same could not be said for his Aunt Rose. Actually three years younger than her celebrated nephew (by marriage), Rose O'Neal Greenhow was one of those women characterised by Pinkerton as 'in the prime of life, frequently beautiful and accomplished'. Her father, John O'Neale, died when she was a baby and the family moved to Poolesville, Maryland, where they dropped the last letter of their surname. While a teenager, Rose, and her elder sister Ellen Elizabeth, moved to Washington to live with an aunt, Mrs H.V. Hill, who ran the Congressional Boardinghouse in the Old Capitol Building where many political figures lodged while Congress was in session. Here Rose, a strikingly beautiful girl with dark eyes, raven hair and olive skin, was introduced to the excitement of the Jackson era. Her wit was sharp and her manner dynamic, and soon this sultry Southern belle was familiarly known on Capitol Hill as 'the Wild Rose'. When Ellen married James Madison Cutts, nephew of the fourth President, in 1833, Rose moved in the very highest circles. In 1835, at the age of twenty, she married Robert Greenhow of Virginia, the librarian and translator for the State Department. They had four daughters, Florence, Gertrude, Leila and the baby of the family, young Rose.

Greenhow, trained in medicine and law before turning to librarianship, was one of American's most accomplished linguists, but is best remembered nowadays for his definitive *History of Oregon and California* (1844) which served as the basis for the United States claim to that vast territory a few years later. In 1850 the Greenhows moved west and Robert opened a law office in San Francisco. In March 1854 he was killed as a result of falling into a street excavation. His grieving widow collected $10,000 in damages from the city and returned to Washington where she soon established herself as a political hostess working for James Buchanan. Indeed, by persuading Buchanan to declare himself in favour of a transcontinental railroad, she secured for him the Californian vote that helped to propel him into the White House in 1857. During the Buchanan presidency Rose was 'a bright and shining light', dubbed by the New York *Herald* as 'Queen of the Rose Water Administration',[2] though somewhat overshadowed by her attractive niece, Adele Cutts, who married Stephen Douglas.

While cultivating friendship with such prominent Northerners as Secretary of State William Seward and Henry Wilson, the Chairman of the influential Military Affairs Committee (with whom, it was rumoured, she was having a passionate affair), Rose sympathised with the South. On the outbreak of war she was recruited into the Confederate ring of female spies, along with Belle Boyd and Madame Velasquez, by Colonel Thomas Jordan, Beauregard's adjutant general. Rose's greatest coup came early in July 1861 when she transmitted two messages by courier, giving full details of General Irvin McDowell's plans, thus enabling the Confederates to prepare for the first battle of Bull Run. For a further month Mrs Greenhow operated boldly and with impunity from her mansion at 398 Sixteenth Street, continuing to transmit the innermost secrets of the Federal government to General Beauregard. She who had known nine Presidents intimately was so well connected that she arrogantly assumed she was untouchable. Possessed of regal manners and given to theatrical gestures, she captivated statesmen and diplomats, legislators and generals alike. Within weeks, Rose's network of spies and informers extended as far as Texas and inculpated militia officers, bankers, politicians and civil servants.

The first inkling that the society belle was a possible leaker of secrets came to Allan Pinkerton from Timothy Webster who had been sent at the end of June to Baltimore 'to lay pipe with the Disloyalists'. Allan had ensured that neither Luckett nor Ferrandini was arrested after their assassination plot was foiled, and they were consequently still going about their nefarious activities, though under the discreet surveillance of Pinkerton agents. Now Webster resumed contact with Ferrandini who introduced him to an arms dealer named Merrill who divulged details of an uprising in Maryland, as soon as Confederate forces were in position. From Merrill Webster also got useful information on Confederate agents operating in Washington, such as Charles Butler who kept a china store on F Street and forged passes. Rose Greenhow's name kept cropping up in conversation, and Webster alerted his boss, who had her house constantly watched by a roster of five operatives.

For a spy, Rose was beginning to behave recklessly. On one occasion, late in July 1861, she paid a visit to the Confederate prisoners-of-war held in the Old Capitol to deliver baskets of food. When she found the superintendent haranguing the prisoners about the treason of the South, Rose interrupted him, saying, 'The South has prisoners hundred to one if the North wants to retaliate.' The dejected prisoners gave her a rousing cheer and left Superintendent William P. Wood speechless with anger. Wood reported the incident to Pinkerton the same afternoon.[3] Subsequently, Allan's operatives tailed Rose and her ladies as they went on a Sunday afternoon picnic near Fort Ellsworth, whose defences were then in course of completion. Rose even obtained the blueprints for the defences at Forts Corcoran and Ellsworth and sent them to Jordan on 1 August with a memorandum detailing her masterplan to spike their guns, kidnap McClellan, cut the telegraph wires and generally create mayhem in an already demoralised city. Her report, preserved to this day in the National Archives, is a masterpiece of detail. Weaknesses in the defensive system of the forts were carefully analysed, while the number, calibre and range of the artillery pieces were listed down to the last six-pounder.

When Rose and her ladies found themselves under surveillance they treated it as a game, resorting to all kinds of ruses to throw the Pinkertons off the scent. Rose even pulled strings at the highest level to have the operatives taken off. She complained bitterly of the ruffians and lawless men who were harassing her, and reserved her special invective for Allan whom she denounced as 'that German Jew detective'. Over the years, the myth has developed of the puritanical lawman falling under the spell of this Southern siren,[4] but Allan's own account in *The Spy of the Rebellion* puts this in stark perspective. His book describes in vivid language how, in mid-August, he managed to break into Rose's mansion while she was away from home. This highly illegal act shows how desperate he was to obtain evidence of her complicity in Southern espionage. He found nothing incriminating, apparently missing a note in the handwriting of Confederate President Jefferson Davis no less, thanking her for the information she had supplied before Bull Run.

Then Allan discovered that a young officer named Captain Ellison had been abstracting papers from confidential files and decided to have him followed. On the evening of 21 August Allan himself, accompanied by Pryce Lewis, Sam Bridgeman and John Scully, followed Ellison around the city. Storm clouds were gathering on this sultry evening and by the time they tailed their man to Sixteenth Street the rain was coming down in torrents. Ellison suddenly darted into the doorway of the Greenhow mansion. Allan and his men sheltered under the dripping trees across the street, in front of St John's Church. Presently a lamp was lit in a front room, so they furtively crossed the street to get a closer look. Allan took off his boots and, on the husky shoulders of Lewis and Bridgeman, clambered up to peer through the blinds. There, in Mrs Greenhow's sumptuously furnished drawing-room, he saw the young officer hand over a map and heard him describe the fortifications in detail. Rose and Ellison then left the room for about an hour; when they returned arm in arm it seemed obvious that Ellison had received his reward in Rose's bedroom. Lewis later stated that, on the doorstep, Rose kissed the gallant captain.

While Lewis and Bridgeman maintained their damp vigil on the Greenhow mansion, Allan, still in his stockinged feet, took off after the rapidly retreating figure. Ellison, realising that he was being followed, paused at the barrack gate and ordered the provost to arrest the man who was chasing him. Allan, shoeless, mud-spattered and soaked to the skin, refused to identify himself and was promptly thrown into the cells. In the course of the night, however, he managed to bribe one of the guards to take a message to Simon Cameron, who immediately ordered that the mysterious detainee be brought to the War Department for personal interrogation. Looking more like something that had just been fished out of the Potomac than the great spymaster, Allan hurriedly gave his report. Captain Ellison was then summoned to the War Department and immediately arrested. A search of his quarters revealed 'sufficient evidence to prove he was engaged in furnishing information to the enemy'. He was placed in close confinement at Fort McHenry where he hanged himself the following day, before Allan could interrogate him.

For forty-eight hours the Greenhow mansion was discreetly watched round the clock. Allan's subsequent report to Winfield Scott proved highly embarrassing to the general-in-chief, for several of his most senior officers were found to have visited Rose in that crucial period. Some of these men had owed their appointments to their political influence, but as a result there was a thorough shake-up of the War Department. On the morning of 23 August a civil warrant for Rose's arrest was issued under Cameron's authority. Allan and the three men assigned to the case, accompanied by Hattie Lawton, went to Sixteenth Street and knocked on the door. Rose herself answered and, on finding 'the German Jew detective' on the step, promptly tried to swallow the paper she was holding. Allan brutally retrieved it from her beautiful mouth and found the saliva-sodden flimsy covered with a message in code. This alone would have been enough to convict her but a thorough search of the house yielded secret papers, maps and Beauregard's code-book. While Allan and his 'uncouth ruffians' ransacked her house, Rose sat calmly in her drawing-room, under the watchful eye of Pryce Lewis. She took the measure of the elegant young man and focused her dazzling charm on him; at one point she begged him to let her go upstairs. Eventually he agreed, so long as he could accompany her. In her boudoir Rose grabbed a pistol from the mantelpiece and in a typically theatrical gesture, twirled around and pointed the barrel at Lewis's head. 'If I had known who you were when you came in, I would have shot you dead!'

Lewis smiled wryly and riposted, 'Madam, you will first have to cock that pistol to fire it.'[5]

He easily disarmed her and frogmarched her downstairs, where the others were completing their work. By now Allan and his team had unearthed a vast quantity of material, ranging from regimental sick reports to Rose's own very perceptive pen portraits of the prominent men she had seduced in the course of her intelligence-gathering. There were ordnance records detailing arms and ammunition, and copies of troop orders giving the strength and disposition of Union forces in and around the capital. Allan found her diary, containing the names of her agents and couriers which, in places, read like an excerpt from the Washington social register. In all, it was a damning record of her fanatical devotion to the South. The little red-bound diary alone incriminated an astonishing array of politicians, lawyers, bankers, railroad officials, businessmen, civil servants, drunkards, drug-addicts, psychopaths and extremists, not to mention the ladies of Rose's inner circle. The resultant scandal reverberated around Washington and led to wholesale arrests right up to the highest level. One casualty of this scandal was James G. Berret, the mayor of Washington, whom Allan arrested when he was found to be implicated in a plot to detach Maryland from the Union. He was imprisoned for several weeks before he was released, after taking an oath of loyalty to the Union and resigning from office.

While Mayor Berret and other traitors, real or suspect, languished in Fort Lafayette, Rose Greenhow herself was treated with astounding leniency. She was not formally charged with treason or any other crimes, but kept under house arrest in her own home. The official version of what happened next is that, despite being under constant guard, Rose somehow managed to continue to communicate with the enemy, Allan reporting that her mansion was still serving as a 'rendezvous for the most violent enemies of the Government'. More probably, she was lulled into thinking that her influence in the highest quarters had let her off so lightly. She continued her activities, naïvely unaware that she was under Allan's eagle eye all the time. This cat-and-mouse technique paid off when Allan detected her in contact with Augusta Morris, whom he described as 'a gay and sprightly widow', who was trying to pass messages to the Confederacy.

By means of Jordan's code-book Allan concocted despatches with false information and got Kate Warne to copy them out in a fair imitation of Rose's handwriting. He then arranged for one of his own agents, possibly Webster, to get the messages to Colonel Jordan in the hope of opening a regular channel of disinformation to the Confederate capital. Jordan, however, was too old a hand at this game to be taken in and decided to change the code. When he later heard that Washington was offering a huge reward to anyone who could break the Confederate code, he jokingly told Beauregard that he was inclined to 'furnish a key to a friend of mine in Washington and let him have the consideration'.

The unmasking of Rose Greenhow proved extremely embarrassing to the Lincoln administration, and Allan was obliged to meet frequently with Simon Cameron and William Seward while they debated what to do with such a dangerous menace. As 1861 drew to a close, diplomatic pressure from as far afield as France and Britain was being brought to bear on Lincoln to release her. The newspapers did not help matters either. In Washington and New York she was at first grudgingly admired for her plucky exploits, but later hyped as America's most beautiful spy. In Richmond she was lauded as the heroine of the hour. A succession of high-powered political figures came to Pinkerton to plead on her behalf, but he merely glowered at them when they suggested that he would be better employed elsewhere and should stop harassing the poor woman. On one occasion Colonel Thomas Key, McClellan's aide-de-camp no less, came to Allan to plead her cause, after he had visited her home and been completely won over by her. Allan reduced the gallant colonel to a quivering jelly with a severe dressing-down for his misplaced chivalry and a stern lecture on security.

Not long after Rose was placed under house arrest, two of her most important agents paid her visits – only to fall straight into Allan's hands. The first was William J. Walker of the Post Office Department who was found to have been in direct communication with Colonel Jordan, Rose's controller. The other was a South Carolina lawyer named Michael Thompson (codenamed 'Colonel Empty', a play on his initials, M.T.) whom Allan described as 'a man of subtle intellect, finished education, practical energy, polished manners and an attractive address'. Following his arrest his house was searched and yielded a fine harvest of incriminating material, including a copy of Jordan's cipher.

Allan's persistence uncovered unexpected connections, and by the end of the year the scale of the spy ring was staggering in its immensity. There was hardly a prominent family in Washington and the vicinity which was not implicated. One of Allan's coups was the arrest of Rutson Maury, who was found to have been the South's principal conduit of letters and despatches to and from Confederate agents in Washington, and also to have been implicated with the British embassy in intriguing against the Union. The British government, reflecting public opinion in the United Kingdom, was very sympathetic to the South. Clyde-built steamships blatantly ran the Federal blockade taking vital supplies into Wilmington and Charleston, and Maury was involved in secret negotiations to export the South's cotton crop to England. The immediate outcome of this investigation was a formal protest to Lord John Russell, the British Foreign Secretary, who was accused of being on the point of recognising the Confederate States. Ironically, Russell had long been a champion of liberty, a proponent of Catholic emancipation and an enlightened liberal who, as Home Secretary, had mitigated the severity of the sentences originally passed on the ringleaders of the Newport Rising.

The arrest of Michael Thompson led Allan to William T. Smithson, one of Washington's leading financiers, an intimate friend of Rose who continued to call on her after her house arrest. For several months Allan's detectives tailed the banker until he was arrested in January 1862. Smithson had devised an ingenious method of getting vital information to Richmond, his coded flimsies, addressed direct to Judah P. Benjamin, the Confederate War Secretary, being screwed up and concealed in plugs of tobacco. Allan described Smithson as 'one of the most prominent and dangerous Rebel sympathisers in Washington'. Despite Allan's objections, Smithson was released after twelve weeks' detention in the Old Capitol, but in 1863 was re-arrested when he was implicated in illegal currency smuggling and banking operations on behalf of the Confederacy.

Allan persistently demanded that Rose Greenhow should not be left at liberty, and as the scope of her activities was more fully revealed his view prevailed. In January she and eight-year-old Rose, the only daughter still at home, were removed with the other female spies from her mansion, which was jocularly known at the time as Fort Greenhow, and transferred to far less comfortable quarters in the Old Capitol. This had been the seat of Congress for half a century from 1800, but it was vacated when the present building was completed. It stood empty and neglected for several years before it was pressed into service as a prison for political detainees who had been rounded up and held without trial. At first only secessionists from Washington and its environs were held there, but by the end of 1861 it was a concentration camp for suspects from as far afield as Illinois and Iowa. Allan had planned to spirit Rose off to prison in secret, but, as usual, she was one jump ahead. Having been warned of her imminent transfer she managed to get word out to her friends and sympathisers. On the appointed day, when she was led out into the street by the unsmiling detective, she found the street lined with hundreds of people; even the lamp-posts and trees swarmed with men and boys eager to get a better look at the heroine. With a cold, disdainful look at Pinkerton, Rose gathered her skirts in one hand and held her daughter in the other, and slowly, majestically, descended the steps to the street. At the foot of the steps she was met by a young lieutenant with his squad of riflemen. 'I hope in the future your men will have a nobler employment,' she said coolly.

Rose permitted herself a wry grin when she surveyed her new prison, for it was none other than the Old Congressional Boardinghouse where, two decades earlier, she had spent happy years with her aunt. She and her daughter were ushered into the office of the prison superintendent, William P. Wood, who was taken aback when the little girl greeted him with defiance and the assurance, 'You have one of the darnedest Rebels here you ever saw!'

Wood, a rather sinister figure, had had a colourful career. Shortly before the Civil War he had been with William Walker's mercenaries in Nicaragua, but when their leader was captured by the Royal Navy and handed over to the local authorities for execution, Wood made his escape back to the United States. For a time he worked as a modelmaker in Washington and was the expert witness in a much-publicised case when Cyrus Hall McCormick, inventor of the reaping machine, sued John H. Manny for infringement of patent. Manny engaged an up-and-coming lawyer, Abraham Lincoln, to defend the $400,000 action. When Lincoln arrived in Cincinnati for the trial, however, he found that another, more experienced, lawyer had been hired by Manny – Edwin M. Stanton. Lincoln, the original counsel, was crowded out of his own case. Lincoln's partner, William Herndon, later stated that Lincoln felt that Stanton had purposely ignored him, and had overheard Stanton speak of him in a very slighting manner. The outcome of the case hinged entirely on the technical evidence. An early model of a McCormick reaper was produced to show that there had been no infringement of patent, but on his deathbed Wood swore an affidavit that he had deliberately altered the machine, on Stanton's instructions, and perjured himself – with the result that McCormick lost the case. Stanton later repaid Wood when, as Attorney General in the Cabinet of President Buchanan, he secured the quondam modelmaker's appointment as prison superintendent.

Stanton, a Democrat, curried favour with the Republicans in anticipation of a place in the incoming administration, but when Lincoln failed to send for him, the disappointed office-seeker reacted by bitterly abusing the new President, whom he referred to sneeringly as 'the Original Gorilla', and constantly intrigued behind his back. In January 1862 Stanton succeeded Simon Cameron as War Secretary in ironic and extremely suspicious circumstances. As his attorney, Stanton advised Cameron to include in his annual report a statement that 'it is clearly the right of this Government to arm slaves when it may become necessary'. In this Stanton was both furthering the case of the radical Republicans and driving a wedge between Lincoln and Cameron. Lincoln reacted promptly by dismissing Cameron, who was packed off to Europe as Minister to Russia. It was in a desperate bid to neutralise Stanton that Lincoln now brought him into his Cabinet in place of Cameron, little suspecting that the new War Secretary favoured arming the slaves even more strongly than the man he was replacing. Simon Cameron was no angel – his maxim was that 'an honest politician is one who, having been bought, stays bought' – but compared to his successor he was a paragon of virtue. With Stanton now at the head of the War Department, Wood's advancement was remarkable. While continuing as superintendent at the Old Capitol Prison he was given a colonelcy and became second-in-command to Lafe Baker in the rapidly mushrooming Detective Bureau. Colonel William E. Doster, who was Provost Marshal of Washington in 1862, worked closely with both Stanton and Wood and left a shrewd portrait of the prison superintendent:

He was in many respects a remarkable man – short, ugly and slovenly in dress while in manner affecting stupidity and humility, but at the bottom the craftiest of men. For some reason, which no one could fathom, he was deeper in the War Department than any man in Washington, and it was commonly said that Stanton was at the head of the War Office and Wood was at the head of Stanton.[6]

During this period Allan Pinkerton worked closely with Wood, but treated him with reserve and regarded him as 'a rather crafty man', which seems like a masterpiece of understatement.

Allan himself selected the room in which Rose and her daughter were incarcerated. Later she would describe her prison in her book. It was quite a large room on the second floor, with a solitary window overlooking the exercise yard. An eighteen-foot-high palisade had been hastily erected to prevent prisoners escaping, and also to blot out the view of the city. The dirty room, smelling strongly of damp, was sparsely furnished, with a bed, chair, small mirror and a sewing-machine, but it was only too familiar to Rose. In that very bedroom, twelve years earlier, Rose had tended one of her dearest friends, Senator John Caldwell Calhoun, the ardent champion of the free extension of slavery to the new territories. Calhoun's death, at the height of the bitter debates in the Senate over the admission of California as a Free State, was the main reason why the Greenhows left Washington and settled out west. Now the chamber in which her great hero had died in her arms would be her prison for five dreary months.

This move, far from quenching Rose's spirit, merely hardened her resolve. Incredibly, from this gloomy prison she continued her espionage activities. Meanwhile Southern newspapers, and not a few in the North and abroad, ran touching stories about little Rose sharing her mother's halo of martyrdom. Even the young lieutenant in charge of the guard detail was so bewitched by the spy that he agreed to take messages to her and then hand her replies on to her friends. This grave breach of security was not detected till some months later.

One of the most embarrassing revelations from Allan's investigation of Rose Greenhow was that she was carrying on a very passionate affair with none other than Henry Wilson. Three years her senior, Wilson was of excellent Yankee stock, having been born in New Hampshire and raised in Massachusetts, which state he represented in the Senate from 1855 till 1873. He had an uncompromising opposition to slavery and soon became one of the foremost anti-slavery orators in the United States. On the outbreak of the war Lincoln appointed him Chairman of the Senate Military Committee, one of the most crucial positions in the government. It was Wilson who had the Chief Justice removed from office on suspicion of treason and engineered the abolition of the existing judicial structure as a wartime measure. He was widely regarded as second only to the President himself as the upholder of the Union.[7]

In light of this, Allan's discovery of a bundle of torrid love letters from the Senator in Rose's boudoir was nothing short of sensational. The bundle, docketed 'Love Letters from Henry Wilson, US Senator from Massachusetts' and preserved in the National Archives to this day, consisted mainly of brief, feverish notes with declarations of undying love and devotion as well as assignations that left no doubt as to their passionate nature. The letters were signed 'ever yours – H' but the handwriting was unmistakable. Allan turned the letters over to McClellan and he, in turn, showed them to General Scott. In due course the H Letters, as they were discreetly known, became the subject of a stormy Cabinet meeting when Senator Wilson was carpeted by the President. The Cabinet seems to have been incredibly naïve, as the consensus was that Wilson's patriotism was not in doubt, and if it had been a crime to be ensnared by Rose then half the Cabinet might be joining Wilson in a prison cell! At any rate his intimate association with the beautiful spy did not jeopardise his career and within a few years he would become Vice-President in the administration of Ulysses S. Grant.

Whether he received so much as a rebuke from Lincoln is not recorded, but shortly afterwards the unrepentant lover was visiting Rose in the Old Capitol, blandly informing an embarrassed Wood that he was there in his senatorial capacity. Rose later recalled that Wilson told her that he was moving heaven and earth to secure her release, but that McClellan, influenced by Pinkerton, had recommended to Lincoln that she be confined for the duration of the war. The news that her capture was exercising the White House and the Cabinet was a crumb of comfort, but she reserved her invective for Pinkerton. Wilson was deeply moved by the sight of his mistress; the sadistic Wood took delight in depriving her and little Rose of their most basic creature comforts, while the inadequacy of bedding and clothing during the harsh weather in January and February added to their privations.

Meanwhile, a galaxy of prominent politicians and socialites were orchestrating a campaign on Rose's behalf, but Allan remained obdurate. Bluntly he informed McClellan, Scott and Stanton that she was a dangerous enemy agent, a threat to the Union and a bad, bad woman who must be confined till the cessation of hostilities. In a report to Thomas Scott, the Assistant Secretary of War, Allan wrote forcibly:

> She has made use of whomever and whatever she could as mediums to carry into effect her unholy purpose . . . She has not used her powers in vain among the officers of the Army and Navy, not a few of whom she had robbed of their patriotic hearts and transformed them into sympathizers with the enemies of the country which had made them all they are . . . Mrs Greenhow is a willing instrument in plotting the overthrow of the United States government.[8]

Confirming this view, Allan later discovered that Rose and one of her agents confined in the Old Capitol, Roberta Hasler, were still trying to get messages out to Colonel Jordan. The messages were intercepted by a Pinkerton agent but Rose somehow got word through to Jordan and put him on his guard lest

Pinkerton should try to foist false information on the Confederates. On one occasion Gustavus Vasa Fox, now Assistant Secretary of the Navy, paid Rose a visit and told her that she would be allowed to go to Richmond if she took an oath of allegiance to the United States. Rose ignored this rather contradictory promise; instead, she turned on the charm to such effect that she actually tricked the gullible officer into divulging details of McClellan's imminent campaign. That very night she encoded a despatch to Jordan, even giving as her source 'Fox of the Navy Department'. When the text was actually published for all to see in the Richmond *Whig*, Allan was livid with anger. To make matters worse, it was reprinted soon afterwards in the New York *Tribune* whose editor, Horace Greeley, had previously argued in favour of letting the South secede. Allan never found out how Rose smuggled out this damaging despatch, but he suspected that the message was embroidered in one of the pieces of tapestry which she sent out, via the Provost Marshal's office, to friends as gifts. By the time the document was republished in New York it, too, had been embroidered. Rose's impassioned letter spoke venomously of Pinkerton and his ruffians who had 'torn letters from my bosom'. This latest episode was intensely embarrassing to Lincoln and his Cabinet.

Allan probably earned a rebuke from his political masters as a result, for he, in turn, gave Wood a stiff talking-to and thereafter security within the Old Capitol was severely tightened. Little Rose, who had been allowed to play in the prison yard, was now confined to the room. All laundry was minutely examined, going in and out. When a sprig of jasmine, Rose's favourite flower, 'reached her without examination', Allan flew into a rage.

Then one day, without warning, Rose was taken to Senator William Gwin's palatial mansion on Nineteenth Street for examination by the War Department's Political Prisoners Commission. She was kept waiting in an unheated antechamber for over an hour before being ushered into the dining-room, where, in happier times, she had often been an honoured guest. The interrogation was conducted by General John Dix who, as Secretary of the Treasury in the Buchanan administration, had known Rose intimately. When Rose was brought in, Dix and his fellow commissioner, Judge Edward Pierrepoint, politely rose to their feet. With regal aplomb Rose waved majestically to them saying, 'Gentlemen, please be seated'. The interview started in a low-key, even fairly amicable, atmosphere; but Rose was hostile, condescending and uncompromising from the outset, and as the damning evidence of her espionage unfolded, the manner of Dix and Pierrepoint gradually changed. At the end, Dix turned to Pinkerton and brandished one of her intercepted letters, crying out that it was 'equal to declaring determined hostility to the government'.

The questioning completed, Rose was returned to her prison to await her fate. In the ensuing weeks, however, further evidence came to light as Allan connected Rose's spy ring to yet another prominent socialite, the wife of Senator Jackson Morton of Florida. The Morton mansion was subjected to a thorough four-day search by Pryce Lewis and other Pinkerton agents, but although many letters indicating the Mortons' Southern sympathies were discovered, nothing tangible to incriminate Mrs Morton was forthcoming.

Rose's influential friends continued to agitate for her parole. These petitions inevitably landed on Allan's desk and he wearied of reminding Stanton that his operatives were daily risking their lives behind enemy lines, and to let Rose go would be an affront to their bravery. In the end, however, he was overruled. Much to his annoyance, Rose was offered parole on condition that she sign an oath promising not to aid the enemy. She refused, but in June 1862 she was released anyway. Under escort, she and two other women accused of spying, were taken through the lines and handed over under a flag of truce, after promising not to return to the North for the remainder of the war.

She was immediately whisked off to Richmond where she was treated like royalty. President Davis called personally on her, presenting her with $2,500 for her services to the Confederacy. In Charleston Pierre Beauregard and his staff gave her a hero's welcome. That winter she speculated in railroad stock, cotton and tobacco futures, and put her prison diary in order for publication in England. In August 1863 she went abroad as unofficial ambassador for the Confederacy. Her book *My Imprisonment and the First Year of Abolition Rule at Washington* was published at London in November and was an overnight best-seller. Rose was now an even bigger celebrity than ever. In Paris she was presented to Napoleon III (whose son was, at the time, on McClellan's staff), and back in London she dined with Queen Victoria and captivated her by her ready wit. Among those who came under her spell was the second Earl Granville, President of the Council and one of the most powerful political figures in Britain. The Earl was a widower, of the same age as Rose, and after a whirlwind romance they became engaged. Little Rose was deposited in a French convent, and her mother planned a brief trip to the Confederacy to deliver her diplomatic report to Jefferson Davis before returning to London for the impending nuptials. She took passage, with two other Confederate agents, aboard the British steamship *Condor*, which ran aground in a fearful storm off Wilmington, North Carolina, on 30 September 1864. When a Federal gunboat hove in sight Rose insisted that the ship's captain lower a boat so that she and the other agents could effect their escape. Near the shore, however, the boat capsized. The two men managed to swim ashore but Rose had sewn hundreds of gold sovereigns (the royalties from her book) into her corset and underclothing and, thus weighted down, she sank and was drowned. Later her body was recovered; she was given a state funeral with full military honours and laid to rest in Oakdale Cemetery, Wilmington. Her dramatic death had the epic touch in which she would have revelled. Little Rose, incidentally, grew up to be a professional actress.[9]

Pinkerton's National Detective Agency, Chicago.

Timothy Webster, one of Allan's most trusted operatives, was executed as a spy by the
Confederates on 29 April 1862

Pryce Lewis, another Pinkerton man caught behind enemy lines

George Bangs was the National Detective Agency's general superintendent for many years

Pinkerton Police Patrol, Chicago. The uniformed security guards recruited to protect factories, warehouses and railroad deposits

Four of the Molly Maguires convicted following the Pinkerton undercover investigation: (top left) James Kerrigan, one of the murderers of John P. Jones, turned state's witness; (top right) Alex Campbell, hanged for the murder of John P. Jones; (bottom) James Roarty and James Boyle, who were hanged for the murder of Benjamin Yost

James McParland, who spent two years undercover as a miner named Jim McKenna to infiltrate the Molly Maguires

BELOW
(left) A Molly Maguire coffin notice

(right) Franklin B. Gowen, president of the Philadelphia and Reading Coal and Iron Company, who asked Pinkerton to investigate the Molly Maguires

Frank Reno, whose gang were brought to justice by the Pinkerton Agency

Jesse James at seventeen

Pinkerton agents heading for Kansas City, Missouri, during the campaign against the James gang

Below appear the photographs, descriptions and histories of GEORGE PARKER, alias "BUTCH" CASSIDY, alias GEORGE CASSIDY, alias INGERFIELD and HARRY LONGBAUGH alias HARRY ALONZO.

GEORGE PARKER.
First photograph taken July 11, 1894.

Name..George Parker, alias "Butch" Cassidy, alias George Cassidy, alias Ingerfield.
Nationality....................American
Occupation..............Cowboy; rustler
Criminal Occupation.....Bank robber and highwayman, cattle and horse thief
Age..36 yrs. (1901)..*Height*....5 feet 9 in
Weight..165 lbs., ...*Build*......Medium
Complexion..Light..*Color of Hair*.Flaxen
Eyes....Blue......*Mustache*.Sandy, if any
Remarks:—Two cut scars back of head, small scar under left eye, small brown mole calf of leg. "Butch" Cassidy is known as a criminal principally in Wyoming, Utah, Idaho, Colorado and Nevada and has served time in Wyoming State penitentiary at Laramie for grand larceny, but was pardoned January 19th, 1896.

GEORGE PARKER.
Last photograph taken Nov. 21, 1900.

Name..........Harry Longbaugh, alias "Kid" Longbaugh, alias Harry Alonzo alias Frank Jones, alias Frank Boyd, alias the "Sundance Kid".
Nationality........Swedish-American..*Occupation*............Cowboy; rustler
Criminal Occupation ....Highwayman, bank burglar, cattle and horse thief
Age........35 years..........*Height*.................5 feet 10 in
Weight...165 to 175 lbs............*Build*....................Good
Eyes....Blue or gray............*Complexion*................Medium
Mustache or Beard..............(if any), natural color brown, reddish tinge
Features......Grecian type..........*Nose*......................Rather long
Color of Hair.........Natural color brown, may be dyed ; combs it pompadour.

IS BOW-LEGGED AND HIS FEET FAR APART.

Remarks:—Harry Longbaugh served 18 months in jail at Sundance, Cook Co., Wyoming, when a boy, for horse stealing. In December, 1892, Harry Longbaugh, Bill Madden and Henry Bass "held up" a Great Northern train at Malta, Montana. Bass and Madden were tried for this crime, convicted and sentenced to 10 and 14 years respectively; Longbaugh escaped and since has been a fugitive. June 28, 1897, under the name of Frank Jones, Longbaugh participated with Harvey Logan, alias Curry, Tom Day and Walter Putney, in the Belle Fourche, South Dakota, bank robbery. All were arrested, but Longbaugh and Harvey Logan escaped from jail at Deadwood, October 31, the same year. Longbaugh has not since been arrested.

HARRY LONGBAUGH.
Photograph taken Nov. 21, 1900.

We also publish below a photograph, history and description of CAMILLA HANKS, alias O. C. HANKS, alias CHARLEY JONES, alias "DEAF" CHARLEY, who may be found in the company of either PARKER, alias CASSIDY or LONGBAUGH, alias ALONZO, and for whom a proportionate amount of a $8,000.00 Reward is offered by the GREAT NORTHERN EXPRESS COMPANY upon arrest and conviction for participation in the Great Northern (Railway) Express robbery near Wagner, Mont., July 3rd, 1901.

Name..O. C. Hanks, alias Camilla Hanks, alias Charley Jones, alias Deaf Charley
Nationality.....American..........*Occupation*................Cowboy
Criminal Occupation ....Train robber ; an ex-convict
Age..........38 years (1901).........*Height*..................5 feet 10 in
Weight....156 lbs...............*Build*..................Good
Complexion......Sandy.............*Color of Hair*................Auburn
Eyes..........Blue..............*Mustache or Beard*......(if any), natural color sandy

Remarks:—Scar from burn, size 25c piece, on right forearm. Small scar right leg, above ankle. Mole near right nipple. Leans his head slightly to the left. Somewhat deaf. Raised at Yorktown, Texas, fugitive from there charged with rape ; also wanted in New Mexico on charge of murder. Arrested in Teton County, Montana, 1892, and sentenced to 10 years in the penitentiary at Deer Lodge, for holding up Northern Pacific train near Big Timber, Montana. Released April 30th, 1901.

CAMILLA HANKS.
Photograph taken 1892.

HARVEY LOGAN. alias **"KID" CURRY.** referred to in our first circular issued from Denver on May 15, 1901, is now under arrest at Knoxville, Tenn., charged with shooting two police officers who were attempting his arrest.

BEN KILPATRICK. alias **JOHN ARNOLD.** alias **"THE TALL TEXAN"** of Concho County, Texas, another member of the "Harvey Logan band" of outlaws, was arrested at St. Louis, Mo., on November 8th, 1901, tried, convicted and sentenced to 15 years imprisonment for participation in the robbery of the GREAT NORTHERN EXPRESS COMPANY, near Wagner, Mont.

WILLIAM CARVER. alias **"BILL" CARVER.** of Sonora, Sutton County, Texas, another member of this band, was killed at Sonora, Texas, April 2nd, 1901, by Sheriff E. S. Bryant, while resisting arrest on charge of murder.

IN CASE OF AN ARREST immediately notify PINKERTON'S NATIONAL DETECTIVE AGENCY at the nearest of the above listed offices.

Or
JOHN C. FRASER.
Resident Sup't., DENVER, COLO.

Pinkerton's National Detective Agency,
Opera House Block, Denver, Colo.

requested to give this circular to the police of their city or district.
Police official, Marshal, Constable, Sheriff or Deputy, or a Peace officer.

Example of information provided by Pinkerton's

William Pinkerton (seated) with Pat Connell, special agent for the Southern Express Company, and Sam Finlay, assistant special agent, during the campaign against the James gang

• 8 •

Behind Enemy Lines
1861–62

Ye are spies; to see the nakedness of the land ye are come.

GENESIS, XLII, 9.

On 11 September 1861 Allan Pinkerton 'opened the pipes laid in Baltimore'. Later that month he reported to William Seward:

> On the 11th instant in pursuance of the orders of the Hon. Simon Cameron, Sec. of War, and Major Gen. McClellan, I went to Baltimore, accompanied by a sufficient number of my detective force and Lt. W.M. Wilson of the 4th U.S. Cavalry. On arriving in Baltimore I proceeded to Fort McHenry and delivered to Major Gen Dix an order from the War Dept. for the arrest of T. Parkin Scott, S. Teakle Wallis, Frank Key Howard, T.W. Hall, Henry May and H.M. Warfield.[1] The said order mentioned to Gen. Dix that I was instructed to conduct the arrests, also to search for and seize the correspondence of the above named parties. On consultation with Gen. Dix it was deemed advisable, as it was now about midnight, to postpone the attempt to arrest until the following night, as it was impossible to tell if the parties to be arrested were in town or at their respective houses.
>
> At about midnight the several divisions moved simultaneously upon the places where we had discovered Scott, Wallis, F. Key Howard, Hall, May and Warfield and at that time all the above-named were arrested within fifteen minutes, their clothing thoroughly searched and immediately afterwards they were forwarded to Fort McHenry in separate carriages. My force made diligent search of all correspondence on the premises of each of the parties, all of which was seized.
>
> Frank Key Howard being one of the editors of the Baltimore *Exchange* newspaper and T.W. Hall, editor of *The South*, I construed the order to search

for and seize correspondence of a treasonable nature in the possession of the parties arrested a sufficient warrant for me to enter and search the editorial and press rooms of the *Exchange* and *South*, which I did, seizing the correspondence found therein.[2]

These Copperheads and Butternuts (who included the grandfather of the future Duchess of Windsor) were fingered by Timothy Webster, who had been operating in Baltimore for several months, with Hattie Lawton posing as his wife. Significantly, other Southern sympathisers were left alone because they were Webster's valuable contacts. Through the gun-dealer Merrill, Webster gained access to a secret society calling itself the Order of the Sons of Liberty, from whom he learned that plans were afoot for a mass insurrection in Maryland. At a signal from Washington, the Baltimore rebels would rise in arms and attack the capital from the north while Confederate forces crossed the Potomac. After a dry summer the river was dangerously low and easily fordable, a matter which gave General McClellan a great many sleepless nights.

On receipt of these reports from Tim Webster, Allan sent a further two agents to Baltimore with orders to infiltrate the organisation. Webster was not told of this, and these operatives were instructed to work quite independently so as not to compromise Webster. Meetings of the Sons of Liberty were held in conditions of the strictest security, with an elaborate system of passwords changed at frequent intervals and checked rigorously by two guards posted at the door. Allan ordered his agents to volunteer for this, notifying him when they would be on duty. In due course they sent word, advising Allan that they would be on the door at a meeting that evening, when the principal speaker was to be a notorious Copperhead, who turned out to be none other than Tim Webster. Allan told them that the meeting would be raided, and asked them to give a signal when Webster reached the climax of his speech. This was a nice touch, calculated to dispel any suspicion that might attach to Webster.

Thus it was that Allan and a team of detectives, backed by several companies of well-armed troops, broke in on the meeting on the evening of 11 September and arrested the ringleaders. Disappointingly, the raid yielded little hard evidence in support of the alleged insurrection, but one titbit which emerged was that William Yancey, the Confederate Minister in London, had given Jefferson Davis assurance that Britain proposed to give formal recognition to the Confederacy on 1 November.

Webster tarried in Baltimore a month after the raid, then made his way south on 14 October. Pausing only briefly to report to Allan in Washington, he kept going and crossed into Rebel-held territory. A day later he was in Richmond delivering his report to Judah Benjamin. Timothy Webster was now playing the dangerous role of double agent. He was fully accepted by the South and acted as a courier between Benjamin and the Confederate agents in Maryland. He took a room at the Spotswood Hotel near the centre of Richmond so that he might serve his Southern masters all the better. On 15 November he smuggled a report to Allan in his neat handwriting, covering some thirty-seven pages, which took Allan and two clerks all night to transcribe. Reading between the fading lines one can appreciate the courage and endurance of the man who compiled it in such detail. It told how he had travelled south aboard a Confederate mail sloop, and how he had met Benjamin in the company of John Beauchamp Jones, the Rebel War Clerk.[3] As usual, Tim's eye for detail was astonishing. The breastworks were of 'split pine logs with a 64-pounder with a traverse of 180 degrees'; the Yorktown landing was 'in front of a hill with a slope 5 feet above the beach'; there were seventeen batteries ringing Richmond and troops were equipped with Enfield rifles smuggled from England via Bermuda. Webster noted that the incidence of sickness in the Confederate ranks was rising and that the conscripts were suffering from the onset of winter, due to lack of overcoats and proper footwear. He even included the prices in Confederate currency of foodstuffs and fodder, adding 'hay very scarce, all sorts of prices'.

In this lengthy report there was only one inaccuracy, but it was one that would have dire consequences for McClellan, and consequently for Allan Pinkerton. Webster estimated the strength of Confederate forces in and around Richmond at 116,430. Despite the precise nature of this figure, it was more than 40,000 too high. Allan, of course, merely transmitted Webster's report to McClellan as it stood, without comment, and the accuracy of the troop strength was not questioned. On the assumption that this figure was correct, McClellan delayed launching an offensive campaign, thereby incurring the wrath of Lincoln and Stanton, not to mention General McDowall (whom he had replaced) and 'Old Fuss and Feathers' Scott himself. Ironically, McClellan blamed the general-in-chief for the inordinate delay in taking the offensive. Scott himself, now aged seventy-five and suffering from dropsy and vertigo, asked to be relieved of his command, and on 1 November he was succeeded by McClellan. Although the thirty-five-year-old general was now in command of all United States armies, he retained the rank of major-general – the same as several other generals who were much older and more experienced but who were his subordinates. Unlike the Confederacy, where brigadier-generals, major-generals and lieutenant-generals commanded brigades, divisions and corps respectively, the Union did not adopt a proper command structure until 1863, and this inevitably created immense problems for the young general-in-chief.

McClellan's delaying tactics – insisting on the need for more artillery and cavalry and improving the equipment and training of existing troops – paid off when, in February 1862, Fort Henry and Fort Donelson (commanded by General Buckner) in Tennessee surrendered to Federal troops after a ferocious siege.

There seems to have been one other discrepancy in Webster's report. His account of his meeting with John B. Jones in October 1861 is at variance with the details given in Jones's diary, published years later. Under 11 December 1861 the War Clerk recorded:

> Several of General Winder's detectives came to me with a man named Webster who it appears has been going between Richmond and Baltimore, conveying letters, money, etc. I refused him a passport. He said he could get it from the Secretary [Benjamin] himself, but that it was sometimes difficult in gaining access to him. I told him to get it then; I would give him none.[4]

It is interesting to note that Webster was quite openly using his real name. He had unwisely used it among his Secessionist friends in Baltimore from the outset and could not now adopt an alias. Jones was a naturally suspicious individual whose gimlet eye missed nothing. On one occasion Webster turned up with a diminutive figure in lieutenant's uniform, but the War Clerk, sensing something not quite right about the lieutenant's 'fullness of breast', refused to grant him a pass. Jones even had the lieutenant arrested but to his chagrin Judah Benjamin ordered the man's release and sent him on his way. The lieutenant was, in fact, Hattie Lawton in disguise.

Tim was back in Richmond on Christmas Day, having slipped through the lines with the wife and children of a Rebel officer from Baltimore. Although the lady was annoyed at the indignities and hardships she had endured along the hazardous journey, her husband was extremely grateful to Webster, and his standing among the Confederates rose considerably as a result. He was allowed to move more freely, and at the New Year visited the Tredegar Iron Works whose output was duly reported back to Washington.

Meanwhile, the weasel-faced Jones was becoming increasingly alarmed at the number of persons seeking passes to travel through the lines to the North. Jones was a typical clerk, doing everything by the book. So apprehensive had he become regarding the escalation in passes that on 16 January 1862 he overcame his natural timidity and broached the subject with Benjamin himself. Benjamin was irritated at the clerk's remonstration and told him brusquely, 'I don't grant any passports to leave the country, except to a few men on business for the government.' Back in his office, however, Jones counted over fifty names to whom Benjamin had given passes since Christmas. His diary entry for 30 January contains the ominous comment:

Some of the mysterious letter carriers who have just returned from their jaunt into Tennessee are applying again for passports to Baltimore, Washington, etc. I refuse them though they are recommended by General Winder's men; but they will obtain what they want from the Secretary himself.

While the South was reeling over the fall of Forts Henry and Donelson, the regular reports from Webster came to a halt, and a few days later Allan learned that his most trusted agent was seriously ill with rheumatic fever. Hattie Lawton was sent to Richmond to nurse him back to health, while Pryce Lewis was assigned the task of carrying on Webster's field work. Perhaps Lewis had some premonition, for he was extremely reluctant, and even threatened to leave the Agency and enlist as a common soldier if Allan persisted; but in the end he relented purely out of concern for his stricken comrade. When Allan casually mentioned that he was sending John Scully along as well, Lewis dug his heels in again. The assignment was far too risky for two. 'One man can remember a story and stick to it but two will be sure to suffer,' Lewis told his boss. Allan talked him round by saying that Scully's duties would consist solely of acting as messenger and bringing Webster's reports back to Washington. At the end of that assignment, when Scully returned to the North, Lewis was to proceed alone 'to Chattanooga, ascertaining the condition of the railroads and rolling stock and gathering information for General McClellan'. Their cover story was that they were contraband traders delivering a letter to Webster from a Copperhead friend in Baltimore. Allan's insistence on Scully being part of this operation, however, was to have tragic consequences.

On a beautiful sunny afternoon in late February Lewis and Scully took leave of their boss. Allan had kitted them out with new clothes, luggage, a Navy Colt pistol apiece and a bag of gold coins. Armed with a personal letter from Pinkerton to General Joe Hooker at Cobb's Point on the Potomac they passed through the Union patrols and almost drowned when their rowing-boat was swamped in a squall in the estuary. With great difficulty they reached the Virginia shore and buried personal letters and other documents which might have incriminated them. In a nearby village they learned that the ferry to Leesburg had been sunk by a Federal gunboat but that another was expected the following day. Dodging Confederate patrols, they made their way into Richmond on 26 February and checked in at the Ballard House. There they waited for Webster to 'make up the mail', as they called their intelligence reports.

They could hardly have chosen a worse time to return to the South. After Fort Donelson, Nashville had fallen, and a Union army under the command of a former store-clerk named Ulysses Grant was moving up the Tennessee River and camping around Shiloh Church. The main army of Northern Virginia was falling back from Manassas to the Rappahannock line. Security in Richmond was tightened, and as a precaution General Winder had the passport office moved to a basement at Ninth and Broad Streets where, Jones noted, 'the clerks were all Marylanders'.

At four o'clock on the following day Lewis and Scully were visiting the bedridden Webster and his nurse when Captain Sam McCubbin, head of General Winder's detective force, strolled into the room. Later Lewis would recall how he blanched as the young captain coolly appraised him, but McCubbin was only concerned for Tim's health. Unfortunately, McCubbin was accompanied by Lieutenant Chase Morton who, as luck would have it, was the younger son of Senator Jackson Morton whom Lewis and Scully had guarded while the Morton family were arrested on Pinkerton's orders. Lewis tried to remain as suave as ever, but the terrified Scully avoided the young man's penetrating gaze. While the puzzled Webster was wondering what was going on, Lewis and Scully made their excuses and slipped out of the room, but before they could leave the hotel they were stopped and arrested.

Interrogated by Winder and McCubbin, the two agents stoutly maintained that they were old friends of Webster and just happened to be passing through Richmond, but when both of Morton's sons appeared and identified them as Union agents Lewis and Scully were appalled to see Winder and McCubbin consult a list of Pinkerton operatives, with their names at the top!

They were immediately handcuffed and escorted to Henrico County gaol, where they tried to escape. Somehow they got hold of a well-tempered kitchen knife and used the blade to saw through the steel bars. This was a painfully slow process; during the day the saw marks were concealed with a paste of brown soap mixed with ashes. Knife-blades broke and others had to be stolen. Meanwhile their cell was regularly searched by the guards and their meagre straw palliasses examined for weapons. At last, on 15 March, the sawing was completed. The following night Lewis and ten other prisoners broke out. While they tiptoed down the creaking wooden staircase the Negro inmates sang spirituals at the top of their voices to conceal the noise. After scaling the outer wall they evaded the provost's patrols in the city and eventually found their way into open country. Lewis endured the worst hour of his life when they traversed a swamp, often slipping into the treacherous water. Some of the older prisoners, weakened by the starvation diet, had difficulty keeping up, so Lewis and another escapee carried one man between them. Near the Chickahominy River they stumbled upon a hole by an uprooted tree. They took a risk by lighting a small fire, dried their clothes, 'and walked about to keep off the chill'. During the night they staggered on, to put as much distance between them and Richmond as possible. As the sky lightened they collapsed, exhausted, on piles of brushwood. When he awoke, Lewis found he was like a man encased in iron: his still damp clothes had frozen to his body.

Resting by day, they struggled on by night, guided by a frosty moon. Again they had to endure immersion in the icy water of a creek, then lit a fire to thaw their frozen limbs. On the following day they had the misfortune to run into a Confederate patrol. To his chagrin Lewis discovered that they were twenty miles from Richmond and not far from the Union lines at Fredericksburg. By the time they were carted back to Richmond, the 'Yankee Jail Breakers' had hit the Richmond headlines. The *Times Despatch* even reckoned that the crowds that turned out to see them being led back to prison were larger than those which had greeted the Prince of Wales two years earlier. Lewis, as the ringleader of the gaol break, was put in leg irons on General Winder's orders, leaving him 'as helpless as a man could be'.[5]

Lewis and Scully were now incarcerated in Castle Goodwin, a filthy fortress that had once been a slave pen. Lewis was thrown into a windowless cell with a group of Confederate deserters. He had been there less than an hour when he was involved in his second escape. The deserters had been tunnelling from their cell to the street outside and the last few feet were excavated. Unfortunately the escapees were caught in the act of breaking out and Lewis found himself charged with leading the escape. He was transferred to a small cell and manacled in solitary confinement. Soon afterwards he learned that Scully had been tried for espionage; while the verdict was awaited, Lewis himself went on trial lasting three days. On 1 April he was taken to Scully's cell where the verdict was formally read to them. They had been found guilty of spying and were to be hanged on 4 April, between 10 a.m. and 2 p.m. Jones noted in his diary, 'Two spies have been arrested here, tried by court martial and condemned to be hung. There is an awful silence among the Baltimore detectives [Winder's men] which bodes no harm to the condemned. They will not be executed, though guilty.'

Lewis remained impassive but Scully broke down completely. There was one glimmer of hope, though, born of a casual remark by Judge Crump, president of the court-martial, who had muttered, 'I wish you were Yankees.' Both men had been born in England and were still technically British subjects; and through a priest, Father McMullen, Lewis got out a message to the British consulate. Late the following day the prisoners were visited by John Frederick Cridland, the Acting British Consul, whom Lewis described as 'a short, fussy man'. Cridland questioned Lewis closely about his family and where they lived in England, but also added that General Winder had told him that he had 'evidence enough to hang a hundred Pinkerton detectives'. Cridland admitted that he had not seen the evidence against Lewis and Scully and, in fact, had been denied access to it. Lewis's hopes were rising, when Scully blurted out that he had told Father McMullen that he was prepared to reveal all to Winder if he were pardoned.

Sure enough, Lewis was taken off to another cell and later, from the window in the door, he saw one of Winder's detectives with a man whom he later learned was Randolph Tucker, the state attorney of Virginia, scurrying along the corridor to Scully's cell. On 3 April, around one o'clock, Lewis looked out of the cell window and saw two of Winder's men helping a third out of a carriage. The third man was well dressed but pale and ill. It was Tim Webster, and just behind him was a very dejected Hattie Lawton. So Scully had betrayed them all.

Later that afternoon Lewis was removed to the condemned cell, 'a miserable damp room', where he read till midnight. Eventually he fell into 'a fitful sort of slumber, full of dreams', waking up as dawn broke. His heart sank as he heard hammering and sawing in the prison yard, as the gallows was erected. The cell door opened at eleven o'clock, and there was the priest beaming, 'I have good news for you, Lewis. President Davis has respited you for two weeks.' But he added, 'It still looks dark for you. I think you should tell the authorities all you know.'

Lewis stood firm, but the next fourteen days dragged interminably. In the meantime Cridland pulled out all the stops, reporting to Lord Lyons, the British Minister in Washington, and filing a lengthy petition with Judah Benjamin. The Confederate Secretary of War was, first and foremost, a lawyer, and he himself was troubled by aspects of the case, notably that the prisoners had been tried and convicted before they could gather evidence for their defence. He therefore acted promptly to overrule the court-martial and postpone the execution of sentence, hence the two-week respite.

This was a nail-biting period, made more stressful when Lewis learned that General Wise, whom he had wined and dined as Lord Tracy in West Virginia, was now in Richmond. As Scully was now singing like a canary to save his own skin, Lewis was in agony lest his one-time comrade revealed details of their previous exploits. Judge Crump also interviewed Lewis at length, and by way of getting him to betray Pinkerton's spy network, he painted a brutal picture of 'a cold, unfeeling bureaucracy which had abandoned a young, misguided man to his fate'. Lewis resolutely stuck to his cover story and denied that he had known Webster to be a Federal agent working for Allan Pinkerton. Over several days Crump kept up his interrogation but Lewis was adamant, saying that he had heard a rumour that Webster carried mails, and for that reason he had brought a letter to him from a friend in Baltimore. Later Lewis was moved back to a cell with Scully who, likewise, worked on him by blaming Pinkerton 'who lied to us'. Lewis retorted, 'Damn Pinkerton! What about Webster? I would not suffer for Pinkerton, but I would for Webster!'

Scully, however, revealed that Winder's detectives had apparently suspected Webster for some time. Like Rose Greenhow, he was so well connected that

Winder could not believe that Webster was a Federal agent, and it was only Scully's confession that betrayed him in the end. A few days later a guard told them that Webster had been found guilty and would hang. Hattie Lawton was given a stiff sentence, and would spend a year in prison before she was exchanged for Confederate prisoner. Lewis and Scully remained in captivity until 1863.

According to Allan's own account, he was with McClellan in the field on 6 April when he first heard that his agents had been captured and sentenced by court-martial to die by hanging. Four days earlier, at dawn on 2 April, the huge Federal army under McClellan's command landed on the peninsula south-east of Richmond and began the advance on Yorktown. Allan was reading a captured Richmond newspaper in his tent when he came across the report. 'My blood seemed to run cold, my heart stood still. I was speechless.'[6] Allan immediately went to the general's tent. McClellan, 'whose sorrow was as acute as though the men had been joined to him by ties of blood', promised to do everything possible to get the three men exchanged. Allan could not sleep that night, but paced up and down his tent till sun-up when he telegraphed to Milward, the harbour-master at Fort Monroe, for news.

McClellan was confident that Yorktown would fall to him by 4 April, but the Union advance was unexpectedly checked by the spirited defence put up by General J.B. McGruder, and what should have been a lightning campaign got bogged down by 17 April when General Joseph E. Johnston took command of the Confederate forces in the peninsula. That day Allan learned that the execution of Lewis and Scully had been delayed, but that Webster was scheduled to hang. This message stated erroneously that both Lewis and Scully had turned informer and testified against Webster. The error was later compounded by Hattie Lawton on her release, and explains why Allan, in his book, averred that Lewis, as well as Scully, had betrayed Webster. Therein Allan wrote:

They were simply men who after having performed many brave acts of loyalty and duty to their country, failed in a moment of grand and great self sacrifice. Their trial was a sore one and they were in great distress.[7]

Webster was not the only casualty of this sorry episode; Pryce Lewis was also a victim. Although his honour was belatedly vindicated by the Agency when it published a pamphlet on the subject in 1903(in which it was clearly stated that 'Lewis remained staunch and did not confess'), the detective had to fight long and hard to clear his name, and in fact the stigma of betrayal hounded him to his suicide in 1910, when he jumped off the top of the Times Building in New York. His memoirs of the Civil War period were found among his personal effects but were not published by his daughter Mary till many years later, .

In desperation, Allan begged McClellan to send a deputation to Richmond under a flag of truce to bargain for the lives of the three men, but the general refused, saying that to do so would be a tacit admission that they were spies, and that this might result in their instant execution. A compromise was effected when Allan and Colonel Thomas Key were sent post haste back to Washington on 21 April to ask the President to summon a special Cabinet meeting that evening. Allan also had a separate interview with Edwin Stanton, 'who promised to do everything in his power to save Webster's life'. Stanton told Allan, however, 'I am little disposed to assist the others who betrayed their companion to save their own lives'. The Cabinet authorised Stanton to send a flag of truce to Jefferson Davis. On the morning of 23 April Pinkerton and Key returned to Fort Monroe with the Cabinet despatch, the text of which, signed by Stanton, was telegraphed to Norfolk whence it was forwarded to Richmond. The despatch pointedly reminded the Confederacy of Washington's lenient attitude toward its spies, who had been punished by brief spells in the Old Capitol, without death sentences so far. The signal to the Confederates was clear: 'Hang our people and we will hang yours'.

President Davis was unmoved by the plea. While he agreed to commute the death sentences on Lewis and Scully he felt that an example would have to be made. When Sam McCubbin delivered the President's decision to Webster, the condemned man asked to be shot by firing squad, a more honourable end for a spy than dangling in a noose. General Winder refused this last request, saying that he could not alter the court's sentence. Hattie Lawton, at Webster's bedside when Winder told the sick man, pleaded with the general but to no avail. Hattie then told Winder in no uncertain terms that Tim would show them all how a Union man could die, but she also delivered a grim warning that Washington would neither forget nor forgive this bitter hour. Her threat was underscored three years later when the South appealed for clemency on behalf of John Beall and Robert Kennedy, Confederate agents who had committed an arson attack on New York City. They were hanged at Governor's Island after their request to be shot was turned down. At that time General Dix threatened to hang Confederate agents from the lamp-posts of Broadway, saying, 'The Rebels should remember Tim Webster.'

At 8 a.m. on 28 April Tim Webster went to his death. He spent his last hours writing letters to family and friends, which he entrusted to Hattie. At five o'clock in the morning Captain A.G. Alexander commanding the provost patrol came to read the death warrant. Later Hattie Lawton described to Allan their last moments together, when Webster had said to her, 'Tell the major I can meet death with a brave heart and a clear conscience.' The two agents embraced for the last time, then Tim stepped between the guards and hobbled painfully out of his cell and down the corridor.

Instead of a gallows in the prison yard, the execution of the Union spy was to be a public spectacle at Camp Lee, which in happier times had been Richmond's fairground. Because Webster was in very poor shape and unable to walk more than a few steps, a carriage was ordered to take him, with the ever-faithful Hattie still in attendance, out to Camp Lee. There he was handed over to the camp commandant, Captain Alexander, and Mrs Lawton was returned to her cell.

Not since September 1776, when Nathan Hale had been hanged as a spy by the British during the War of Independence, had an American been executed for espionage, and the Richmond crowds were determined to make the most of the entertainment. From dawn countless thousands from Richmond and the surrounding towns, villages and farms had crowded into the city and made their way out to the old fairground. There was a nip in the air that sunny spring morning when a party of soldiers helped Webster up the steps of the gallows. Contemporary accounts in the Richmond newspapers of Webster's behaviour on the scaffold were contradictory and biased. In one account he snarled and cursed his guards, 'treating his approaching death with scorn and derision'. Another said that he wept and begged piteously for mercy. Pryce Lewis later reported, however, that his guards had told him that his comrade had died with dignity, like a man, and this was Hattie's version also, despite the fact that the execution was grotesquely bungled. Richmond did not have an official executioner, so the work was entrusted to Kapard, the gaoler at Castle Thunder. Somehow the noose slipped and when the trap was sprung poor Webster fell to the ground below. He lay there, a desperately sick man, badly injured by the fall, yet struggling feebly with his legs and arms pinioned and a hood over his face.

Alexander's men picked him up and roughly manhandled him back up the steps for a second time. They held him upright as Kapard put another noose around his neck and pulled it so tight that Webster throttled, gasping, 'I suffer a double death.' His agony was unduly prolonged, as Kapard measured the rope and one of the officers below the gallows called up, 'The rope's too short'.

'It'll do,' said Kapard casually, as he checked the knot again, then stepped back and released the trap. Mercifully the rope must have been right this time, for Tim died instantly, without a sound. 'There was not a motion of the body or a quiver of a muscle,' gloated one paper.[8] The body was left dangling for thirty minutes, then cut down and taken back to Richmond in a prison wagon. The newspaper also recorded that Winder's men, who escorted the corpse, cut up the hangman's noose among themselves as grisly souvenirs of the occasion.

News of the execution was brought to Hattie by Captain Alexander. Lewis described this man in his memoirs as 'a pompous fool who was either reciting his own horrible poetry or walking about his warehouse prison, a huge black dog trotting at his heels'. Resplendent in a scarlet-and-grey uniform, the gallant captain escorted Hattie to the Richmond funeral parlour where Tim's body lay. There she arranged for it to be placed in a metal coffin. Several Confederate officers were present when Hattie entered the room. When she denounced them as murderers, Alexander theatrically put his hand on the dead man's forehead and swore, 'I did nothing to bring this about . . . I simply obeyed orders to bring him from the prison to the place of execution.'

When word of Tim's execution reached the Union lines, Allan was beside himself with grief. He tried to arrange with his opposite number, General Winder, to have the coffin sent through the lines, but Winder refused. A second petition from Allan, requesting that a vault be rented for the repose of the coffin till the cessation of hostilities, was likewise turned down by Winder. In the dead of night Winder's men buried Webster's body in the paupers' section of the Richmond cemetery. There was no stone to mark the spot, and the earth was trampled down. In his front-line tent, not many miles away, Allan vowed bitterly that someday he would find Webster's body and 'have it buried in Northern soil'.

True to his vow, Allan sent George Bangs to Richmond after the war to locate the unmarked grave. Eventually the coffin was disinterred and Tim's remains brought back to the North, for a funeral befitting the hero he was. At Allan's personal expense, Webster was laid to rest in the cemetery at Onarga, Illinois, next to the body of his son, who had been killed in the war shortly before the cessation of hostilities. Some confusion over Webster's last resting place arose because Allan had a memorial to Webster erected on the Pinkerton family plot in Graceland Cemetery, Chicago. This elaborate stone bears an extraordinary seventeen-line inscription which recounted the life story of the 'patriot and martyr', even mentioning his part in foiling the Baltimore Plot (and naming Allan Pinkerton and Kate Warne *en passant*). This eloquent epitaph ended, 'He enjoyed the confidence of Abraham Lincoln and sealed his fidelity with his Blood'.

◆ 9 ◆

Major Allen
1862–64

All the business of war, and indeed all the business of life, is to endeavour
to find out what you don't know by what you do; that's what I called
'guessing what was at the other side of the hill'.

DUKE OF WELLINGTON, *CROKER PAPERS*, VOL. III, p.276.

The young general-in-chief was not left long in his exalted position. Six weeks after assuming supreme command, on 20 December 1861, McClellan was struck down by typhoid fever. The attack was severe and for several days he was critically ill, but by 13 January 1862 he was sufficiently recovered to return to his office, though it was some time before he recovered his strength and full mental vigour. Through the whole of 1861 he had been working at top capacity, snatching food at an odd hour or not at all, working sometimes sixteen hours a day, and nature took revenge for his excesses.

McClellan's state of health probably contributed to his delay in launching the Union offensive, but it would have been unrealistic to expect the Army of the Potomac to take the field in the depths of winter, against an enemy which, if not actually superior in number, was at least numerically similar but fighting a defensive campaign on its own familiar territory – a fact which seemed to escape most of the armchair warriors, from Lincoln and Stanton downward. While the politicians were clamouring for action – even action that might (and would almost certainly) end in a defeat – the general turned a deaf ear to their entreaties and calmly got on with the superhuman task of welding his torrent of recruits into an efficient fighting machine. McClellan had gained invaluable experience in the Crimea, and from his close study of the Prussian and other Continental armies, he appreciated that training was vitally important. The peacetime army of the United States numbered about 17,000 men. The short-lived experiment with militia levies raised by the states for ninety days' service proved wholly inadequate and was replaced by a system of volunteers for three years. These recruits, streaming down from the north-east to Washington from August 1861 onwards, could not be equipped and trained overnight. It was largely due to McClellan that these raw troops were licked into excellent shape by the spring of 1862. Yet, at the time, poor McClellan was almost universally stigmatised for what seemed inordinate and inexcusable delays. Half a century later, when the United States mobilised a large army to fight in France, it took much longer to get this expeditionary force ready for combat; then the results achieved by McClellan were seen in their true perspective, but at the time he was hounded by politicians and the press and intrigued against by everyone from the Secretary of War down to his brother major-generals. This culminated in a half-hearted attempt to introduce a vote of no-confidence in the House of Representatives, but Lincoln succeeded in getting the matter suspended.

Lincoln and Stanton were actually in McClellan's sitting-room on 9 March when word came that the Rebels had abandoned their lines at Manassas and were retreating toward Richmond. This was due almost entirely to the formidable Union force now ranged against them and about to take the offensive at any moment. Lincoln, however, was unimpressed, for only two days later he issued the order relieving McClellan of supreme command. He was not immediately replaced, merely ordered to confine his command to the Army of the Potomac. When Major-General Henry Halleck was eventually appointed general-in-chief, he was little more than Lincoln's chief of staff. What was especially galling and insulting to McClellan was the fact that he was actually at his field headquarters near Fairfax Court House, Virginia when he received word, through the newspapers. He was never in his Washington office again; Stanton took charge of it immediately and McClellan never knew what became of his papers, official and personal, which were in his desk. There is no doubt that the effective demotion of McClellan was politically inspired, and had no sound military reason. Even as army commander in the Peninsular Campaign, he was hampered at every turn, vital divisions being detached from his army on the merest whim of Stanton.

On 2 April McClellan's Army of the Potomac began to land on the peninsula near Richmond, while McDowall at Fredericksburg was executing a pincer movement. Gradually the Federal ring of steel round the Confederate capital began to tighten. Much has been made of the supposedly poor intelligence which led McClellan into making the wrong decision, or not pressing the attack when he should have. Here again, this canard rests largely on the monumental biography of Lincoln by Nicolay and Hay, who devoted ten chapters to assassinating McClellan's character, and have coloured so much of the general history of the Civil War ever since.[1] Far from having the army of over 150,000 men often claimed in general works, McClellan now had only 85,000. No fewer than 134,000 troops were held back by Halleck for the defence of Washington itself, although the forts and breastworks erected by McClellan for that purpose could have been more efficiently manned by a fraction of that number.

The Peninsular Campaign can be briefly summarised. The Confederates fought a brilliant rearguard action, holding up the Union advance at Big Bethel, Yorktown and Williamsburg. Nevertheless, by 21 May, McClellan's forces were within seven miles of Richmond, though they were now held up by the Chickahominy River with its treacherous swampland. The following day McClellan's reconnaissance patrols had forded the river at Bottom's Bridge east of Richmond and encountered only light resistance. Had McClellan pressed forward that fateful day his troops might have overrun Richmond within hours and the Confederacy would have been dealt its death blow; but he hesitated and the opportunity to bring the war to a speedy and decisive conclusion was lost. 'With the force actually at my disposal,' he later wrote, 'such an attempt would simply have exposed the Army of the Potomac to destruction in detail, and the total loss of its communications.'

In McClellan's defence it should be stated that his repeated pleas for reinforcements were ignored. The last straw had been Lincoln's removal of General McDowell's forces, 40,000-strong, to cover Washington,[2] leaving McClellan in the impossible position of launching an attack on the enemy capital with numbers equal to those opposing him. The combined forces of Lee and 'Stonewall' Jackson have been estimated at 85,000 'all arms', while McClellan's forces at that point numbered 98,000. McClellan continued to move forward, seizing Mechanicsville, only five miles from Richmond, on 24 May. That same day there was a very spirited and successful skirmish at New Bridge a few miles south, and McClellan sent for the young lieutenant who had led the patrol. In this manner he met for the first time George Armstrong Custer whom he appointed an aide-de-camp. 'He was simply a reckless, gallant boy, undeterred by fatigue, unconscious of fear; but his head was always clear in danger, and he always brought me clear and intelligible reports of what he saw under the heaviest fire,' wrote McClellan approvingly. Many of the 'carpet-knights of Washington' who loudly condemned McClellan for his supposed timidity would, fourteen years later, condemn General Custer just as vociferously for his 'reckless rashness' at the Little Big Horn.

Atrocious weather, which made roads impassable and flooded the Chickahominy making bridge-building impossible, held up the Union advance for a week. During this period McClellan was stricken by 'my old Mexican enemy', a debilitating attack of dysentery which lasted several days. At the beginning of June came the twin battles of Seven Pines and Fair Oaks, won by the Confederates and Union forces respectively. At this point General Robert

E. Lee took command of the Confederate army and immediately launched a furious assault on the Union right wing. There ensued the terrible Seven Days or 'the Infernal Week' (26 June to 1 July), during which McClellan was forced to fall back on the James River. This setback was bad enough, but a lengthy telegram from McClellan to Stanton very early on the morning of 28 June, ending petulantly, 'If I save this army now, I tell you plainly that I owe no thanks to you or to any other persons in Washington. You have done your best to sacrifice this army,' incurred the everlasting displeasure of the Secretary of War.

One can forgive this telegram, sent in the heat of battle when McClellan was overwrought; but no such mitigating circumstance attaches to the long letter which McClellan handed to Lincoln personally on 8 July, when the President paid a visit to the general's headquarters at Harrison's Landing. This document, which set out McClellan's political views and urged on the President a more statesmanlike attitude towards the conduct of the war in particular and the southern states in general, was ill-advised to say the least, and engendered a similar feeling of hostility among the members of the Cabinet. It may explain why, only three days later, the post of General-in-Chief of the Army was at long last filled by General Halleck.

Horan asserted that 'Pinkerton knew the contents of, or perhaps had helped McClellan to compose' this letter. This assumption was derived from a letter written from New York by Colonel Thomas Key, McClellan's former aide, to Allan Pinkerton on 29 July 1864. Addressing Allan as 'My Dear Major', Key wrote:

> My friendship for McClellan, my hatred of Stanton & Lincoln, my Democratic views, my anti-slavery sentiments, my abhorrence of the war and the way it is carried on, all combined to separate me politically from everybody that I know but yourself.
>
> We were in the same condition when the Harrison Landing Letter was written, except that then McClellan was with us. What man in the Army but you and myself would have approved of his sending it. Yet [on] it and some military orders and Western and Eastern Va. rests his entire political fabric.

This seems hypothetical and Key's rhetorical question is not the same as saying that he and Allan had actually seen the letter and approved of it. Allan himself made no such claim, referring to the letter (in his own memoirs) merely as 'a review of McClellan's views on the conduct of the war'. From this false premise, therefore, Allan's supposed swallowing of his scruples when McClellan urged Lincoln to avoid 'forcible abolition of slavery', led Horan to comment unfairly, 'Perhaps a man of stronger principles would have seen the light and ditched his general'. There is no internal evidence of Allan having seen the letter, far less helped to write it. On the other hand, McClellan stated to W.C. Prime (who edited *McClellan's Own Story*) that he did not show the letter to his most intimate friends. The letter was marked 'Confidential', was for Lincoln's private consideration, and certainly not intended for publication.

Despite this tactlessness, McClellan continued to command the Army of the Potomac until the late autumn, when his conduct of the battle at Antietam, allowing Lee to retreat safely across the Potomac, was censured. McClellan's delay in pursuing the Confederates exasperated Washington and on 7 November 1862 he was relieved of his command, Major-General Ambrose E. Burnside being appointed to succeed him. Effectively, it was the end of McClellan's military career, and never again would he command troops in the field. Ironically, the strategy which McClellan had advocated in the summer of 1862 was actually adopted by Grant two and a half years later, and his success vindicated McClellan's stance.

Millions of words have been written about McClellan and the controversy over his generalship rages to this day. Horan is alone, however, in putting the blame for McClellan's indecisiveness on Major Allen, alias Allan Pinkerton, his security chief. Horan quotes numbers of troops on both sides at different stages of the 1862 campaigns, in support of his views that McClellan was prone to exaggerate the opposition. That may well have been the case but there is no real evidence, amid the many hundred pages of intelligence reports filed by Allan and his agents, to back up his contention that Allan Pinkerton was responsible for misleading the general, and certainly nothing to justify this sweeping condemnation:

> In the spring and summer of 1862 Allan Pinkerton's headquarters was in the field with the Army of the Potomac. Here he failed miserably both as a front-lines intelligence officer and as a political infighter. The best that can be said of him is that he should have remained in Washington, chasing spies.[3]

A great deal of Allan's work during the spring campaign was taken up with interrogating prisoners, deserters, Union sympathisers and contrabands (runaway slaves). Horan makes much of the fact that Allan imported to the battlefield the working methods of his Chicago detective agency, with disastrous results, although no actual reports are cited in support of this view. Then there was Allan's well-known attitude towards Negro slaves, whom he had been helping for years:

> In the field, Pinkerton, in his sympathy, was uncritical of the excited, uneducated slaves who stood before him in his tent, twisting a ragged hat,

shuffling their feet in the excitement of knowing that at last they were among friends and in sight of food and freedom. Though they were incapable of giving realistic information about what was happening on a grand scale behind Confederate lines, it is evident that Pinkerton believed everything they told him.[4]

The chief reason for taking this critical view lies in a report by McClellan to Stanton on 25 June 1862, saying that several contrabands had just arrived 'to announce that Jackson's forces were in line; that even Beauregard had come up and that the Rebel forces were near 200,000 men'. The combined forces of Lee and Jackson at this time were slightly half that number. Blame for accepting this figure was placed by Horan squarely but unfairly on Pinkerton's shoulders. The mass of reports and despatches quoted so extensively by McClellan in his own story gives the lie to this. Dashing young cavalry officers like Custer were the eyes and ears of McClellan's staff, and he was quite able to test the validity of the information brought in by runaways, deserters and refugees. All the arguments about numbers (magnified by some writers soon after the event, and parroted by many historians to this day) would have been swept aside had McClellan won. As late as 27 June he was urgently wiring Stanton, pleading for just 10,000 fresh troops which would have turned the tide of battle in his favour. It was Stanton's refusal which finally convinced the general that he was being stabbed in the back.

Writing years later, with the benefit of hindsight, Allan never swerved from his faith in his hero:

I followed the fortunes of General McClellan never doubting his ability or his loyalty, always possessing his confidence. I am at this time proud and honored in ranking him foremost among my invaluable friends.

McClellan was, in Allan's view, a man 'struck down at the peak of his career by secret enemies who endeavoured to prejudice the mind of the President against his chosen commander . . . wily politicians . . . jealous-minded officers'. This trenchant assessment was eventually confirmed by the publication of the correspondence of Edwin Stanton, which revealed him as the conniving, treacherous politician he really was, and how he plotted and intrigued against the young general-in-chief.

Allan's old loyalties were sorely tested and divided between the powerful personalities of the two men with whom he had worked before the war. On one occasion he met the President informally and together they reminisced about the old days on the Illinois Central Railroad; but by May 1862 Allan was beginning to see Lincoln in a new light, though he never quite subscribed to

McClellan's view that Honest Abe was now motivated by 'hypocrisy, knavery and folly'. At Easter 1862, shortly before the Peninsular campaign got under way, Allan was joined at field headquarters by his elder son. Willie, aged fifteen, had been allowed to abandon his studies at Notre Dame and join his father. Dressed in a slouch hat and befrogged tunic, the boy served as his father's aide, getting his baptism of fire during the Seven Days when he was employed as a despatch-rider. Because of his light weight, the boy also flew as an observer over the enemy lines in one of Professor Thaddeus Lowe's balloons – the first time that aerial reconnaissance was used in warfare, as a twenty-three-year-old Prussian cavalry volunteer named Ferdinand von Zeppelin was quick to note.

According to the Pinkerton letter-books and journals, Allan was not only co-ordinating military intelligence, with a network of agents all along the front as well as deep within enemy territory, but he was continuing to grapple with myriad security problems in Washington itself. He was also getting to grips with the army of racketeers, black-market operators, crooked contractors and corrupt officials in Washington. Case notes pursued him from the capital to field headquarters and he would often work far into the night, by the light of a lantern, on transcripts and depositions. He was frequently importuned by politicians seeking entrée to McClellan and harassed by unscrupulous defence lawyers. He was often obliged to make the difficult journey back to Washington to testify at courts-martial and loyalty commissions. On one occasion when Lincoln paid a surprise visit to the front line, McClellan made himself scarce and left it to Major Allen to entertain the President. On top of this, he still had the National Detective Agency to run. There was a prolific correspondence between Allan and George Bangs, who continued to hold the fort back in Chicago and who almost ruined his health in the process. Reviewing the prodigious mass of papers in the Pinkerton letter-books, National Archives and the Library of Congress involving Major Allen in all aspects of the war at this crucial period, one can but marvel at Pinkerton's ability to achieve as much as he did.[5]

By 18 August 1862 the Army of the Potomac, which had almost got within shelling distance of Richmond ten weeks earlier, had retreated through the York Peninsula and was now back where it had started on 4 April. During the campaign ten major and extremely bloody battles had been fought and the losses on both sides were appalling. From his field headquarters that day, McClellan sent a despatch to his successor General Halleck imploring him to 'please say a kind word to my army that I can repeat to them in general orders'. Halleck ignored this, and McClellan embarked his battered remnants at Newport News. Three days later, Halleck wired him to maintain a garrison at Yorktown which he promised to reinforce as rapidly as possible; but by that time the last Union soldier was safely back across Chesapeake Bay.

Allan Pinkerton had already left the battlefield and returned to Washington, from where he wrote at great length to McClellan on 20 August. Halleck's despatch to McClellan of 21 August had ended with the words, 'The forces of Burnside and Pope are hard pushed, and require aid as rapidly as you can send it. Come yourself as soon as you can.' Allan's long letter caught up with McClellan at Acquia Creek, on the same day as a second message from Halleck, stating baldly, 'I do not know either where Gen. Pope is or of where the enemy in force is. These are matters which I have all day been most anxious to ascertain.' McClellan viewed this sourly. John Pope was a general whom McClellan despised and held in contempt, not only for his incompetence in the field but for his infamous orders to his men, giving them a free hand to rape and pillage. To his wife, Ellen, McClellan had written on 8 August, 'I will not permit this army to degenerate into a mob of thieves, nor will I return these men of mine to their families as a set of wicked and demoralized robbers.'

The incredible muddle in Washington was described very vividly by Allan in his letter of 20 August. He began by describing Pope's retreat to the Rappahannock in some detail, from information brought to him by one of his agents, adding:

My informant states that Pope reports a force approaching him of two hundred thousand and continually receiving accessions from Jackson, and that since you commenced your retreat the reinforcements have been much larger. But a day or two ago it was officially reported that Jackson had but 21,600 infantry, 2,300 cavalry and 1,000 artillery.

This sort of accurate reporting not only gives the lie to Allan's alleged exaggeration of enemy numbers, but shows how he was quick to assess the situation correctly. Clearly, if McClellan were occasionally guilty of exaggerating numbers, he was by no means the only one. The rest of the letter, however, shows that Allan was now spying on McClellan's behalf on those men in Washington whom he perceived to be the general's enemies:

Yesterday Lincoln, Stanton and Halleck appeared badly. Lincoln was at the War Department by seven a.m., Stanton soon after – and soon Halleck joined them. Guards were placed to keep all persons out of the Department except those with special permits for the day.

Burnside arrived at Fredericksburg yesterday forenoon, and telegraphed that he would be here. About 5 p.m. he arrived, went to Willard's, and kept strictly private. Shortly after his arrival, Stanton went upstairs and soon after, Lincoln. Whether they went to Burnside's room or not my informant cannot tell, but they were there about one hour, each coming down separate stairs (retreating by two ways to blind the observers). Chase [Salmon P. Chase, Secretary of the Treasury] soon afterwards came and remained about two hours, coming down very quietly and vamoosing in same style.

When I was at the Fortress [Monroe] I met Burnside – on his way to meet you. He told me you were all right, and you could have anything you wanted, and agreed to see me after he had reported here. I tried my best to get to see him all last night, but failed. Whether he did not wish to see me, or my messenger did not reach him, I cannot say. If he has not left, I shall try again this morning before he leaves.

I know that all now rests on your being able to reach some point in time to save Pope and by so doing again save the nation. I am still of the opinion that this could best have been accomplished by your original plan – taking Richmond and cutting off Jackson's supplies. But as this was overruled, then it remains to be seen if you can arrive in season to save the nation, as Blücher saved Wellington.

There is something of importance going on with Fox [Gustavus Fox, Assistant Secretary of the Navy] – he is all the time at his house. Yesterday afternoon Lincoln was there for a long time, and Halleck spent four hours there in the evening, and about half-past six this morning Lincoln went there and stayed until about nine o'clock, when he left and went direct to the War Department.

I learn that on Monday a delegation of Illinoisians called on Lincoln and cautioned him against putting Pope forward, remarking, 'Lincoln, you know John Pope well enough,' and I learned that he intimated that he appreciated their sentiments.

In contradiction of what I reported as having been learned from Watson [Peter Watson, Assistant Secretary of War] – that you were to be placed under Pope – I learned last night that Lincoln said to an Illinois friend that you should not be placed under Pope – that it would be a degradation, and he should not do it. That he knew you would not submit to it. At the time he said this, Lincoln must have known that Pope was retreating. May this not account for the milk in the coconut?

Three other letters in similar vein were sent to McClellan in the ensuing week, from which it is abundantly clear that Allan regarded the 'Washington cabal' as less concerned with the successful prosecution of the war as intriguing against McClellan. Over the next few days Allan learned, from his friend Anson Stager of the Federal Telegraph, that Lincoln, Stanton and

Halleck had agreed to give Burnside the Army of the Potomac, leaving McClellan to command Fortress Monroe. 'This will keep you and your friends quiet and thus enable them to get rid of you and your dangerous influence. There would be no orders until all the troops you are to send were gone.' Another agent, however, revealed that Pope was being considered for overall command of the Armies of the Potomac and the Shenandoah Valley, with McClellan reduced to a subordinate role. Allan added, 'From what I can learn, Halleck is vain and egotistical and will spare no effort to ruin you who are the only dangerous rival he has.'

By 25 August many of the regiments withdrawn from the York Peninsula were back in the Washington area and the generals and staff officers were in the capital itself. Allan reported that the tide of opinion was now beginning to swing back in McClellan's favour, the feeling being that he should have been allowed to press on to Richmond *as he had wished*, instead of being pulled back. General Hooker (whose surname would one day enter the language on account of his concern to supply his troops with brothels) was 'mentioned as being very indignant'. '[Major-General William B.] Franklin is said to have had a plain talk with Halleck – and rumors from Alexandria say that the Field and Regimental officers are very outspoken on this point – all of which tends to increase the fears of Lincoln & his coadjutors and this is the only point from now . . .'

On 1 September Allan accompanied his general to Washington, summoned by Lincoln who wished to know why McClellan was not giving General Pope the support he deserved. Salmon Chase had been seeing a great deal of Pope at this time and a day or two previously had reported to Stanton that Pope 'condemned Gen. McClellan's conduct more and in stronger terms than Gen. Halleck, and said that in conversation he found Halleck quite agreed with him, but was averse to precipitate action'.[6] The whispering campaign begun by Stanton and enthusiastically taken up by Chase therefore forced the President's hand. At the interview with Pinkerton and McClellan, the general put his case forcefully, though he agreed to order his subordinates to give the hard-pressed Pope more support. Even so, the President came very close to dismissing McClellan at this time. For a time, Lincoln temporised. As he told John Hay and Gideon Welles, the Navy Secretary, 'We must use what tools we have . . . there is no other man in the army who can man these fortifications and lick these troops of ours into shape half as well as [McClellan] . . . If he can't fight himself, he excels in making others ready to fight.' The President's intention of using McClellan in an administrative role rather than as a field commander was broken by Lee's sudden advance across the Potomac into Maryland. Lincoln offered command of the Army of the Potomac to Burnside, but he knew his limitations and suggested McClellan.

In the end, fear of the Rebels' approach and an increasingly critical public opinion forced Lincoln to reconsider. On 2 September he reinstated McClellan who returned to the battlefront, accompanied by his faithful detective. Allan assigned a new team of operatives, led by George Bangs and Gus Thiel, to monitor the movements of Lee's forces, and by 4 September they were reporting back that they had located Lee's headquarters on the Aldie Turnpike near Dranesville and Jackson's near Fairfax Courthouse. Luck also played a part. A small parcel containing three cigars was found to be wrapped in Lee's field orders; it had been accidentally dropped by one of his aides and later found by a Union patrol. The papers were passed to Allan who brought them immediately to McClellan. The general scanned the documents and exclaimed, 'Here is a paper with which if I cannot whip Bobbie Lee, I will be willing to go home!'

On 17 September McClellan attacked Lee at Antietam. Victory was within McClellan's grasp, with Burnside's corps belatedly coming to his aid; but at the vital moment they ran into A.P. Hill's division and their progress was barred. On the following day the two great armies faced each other. The carnage was the worst of the war up to that time, and although Lee momentarily crossed the Potomac his exhausted troops were soon forced to retreat into Virginia once more. McClellan's forces sustained over 12,000 casualties, but the Army of the Potomac had taken 6,000 prisoners, upwards of 15,000 stands of small arms and thirteen artillery pieces.

While the battle was at its height Allan nearly lost his life. He was with a cavalry squadron when they were targeted by Confederate artillery and came under heavy fire before they gained the safety of deep woodland. Before they reached the trees Allan's favourite sorrel was shot from under him as he was fording a stream. He was thrown from his saddle and concussed when his head hit a boulder. Still half-stunned he managed to stagger out of the water and mounted up behind a cavalry officer. Riding double, they staggered into the woods pursued by enemy gunfire. Although Allan wired Washington that McClellan had secured a 'brilliant victory', Antietam was a victory for neither side. Had Lee been able to press his assault one more time McClellan would have suffered a disastrous rout. While Lee withdrew in reasonably good order, McClellan was in no position to pursue. Instead, he sent Major Allen back to Washington to assess the reaction of the public in general, and of Abraham Lincoln in particular, to the outcome of the battle.

On the morning of Saturday, 22 September, Allan had a meeting with the President and dutifully reported back to McClellan shortly afterwards. He had called at the White House and had seen 'my friend [John] Hay, the Private Secy. He asked if I wanted to see the Pres. I said – no, not particularly. I have nothing new to say, but if the Pres. desired to see me, I should be happy to tell him all I knew . . .' Hay was Nicolay's collaborator in the ten-volume biography of Lincoln, commenced immediately after the President's assassination and, as we have already seen, no friend of McClellan. In the course of Allan's very long and detailed letter it is clear that Lincoln asked numerous searching questions, but that Allan was able to give him a full and factual account. Throughout this lengthy interview Lincoln was perfectly affable, and Allan was forced to conclude:

> For myself, you know I am rather prejudiced against him – but I must confess that he impressed me more at this interview with his honesty towards you & his desire to do you justice than he has ever done before and I would respectfully suggest that whenever you can consistently give him information regarding your movements, skirmishes, etc it would be very acceptable . . .
>
> Previous to seeing the President I had seen Stanton at the Department. He saw me in the hall while waiting to see [Major Thomas] Eckert and invited me into his private room. He evidently wanted to talk – just as he has on one or two occasions done before – but feared to broach the topic, so after a few unimportant statements made by me, in reference to the pursuit of the enemy, our conversation closed. I sat for about ten minutes without speaking and on the entrance of some gentlemen, took the opportunity to leave. While with the President and just as I got through, Stanton came into the room. The Pres. asked him to be seated but S. said no – he supposed he [Lincoln] wanted to see Mr Allen alone – and he left.[7]

Two days after Allan's visit to the White House, Lincoln published the draft of his Emancipation Proclamation. That afternoon serenaders came with a brass band, and the President addressed them from his balcony, saying, 'I can only trust in God I have made no mistake.' While Lincoln was immensely gratified by the plaudits, privately he noted in his diary 'the stocks have declined, and troops come forward more slowly than ever'. In England, half a million men were thrown out of work because of the cotton famine, and 130,000 in one French textile district alone. A wave of fury swept the South; Lincoln was breaking the laws of civilised warfare, outraging private property rights, inviting Negroes to kill, burn and rape – or so the statesmen, orators and newspapers said.

Against this background Horan's claim, that McClellan told Pinkerton that he would resign if he had to serve a government that supported emancipation, has to be examined. McClellan was a Democrat by political persuasion (but so was Stanton and Montgomery Blair, the Postmaster General). McClellan's views on the matter, however, were far more balanced. 'I invariably took the ground that I was thoroughly opposed to slavery, regarding it as a great evil, especially to the whites of the South, but that in my opinion no sweeping measure of emancipation should be carried out, unless accompanied by arrangements providing for the new relations between employer and employed, carefully guarding the rights and interests of both. If there were such a measure framed to my satisfaction I would cordially support it.'[8]

The basis for Horan's assertion lies not in anything published by Pinkerton after the event, but in a remark by the general in a private letter to his wife: 'The President's proclamation, and other troubles, render it almost impossible for me to retain my commission and self-respect at the same time.' Putting this in context, one should note the letter to Ellen written on 20 September, three days after Antietam. He had come to the conclusion that Stanton and Halleck should be got rid of: '. . . no success is possible with them. I am tired of fighting against such disadvantages, and feel that it is now time for the country to come to my help and remove these difficulties from my path.' That evening he added a further passage: '. . . I hope that my future will be determined this week. Thro' certain friends of mine I have taken the stand that Stanton must leave and that Halleck must restore my old place to me. Unless these two conditions are fulfilled I will leave the service.' Three days later he wrote to Mrs McClellan again, ' . . . I cannot make up my mind to fight for such a cursed doctrine as that of a servile insurrection – it is too infamous. Stanton is as great a villain as ever and Halleck as great a fool – he has no brains whatever!'

The proclamation of 22 September had been half-baked and its consequences not thoroughly considered. The Cabinet itself was bitterly divided on the matter. Some thought that the freed slaves should be conscripted into labour battalions to serve in the army; others toyed with the notion of shipping them off to Liberia or Haiti; while there was also a plan to purchase land in Panama and colonise it with the freed slaves. The proclamation sent shockwaves that reverberated across the nation, North and South, and rumours of plot and counter-plot against the government were rife. On 24 September, for example, the journalist L.A. Whiteley wrote to James Gordon Bennett from Washington:

A deep and earnest feeling pervades the army concerning the proclamation. The army is dissatisfied and the air is thick with revolution. It has been not only thought of but talked of and the question now is, where can the man be found. McClellan is idolised but he seems to have no political ambition. The sentiment throughout the whole army seems to be in favor of a change of dynasty . . . if the expression from the army of McClellan corresponds to that of the position of the army round Washington there may be a change in the Government and in the form of Government within a very few days. Your article of a few days ago suggesting that McClellan should dictate to the administration was regarded then as revolutionary, but I have heard a hundred of the same men, who then found fault with it, express today the same opinion.[9]

The Democratic Party, already campaigning for the November elections, raised the issue that the war for the Union had been changed to a war for abolition. It was in light of this that McClellan defused the explosive situation by issuing a general order reminding his officers and men that in a democracy the military was subordinate to the civil authorities and that the objectives of war were not decided by the troops but by civilians. 'The remedy for political errors could be found at the polls.' Horan's extravagant comment on this was:

Pinkerton showed the weakness in his character when he, the one-time rabid abolitionist who had virtually obtained the train fare for John Brown and his runaway slaves by threats and intimidation of Chicago politicians, endorsed his general's egotistical, unbelievable order to the army.[10]

But McClellan's general order was none of these things; and there was nothing in it to which Allan could have taken exception, far less earned such opprobrium or denigration from his unsympathetic biographer. Furthermore, there was no reaction from either Halleck or Stanton, nor, indeed, from Lincoln himself. The order had the desired effect in calming the furore among the front-line troops.

On the morning of 1 October McClellan got a tip-off from Allan that Lincoln, accompanied by Major-General John A. McClernand, John W. Garrett, the Secretary of State of Illinois, and other politicians from that state, was on his way to the battlefront. McClellan left Sharpsburg with Major Allen and went to Harper's Ferry where they caught up with the presidential party. With relief McClellan noted that none of the Cabinet was with Lincoln. McClernand (1812–1900), like Lincoln, had been born in Kentucky but had made his mark as a lawyer in Illinois. He was at this time a major-general of volunteers and had commanded a division at Shiloh. Eighteen months later he would be removed from his command by Grant for dilatoriness, but promptly restored by his crony Lincoln, anxious to conciliate this leader of the Illinois War Democrats.

Lincoln stayed at the front for several days and during the visit McClellan had many long conversations with the President alone. Lincoln reassured him that he had every confidence in him and wished him to continue preparations for a new campaign. 'He repeated that he was entirely satisfied with me; that I should be let alone; that he would stand by me.'[11]

Outside McClellan's tent on South Mountain on 4 October Lincoln posed for a photograph by Matthew Brady, flanked by two of his old friends from the railroad days. On the left stood Allan in mufti with a bowler hat, squinting into the autumn sunlight. On the right stood a heavily bearded McClernand. Towering above them both, his height accentuated by a tall top hat, the President stood to attention. Both Pinkerton and McClernand had their right hands thrust into their chests in the manner of Napoleon. Photographs of McClellan and Lincoln sitting together bareheaded in the general's tent were also taken by Brady.

Later that morning Allan rode back in the train with the President and the Illinois delegation. Soon after his arrival in Washington he wrote at great length to McClellan, reporting that he had had considerable conversation on the journey and concluding on an optimistic note about Lincoln:

> There is no doubt in my mind but that he now appreciates your worth – and at the present time is friendly. How long he may be allowed to continue so is impossible to say. But my opinion is that it will be very difficult to move or change him now. I believe him honest in what he said – and that he feels disposed to give you all you want.
>
> I also had a private conversation with Mr Hatch of Springfield, Illinois, who told me that he knew the President believed you to be the ablest General in the country and the only one capable of fighting a large army.

The letter also gave details of some of the problems Allan was having with the bureaucrats over the payments for the services of his agents. This had been a recurring problem since following McClellan to Washington, Allan often being kept waiting months for settlement of these accounts. On several occasions he was reduced to telegraphing Bangs for drafts in order to pay his operatives and other expenses. Now he was irritated to be questioned by Assistant Secretary Peter Watson over the bills he had submitted for July, August and September. Watson was demanding the names of Allan's operatives in full. Hitherto Allan had identified them merely by initials, and he refused to comply with Watson's demands on the grounds that 'the very nature of this service requires me to keep my men unknown', adding that, on account of the War Department having let certain Confederate sympathisers go South, his agents had been compromised and one of them hanged. Watson was unmoved by this, and insisted that he would not pass the bills for payment unless he had the full names. Allan then retorted that he would prefer to withdraw the bills and lose the amounts, rather than give such a key to his force.

Regarding the session with Matthew Brady, he continued:

I had an interview with my friend Nicolay. He called by request of the President to get some of the pictures which were taken of yourself and the Prest. at your Headquarters. They will be ready tomorrow and I will see he receives them. They are very fine, the best I have ever seen. The anxiety of the President to get them augurs no ill feeling. I will have copies sent to you by first opportunity.

Nicolay (whom we now know to have been unreasonably hostile to McClellan) told Allan that the President 'was much gratified' by his visit to Antietam. 'From what Nicolay said I have no doubt but that after you give the Rebels one more good Battle you will be called here to the command of the whole Army.' This gentle hint was followed by a recital of Watson's grumblings, inferring that the sole reason for Lincoln's visit to the battlefield had been to urge McClellan to action. Although Allan dismissed this as mere newspaper gossip, he added:

By the way I learn that a Brig. Genl. Garfield, or name like that, had been talking in a similar strain as Watson to the Judge Advocate. Garfield is said to belong to the Army of the Potomac. Garfield had said that McClellan had been laying still for a month; that the Army was all anxious to go forward but he (G) supposed it would go into Winter quarters; that the enemy was not over seventy thousand strong and that if you would only move on them you could go straight on to Richmond.

The fire-eating general was James Abram Garfield (1831–81), former canal boatman, carpenter, dirt farmer, teacher, lately Professor of Ancient Languages at the Eclectic Institute in Hiram, Ohio, member of the state senate and commanding officer of the 42nd Ohio Volunteers. He had fought bravely at Shiloh and had recently been promoted to brigadier-general. Like Allan, he was violently opposed to slavery and, as one of the more outspoken politicians on the radical wing of the Republican party, was a staunch advocate of the confiscation of Confederate property. Promoted to major-general for gallantry at Chickamauga, he returned to politics after the war. In 1880 he was elected to the Senate. The following year, on the *thirty-sixth* ballot, he secured the Republican nomination for the presidency and narrowly defeated his Democratic opponent. His tenure of the White House was short-lived. Less than four months after his inauguration he was shot at a Washington railway station by a disappointed office-seeker. He lingered on till 19 September 1881 and was buried in Cleveland, Ohio.

During October McClellan regrouped and consolidated his position, strengthening the defences around Harper's Ferry on the Shenandoah and building great pontoon bridges which would transport his army, wagons and artillery over that river and the Potomac. Far from contemplating a withdrawal to winter quarters, McClellan planned to launch an all-out attack. At the end of the month the army began to move forward but heavy rains hampered its progress. Nevertheless, in the ensuing week the corps and divisions of the army advanced according to McClellan's carefully laid plans. Everything was going well when, at 11.30 p.m. on the night of 7 November, McClellan's letter-writing to his wife was interrupted 'in the shape of dear good old Burnside, accompanied by Gen. Buckingham, the secretary's adjutant-general'. They brought with them the order from Stanton that he was to hand over his command to General Burnside and proceed to Trenton, New Jersey, immediately.

Napoleonic to the last, McClellan issued an emotional farewell to the army from his camp near Rectortown, Virginia. The army as a whole was consternated by the President's decision to sack Little Mac, and there were many who felt like marching on Washington to take possession of the government. McClellan stayed on long enough to calm this dangerous situation and hand over to Burnside in an orderly manner. His farewell parade at Warrenton on 10 November was, by all accounts, an extremely moving occasion, raw recruits and grizzled veterans alike weeping uncontrollably as their favourite general, desperately struggling to maintain his self-control, rode along their ranks. His services of national prominence had lasted barely eighteen months, during which time he had experienced such extremes of good and ill fortune, of success and failure, as seldom have fallen to the lot of any one man. Despite all the verbiage of McClellan's detractors, the plain fact was that no general cared more for his men, or was more loved by them in return. His dismissal was one of the more disgraceful incidents in a war replete with sordid acts.

Lincoln's *volte face*, one of the few discreditable acts of his administration, has been glibly explained away as a reaction to McClellan's tardiness; but this ignores the intensely bitter feelings against the Democrat general shared by many of the politicians of the period. As one observer later recorded, the President realised 'that the bitterness of many influential men in Congress and some filling high official and military offices towards McClellan was such, that to them his success in command would be less endurable than his failure'.[12] Stanton and Chase were bitterly hostile to McClellan and had demanded his dismissal, whereas Seward and Gideon Welles (Secretary of the Navy) were more conservative. The sad truth was that no one in Washington realised just what poor shape the army was in at this time. McClellan, attentive as ever to the welfare of his men, importuned the War Department time and time again for fresh footwear, uniforms, blankets, greatcoats and other stores before the onset of winter, but the politicians refused. There is an abundance of evidence, in the personal letters of generals and field officers as well as regimental troops, that thousands of men were barefoot, and that artillery horses and pack animals were starving.[13]

There is a curious tailpiece to this episode. Brigadier-General Duffield of Pennsylvania, who had been on McClellan's staff at Antietam, claimed later that one afternoon shortly after the battle, a group of Senators and Congressmen had visited headquarters, and urged McClellan to take control of the government and be free to act as he thought best for bringing the war to a close. McClellan called his staff together and sought their views on this proposal. The consensus was that this would present no difficulty, and would be generally welcomed, but that there might be practical difficulties in relinquishing dictatorial powers after peace was established. McClellan thanked them and said that this was his own view of the matter and therefore he proposed to dismiss it without further notice.

In 1915 Captain John R. King, who had commanded a company of the 6th Maryland Infantry during the war, told William Myers (McClellan's biographer) that, immediately after the battle of Antietam, McClellan had written a letter to his Confederate opponent, inviting him to a conference with a view to uniting both their armies and marching on Washington to end the war. McClellan would be dictator and Lee commander-in-chief. General Joe Davidson, who had been on Hooker's staff at Antietam, substantiated this story and arranged a meeting between Captain King and General James Longstreet, the ex-Confederate, who was then in Washington. King brought up the subject of the letter and Longstreet claimed to have seen it. Lee had sent for him, shown him the letter, and asked him what it meant, but Longstreet advised Lee to have nothing to do with it. Lee also showed it to Robert Toombs, who gave the same advice.

The only reference to this affair in McClellan's papers is in a letter from his friend E.H. Wright, dated Washington 11 March 1864, deploring 'the infamous statement of a certain Mr W in reference to an interview between you and the Rebel General Lee, a few days after the battle of Antietam. These are sad times when men can be brought to perjure themselves.'[14] The perjury seems to pertain to an actual meeting (which never took place), but this does not rule out the possibility that McClellan did put out some sort of feeler towards Lee. In ordinary circumstances this might seem treasonable, but these were extraordinary times, and Lee himself was unique, the only man in history who, at the commencement of a war, was offered general command by *both* sides. Though he detested slavery and could imagine no greater calamity than the dissolution of the Union, Lee felt honour-bound to support his native state, Virginia.

After McClellan's sacking, Allan resigned his commission in sympathy and withdrew his operatives from the Army of the Potomac. He did not trust Burnside, who made no move to retain his services. Thereafter Allan returned to Chicago, to be reunited with his wife and family after a gap of eighteen months. Before he left field headquarters at Warrenton, Allan wrote a letter to Pryce Lewis, still in detention at Castle Thunder near Richmond. He told him that he had resigned from the army and was 'returning to the old stand in Chicago'. Both he and McClellan were still trying to procure his release, in exchange for Confederate prisoners. In Washington, Allan had a brief interview with Stanton, who made a half-hearted promise to get the Pinkerton agents released; but there is no evidence that he ever lifted a finger. So far as Stanton was concerned, Lewis and Scully were little better than traitors and were not worth an exchange.

While McClellan was sent to an obscure posting in the North, Allan continued to act on behalf of the War Department, investigating the claims of contractors and others, but never again engaged in espionage or intelligence work. Throughout 1863 Allan and his agents remained in and around Washington, engaged on fraud and other criminal rather than military matters. In July of that year he received a letter from his old commander, written from Orange, New Jersey. On being relieved of his command, McClellan was ordered to proceed to Trenton where he kicked his heels, out of the political limelight. He soon gave up his quarters at Trenton and moved to nearby Orange, where he eventually purchased a fine house. The letter, beginning 'My dear Allan', was in reply to one from Pinkerton a week earlier giving the general an eye-witness account of the battle of Gettysburg and smugly noting that Lee had yet again escaped. 'I wonder whether they will ever learn that a large army is not to be trapped like a rat?'

During that year Allan commuted between Washington and Chicago, gradually picking up the threads of his pre-war business. Much of his civil workload that year came from the railways, ending in the successful prosecution of a dozen conductors on the Philadelphia and Reading Railroad for larceny on a large scale. Only one man contested the evidence and was acquitted, but the others were found guilty and sentenced to long terms of imprisonment.

In the spring of 1864 Allan and his team of agents, including his son William, were transferred to the Department of the Mississippi under Major General Edward R.S. Canby, and sent by Stanton to New Orleans to investigate the massive cotton frauds. The damning evidence of corruption on a grand scale which Allan amassed led to the conviction of a large number of crooked brokers and fraudsters, and the recovery of vast sums of money for the government.

Allan was in New Orleans when news reached him that his daughter Belle, who had been in poor health since early childhood, had died. He and Willie immediately set off on the long journey home for the funeral. The death of this girl, still in her teens, shattered Allan, stricken with remorse that he had neglected his family these past two years and had not been with Belle at the end. The death of one frail child might seem as nothing when men were still being slaughtered in their thousands; but Allan, who had seen more than enough of violent death since the war began, took this blow very hard. After this, he was never the same man again.

In ten days early in May 1864 Grant with 120,000 men confronted Lee with two-thirds that number. By dawn on 13 May the Union forces had lost 26,815 killed and wounded and 4,183 missing. No record of Confederate casualties was ever published, but on the basis of the prisoners taken by Grant it was plain that Lee's army was being mercilessly slashed. Though the ten days' running battle of the Wilderness was hailed as a victory, Grant's reputation waned as the dreadful truth of Union losses emerged. A few days later, at Cold Harbor, within sight of the steeples of Richmond, Grant ordered a frontal attack and lost 3,000 men in twenty minutes. On 3 June, 7,000 Union troops perished, against 1,200 on the Confederate side. The Northern newspapers were loud in their criticism and there was a clamour for the recall of George McClellan. Allan wrote to his old chief from Washington, 'From what I could glean here there is intention of giving you command. Would you accept it?' McClellan, however, now had his sights set on higher things, the presidency of the United States no less.

The Democratic Convention met in Chicago on 29 August 1864. Allan Pinkerton was among the 'disgruntled Republicans' whom the 'war Democrats' wooed. McClellan's platform was remarkably simple, promising to adhere 'with unswerving fidelity to the Union under the Constitution as the only solid foundation of our strength, security, and happiness as a people, and as a framework of government equally conducive to the welfare of all the states, both Northern and Southern'. McClellan roundly condemned the Lincoln administration for a lack of sympathy with prisoners-of-war, and promised 'care, protection and regard' for soldiers and sailors. McClellan won the nomination overwhelmingly – indeed, he was too successful in this respect for some of his most enthusiastic supporters were notorious Copperheads, such as Clement Vallandigham of Ohio.

On the morning of 29 October, McClellan's most trusted aide, Colonel E.H. Wright, travelled to Baltimore for a secret meeting with Allan Pinkerton who told him, in all seriousness, of a plot by McClellan's friends to murder Lincoln. Later Wright reported the gist of this meeting to George Ticknor Curtis:

Every one of the conspirators was known and watched and on the slightest movement on their part all would be arrested and hung. I asked him for the names of these men. He mentioned the names of yourself [Curtis], Colonel [Thomas] Key, Mr [August] Belmont and my own name, with those of others I do not recall. I treated this statement as an absurdity, and asked him if he had anything else to say. Pinkerton then told me that he was a friend of McClellan and wished to serve him in every way he could; that McClellan and his friends might as well give up the fight; that the elections would be carried for Mr Lincoln by just such majorities as they wished; that Pennsylvania would give any majority they called for; that, with the exception of New Jersey, about which they cared nothing, every state would give Mr Lincoln its vote, and it would be seen that the majorities were overwhelming, as to prevent further opposition. That the attempt to get the soldiers to vote for McClellan would not be allowed to get beyond control. That the election was already settled, and that McClellan and his friends would get into serious trouble if they did not abstain from further action.[15]

Allan concluded with the very interesting statement that 'Mr Lincoln knew of this interview, and that it was with a desire to befriend McClellan and save him from possible trouble that he had employed him [Pinkerton] in the matter'. Wright added that McClellan treated this story as absurd when it was reported to him, and remarked that he would not insult any of his friends by repeating such a charge to them. 'The interview did not have the slightest effect on him or his friends. It was agreed that my interview with Pinkerton should not be spoken of to any one,' concluded Wright:

I believe he [Pinkerton] was honest in his assertions of friendship for McClellan; that he knew the desperate men in control at Washington and had their secrets; that he feared the zeal of some of McClellan's friends might be used by his enemies as an excuse for his arrest and trial by the pliant courts and suborned witnesses of Stanton.

Balloting took place on 8 November 1864 and resulted, as Allan had so gloomily predicted, in a crushing majority for Lincoln. McClellan carried only three states, Delaware, Kentucky and New Jersey, with an electoral vote of twenty-one; Lincoln took the remaining twenty-two states with an electoral vote of 212. In fact Little Mac only narrowly lost Connecticut, New Hampshire, New York and Oregon, which had an electoral vote of forty-seven, and was not far behind Lincoln in Illinois, Indiana, Maryland, Minnesota and Pennsylvania, which cast sixty-six electoral votes. A shift of some 60,000 votes in these strategic or marginal states would have made all the difference.

On the day of the election, McClellan sent to Lincoln the resignation of his commission as a major-general in the regular army. Meanwhile Allan returned to New Orleans, taking with him his younger son Robert, then aged seventeen, who was immediately sworn in as one of his father's deputies by a lieutenant of the New Orleans Provost Marshal's office.

◆ 10 ◆

Aftermath of War
1865–68

On 29 September 1863 Lewis and Scully were finally released from Castle Thunder and joined a party of 150 Union prisoners-of-war being repatriated at City Point. When Lewis, ragged and emaciated, stepped out of the railway boxcar and saw the Star-spangled Banner on the mast of the exchange boat, he wept for joy. 'If before this moment I had any English feelings left,' he recollected, 'I was turned into a complete American at that time.' That night they slept on deck, and arrived at Annapolis, Maryland, early the following morning. Instead of the hero's welcome he had anticipated, Lewis found total indifference. Even worse, the transport officer insisted that his orders did not permit free passage of civilians to Washington. Lewis pawned his once-fine jacket for three dollars and got sufficient cash for two one-way tickets and some bread and cheese. Arriving in Washington late that night, the ragged couple wondered who to contact; Allan Pinkerton was now in Chicago and McClellan in New Jersey. Then they remembered William Wood, the superintendent at the Old Capitol. They set off to walk all the way to the prison. Wood was hauled out of bed by the night guard and peered in disbelief through the grating at the human scarecrows, clad in filthy rags. When Wood heard the unmistakable clipped English accent of Pryce Lewis, he gasped. Immediately he summoned the prison doctor and ordered up a sumptuous meal from his own kitchen. Wood almost wept as he watched the two men fall on the food like ravening wolves. 'My God!' he kept saying. 'Why didn't you telegraph me? I would have sent a special locomotive for you!'

The following day Wood took Lewis and Scully to the War Department, but

Stanton refused to see them, believing them both to have sent Webster to his death. Whatever the rights and wrongs of the matter, Stanton should have debriefed the agents, but his prejudice got in the way of his good sense, and much valuable intelligence on the present state of the Confederacy was thereby denied him. Wood telegraphed Allan, who was then in Philadelphia on a case. Lewis preserved the telegram which Pinkerton sent to Wood, using his *nom de guerre*:

> Many thanks for your kind information. Tell Scully and Lewis to come here. I cannot possibly leave just now. Should they require money to come please let them have it. I will return it to you. Give them my address here and tell them to avoid all publicity of their affairs until they see me.[1]

In view of the fact that Allan was, at that time, convinced that both men had betrayed Webster, his magnanimity was remarkable. Lewis did not say what transpired when they met in Philadelphia, recording only that he had 'a hot interview with the old man . . . and we did not spare him for his carelessness in getting us into the enemy's hands'. This was an allusion to the decision by the government to release Confederate agents and sympathisers, including the Morton boys, and permit them to go South. In the Agency pamphlet of 1903 there was a laconic reference to the release of Rose Greenhow and the Mortons from the Old Capitol and their subsequent journey to Richmond – 'a terrible mistake on the part of the War Department'. Both Lewis and Scully were still alive when this was published but there is no record of any comment by them at that time. Allan arranged for $100 in gold to be sent to Richmond to pay Confederate Brigadier-General Humphrey Marshal who had acted as attorney for Lewis and Scully and helped negotiate their release. The bag of gold was entrusted to Belle Boyd, one of Rose's female spies, who was escorted by Captain James Mix of the Old Capitol prison guard, to ensure that she would get safely past General Ben 'the Beast' Butler at Fortress Monroe on 1 December 1863 – one of the more bizarre incidents in this topsy-turvy war.

Neither man ever worked for Pinkerton again. Thanks to Wood, Lewis secured an appointment as bailiff at the Old Capitol. In 1866, when Colonel William Wood was appointed head of the United States Secret Service in succession to General Lafayette Baker, Lewis joined Wood's staff and continued to give good, if clandestine, service to his adopted country for many years. Scully returned to Chicago, where he spent the rest of his working life as a security guard in the City Hall.

While he was only too ready to disburse money on behalf of his former agents, Allan was at this time having a running battle with the Treasury Department in Washington whose auditors were querying his Secret Service accounts, going back over a period of two years. There was a discrepancy of $683 dating from 1861 which was giving immense worry to Third Auditor R.J. Atkinson who wrote repeatedly to both Pinkerton and McClellan earnestly pleading with them to 'submit at the earliest practical period a reply'.[2] Allan's letter to H. Limouse, his New York representative, on this matter casts an interesting light on his work at this time and the curious method by which it was funded. Before he came to Cincinnati in 1861, Allan had sent three operatives 'to Memphis and vicinity' at McClellan's behest. Their pay was to be ten dollars a day, plus expenses.

They returned on May 19 and at the General's order reported to me. I took their statements and on the General's order settled their accounts with them. Taking on direction of Major Marcy [McClellan's father-in-law] separate vouchers from each in duplicate, calculating their time at ten dollars per day, including the 20th and expenses. Receiving from the General's personal check on the Commercial Bank, Cincinnati for $419 which was the amount necessary to settle with them. The General had paid two of them since Marcy at starting out, which amount I included in the settlement. I think it likely you will find some receipt of this in my files or the General has it.

Please call on General McClellan at this office and he will give you the date when these men left, compute their time at ten dollars each day and divide the balance of the amounts paid by General McClellan prior to starting and the $419.00 and disbursed by me to them as for expenses to each $1000.

All these paid [to the agent] were paid by the General into his own funds, and the only way it appears to me is to include those charges in my bill and when the balance is paid I can repay the General. Thus my bill will be his voucher for his operations in the 'Department of Ohio' but in all make out the charges as the General directs and then deliver the bill to the General making a full Journal entry as regards total of the bill and balance.

In the spring of 1865 the war finally dragged to a close. On 9 April Lee surrendered his army to Grant at Appomattox. A day later William Tecumseh Sherman moved out against Joe Johnston and occupied Raleigh, North Carolina, on 13 April. The following day Johnston asked for an armistice. Effectively it was the end of the war, though desultory fighting continued beyond the Mississippi till 26 May. 14 April was Good Friday, and there was a holiday atmosphere in Washington. Mary Todd Lincoln, who had only recently given up mourning the loss of her youngest son William Wallace, urged the President to accompany her to Ford's Theatre for an evening performance of *Our American Cousins*. Around eight o'clock the Lincolns entered their carriage and rolled off down H Street where they called at the home of Senator Ira Harris to pick up twenty-eight-year-old Major Henry Rathbone and his fiancée Clara Harris.

The President's bodyguard that evening was John F. Parker, one of the four officers from the Metropolitan Police of Washington on the White House detail, charged with keeping a close watch on Lincoln at all times. Parker had something of a questionable record. In March and April 1863 he had been tried on various charges which included being asleep in a streetcar when he should have been pounding his beat and conduct unbecoming an officer through five weeks' residence in a brothel where it was alleged he had been habitually drunk and disorderly and had fired a revolver through a window. Parker was clearly a man of loose habits. How he wormed his way on to the White House detail, let alone remained there, is a mystery; but it should be noted that when he received notice of his draft for the army on 3 April 1863 it was Mary Todd Lincoln, no less, who wrote a letter to the District of Columbia Provost Marshal securing Parker's exemption from military service.

At the theatre, coachman Francis Burns reined his horses and valet Charles Forbes opened the carriage door. The party entered the theatre at 8.25 p.m.; the Lincolns were late and the first act was well under way. Parker led the way up to the presidential box and as the Lincolns took their seats the virtually full house of 1,675 stood up and cheered. The performance was halted, while the orchestra played 'Hail to the Chief'. Lincoln, partly concealed from view by heavy drapes, sat with his back to the door, in a black walnut rocking-chair upholstered in red damask. Mary sat on his right, and on the far right Miss Harris and Major Rathbone were seated on a small sofa. Parker, having already checked the box, took up his stance in the corridor leading to the box. Shortly before nine o'clock, bored stiff, Parker left his post, went outside and invited Burns to join him for a drink at Peter Taltavul's saloon next door. Soon afterwards they were joined by Forbes who had left his seat at the back of the presidential box.

Meanwhile Abraham Lincoln relaxed. He was in a genial mood: the war was all but over and soon the army would be demobilised, saving the taxpayers at least half a million dollars a day. To his right, he noted young Rathbone and Clara surreptitiously holding hands. Romance was in the air, for he now did something he had not essayed in many a long year; he reached out and fondly squeezed his wife's hand.

John Wilkes Booth, celebrated actor and the matinee idol of the times, rode up to the theatre at 9.30 p.m., entered the alley at the side and dismounted. A young boy named Joseph Burroughs, nicknamed Johnny Peanut because he used to sell peanuts, agreed to hold Booth's horse for him. Booth went in through the back door and crossed the theatre underneath the stage. He was very familiar with the play, for it had been playing to packed houses for fourteen years, and he knew exactly the right moment when a solo actor would be on stage, getting the loudest laugh of the evening. He had time to kill, so he exited on Tenth Street and went into Taltavul's where he ordered whisky. Outside the saloon later he chatted for a while with two of the theatre staff, presently joined by Captain William Williams of the Mounted Police, a long-time fan of Booth. Williams invited his favourite actor to join him for a drink, but Booth declined, saying he wished to catch Miss Keene's performance. At 10.07 p.m. Booth re-entered the theatre by the main door, nodded to John Buckingham in the ticket booth, and ascended the stairs to the dress circle, paused momentarily and then slipped through the small white door leading to the presidential box.

Through the spy-hole in the door, Booth saw Lincoln in his rocking-chair. When Harry Hawk, playing the part of Asa Trenchard, reached his punch-line, 'Don't know the manners of good society, eh?' Booth noiselessly opened the door inward, crept swiftly and silently across the box, and placed his small-bore Derringer at the back of Lincoln's head just behind the left ear. As the audience erupted with laughter, Booth fired once. '*Sic semper tyrannis*,' he said softly. The words, meaning 'thus always to tyrants', were spoken by Brutus as he stabbed Caesar – and were also the motto of the State of Virginia.

Rathbone grappled with the assassin, but Booth pulled out a Sheffield knife and slashed the major's left arm to the bone. Crying out 'Revenge for the South!', Booth vaulted the balustrade and dropped twelve feet to the stage below. He had a fine reputation as a swashbuckling actor, but on this occasion the spur of his right boot caught on a flag draping the box and he crashed heavily to the boards in an awkward kneeling position. His left leg took the full force and snapped just above the ankle. Despite his injury, Booth stumbled to the wings and made his escape before the audience was aware that this was not part of the play. In the alley he knocked down Johnny Peanut, swung into the saddle and galloped off into the night.

Ten days earlier, William Seward was gravely injured in a riding accident, his right shoulder badly dislocated and his jaw smashed. At about the same time as the President was shot, a Confederate deserter named Lewis Paine burst into the Seward home on Lafayette Square, pistol-whipped Fred Seward and smashed his skull, then attacked the Secretary's daughter Fanny and a soldier-nurse, Sergeant George T. Robinson, who were at Seward's bedside. Seward was asleep, his head encased in a massive iron frame. This undoubtedly saved his life, but his assailant managed to stab him three times in the cheek and neck, before Seward rolled over and fell out of bed, on the floor between the bed and the wall. Paine made his getaway after slashing a State Department messenger, Emrick Hansell, on the staircase, and rode off.

William Bell, the Sewards' young Negro servant, ran after him, screaming 'Murder! Murder!' at the top of his voice. Behind lay five people severely injured.

Abraham Lincoln did not die instantly. He lingered on through the night and expired at 7.21 a.m. on Saturday morning. During the night Edwin Stanton had become the man of the hour, issuing orders to the military and the police, telegraphing Grant and other generals, alerting Chief Justice Chase to be on stand-by to administer the oath of office to Vice-President Andrew Johnson, and wiring Police Chief Kennedy in New York, asking him to send his best detectives immediately.

Allan Pinkerton was with General Canby at general headquarters in New Orleans five days later when he learned that Lincoln had been assassinated. Willie would later recall incorrectly that the news came by wire and that his father wept bitterly as he crumpled the telegram in his hands. Indeed, it was logical to assume that such dreadful news would have been disseminated as widely and as quickly as possible by telegram, if only to warn the security forces everywhere to be on the lookout for the perpetrators. In fact, the first that anyone in New Orleans knew of the tragedy (and even then inaccurately) was when they read it in their newspapers, as Allan himself stated in the telegram which he sent, on 19 April, to the War Department offering his services:

This morning's papers contain the deplorable intelligence of the assassination of President Lincoln and Secretary Seward. Under the providence of God, in February 1861, I was enabled to save him from the fate he has now met. How I regret that I had not been near him previous to the fatal act. I might have had the means to arrest it. If I can be of any service, please let me know. The services of my whole force, or life itself, is at your disposal. I trust you will excuse me for impressing upon you the necessity of great personal caution on your part. At this time the nation cannot spare you.

E.J. ALLEN

In due course Stanton got this telegram on the evening of 23 April, though it seems odd that it should have taken four days to reach Washington. Stanton sent a brief letter the following day, addressed to E.J. Allen as usual:

Accept my thanks for your telegram of the 19th received this evening. Mr Seward is still alive and there is a bare possibility of his recovery. His son's case is hopeless. Booth and two of his accomplices Surratt and Harrold [Herold] are still at large. Some of the others have been secured. Booth may have made his way to the West with a view of getting to Texas or Mexico. I think he has tried to do so. You will please take measures to watch the western rivers and you may get him. The reward offered for him now amounts to One hundred thousand dollars or over. Ask General Canby to give orders in his command for his arrest.

By the time Allan got this message about the end of the month, however, Booth was already dead. He and Herold escaped from Washington and were on the run for ten days before they were tracked down to Garrett's Farm near Port Royal Virginia. Herold surrendered but Booth, holed up in a tobacco barn, was shot and fatally wounded by Sergeant Boston Corbett at 3.15 a.m. on 26 April. Although official instructions from Washington were that Booth should be taken alive, one officer instructed his men to shoot the assassin on sight. That man was Colonel William P. Wood.[3]

Commenting on the assassination, Allan would later pen one of the great might-have-beens of history: 'If only I had been there to protect him as I had done before'. Between the Baltimore Plot and the incident at Ford's Theatre there had been seventy-eight threats to the President's life, but no other actual attempt.

Horan, writing in 1967, printed Stanton's letter to Pinkerton without comment. In light of startling evidence which was only discovered in 1957 but not made fully public till 1966, it seems that Stanton deliberately put Pinkerton off the scent. The case against the Secretary of War may be summarised briefly. A few days earlier Lincoln had visited Richmond and returned to Washington to give the impression that he intended to adopt a conciliatory approach to the defeated Confederacy. This alienated the radical wing of the Republican party which got its revenge when the infamous Reconstruction of the South was inaugurated after Lincoln's death. Vice-President Andrew Johnson, the man who stood to gain most from Lincoln's death, was perceived by the radicals as the right man to exact a 'just peace'. Ironically, Johnson changed tack and began to espouse Lincoln's policy, resulting in his denunciation by the disappointed radicals and accusations that he was implicated in Lincoln's murder.

On the other hand, a damning mass of circumstantial evidence could be presented against one man who had much to gain by the death of Lincoln and Seward, who was exceedingly ambitious, ruthless, devious and totally without scruple. Chief among the 'Washington cabal' who intrigued against McClellan was Edwin McMasters Stanton, of whom the general once wrote to his wife:

I think that (I do not wish to be irreverent) had he lived in the time of the Saviour, Judas Iscariot would have remained a respected member of the fraternity of the Apostles, and that the magnificent treachery and rascality of E.M. Stanton would have caused Judas to have raised his name in holy horrors.

Little Mac was not alone in such extreme views. Gideon Welles, the Secretary of the Navy, also distrusted Stanton intensely. A shrewd judge of character, he once wrote in his diary that the Secretary of War 'has cunning and skill . . . dissembles his feelings . . . is a hypocrite'. As regards the plot to kill Lincoln, Edwin Stanton had both the motive and the means. There is abundant evidence, too detailed to discuss here, that Stanton had prior knowledge of the plot. Stanton went to extraordinary lengths to prevent General Grant joining the theatre party on that fateful night; in hindsight this could be seen as forestalling any move by Grant to save the President's life. Similarly, Stanton contrived that Major Thomas Eckert should not be in the presidential box either. When Lincoln asked for Eckert as his bodyguard Stanton lied, saying that Eckert was engaged in vital work elsewhere. Eckert was subsequently named as one of Stanton's accomplices in the plot.

Stanton took complete control of the manhunt and the subsequent trial of the conspirators. While he endeavoured to let Booth escape, he directed the investigation towards minor players, as well as people such as Dr Samuel Mudd who were completely innocent. Mudd's only crime was to set Booth's broken leg, but he was quite ignorant of the identity of his patient, and even informed the proper authorities afterwards when his suspicions were roused. None of that saved him from a savage sentence of life imprisonment with hard labour in the infamous Dry Tortugas. Incidentally, the three detectives who questioned Mudd and subsequently arrested him were Secret Service agents, acting under the direct orders of William Wood. When Stanton learned that Booth was crippled and certain to be captured, he secretly arranged, through Wood, that Booth would not be taken alive, far less be able to give evidence against his accomplices. Wood's intimate connection with Stanton, going back ten years, has already been outlined.

Privy to Stanton's plot was Brigadier-General Lafayette C. Baker, the one-time Californian vigilante who became the first head of the United States Secret Service. Baker sent for two of his most trusted subordinates, Lieutenant-Colonel Everton J. Conger, and Lieutenant Luther Byron Baker (his cousin), and directed them precisely to Garrett's Farm where the injured Booth was holed up. Boston Corbett, the man who actually shot Booth, was charged with a breach of military discipline and sent to Washington for court-martial, but Stanton dismissed the charge. Booth's body was sewn up in a grey army blanket and, at Stanton's command, was buried at night in great secrecy. General Baker and his cousin went to incredible lengths to conceal the whereabouts of the corpse. A hole was dug in the floor of a cell in the Old Penitentiary Building and Booth interred in an unmarked grave. The cell was locked and the key given to Stanton.

Booth left a mysterious note at Vice-President Johnson's house on the afternoon of Good Friday: 'Don't wish to disturb you. Are you at home? – J. Wilkes Booth.' After Booth's death there was no way of explaining this note, but it seems to have been intended to compromise Johnson. With Lincoln and Seward dead and Johnson incriminated, the three men ranking above Stanton would be removed.

Subsequently Stanton got hold of the assassin's diary. Later General Baker would testify under oath that the diary had been mutilated since it was taken from Booth's body, eighteen pages being cut out. What was written thereon will never be known, but it is not improbable that Booth left details of Stanton's complicity.

Stanton went to extraordinary lengths to ensure the silence of the accused lest they might reveal information of conspiracy in high places. The eight suspects, ranging from Paine, who had tried to kill the Seward family, to the hapless Dr Mudd, were held in solitary confinement, with empty cells between them to prevent communication through the walls. At all times, right up until their appearance in court, they were heavily chained and compelled to wear hideous padded masks that totally enveloped their heads, making breathing, let alone eating, exceedingly difficult. These sadistic helmets were devised by Stanton himself, who took fiendish delight in speculating that such confinement in the sweltering heat would drive the conspirators out of their minds before they came to trial. When four of them were sentenced to life imprisonment, it was Stanton who engineered their confinement in the living hell of the Dry Tortugas, rather than the state penitentiary at Albany. The trial, masterminded by Stanton, was a farce, the prisoners being prevented from uttering a single word in their defence. Stanton demanded the death penalty for all eight, but only four were hanged, including Mary Surratt whose only crime was to have been the landlady of the boarding-house where three of the conspirators had lodged. Her son John escaped to Canada and then to Europe before he was apprehended in Egypt in 1867. When rumours of a plot hardened into actual evidence of a conspiracy, in March 1865, it was Stanton who suppressed Louis Weichmann's testimony against his fellow-boarders at Mary Surratt's lodging-house. On the other hand, John F. Parker, the White House bodyguard whose thirst led him to desert his post, was never punished nor called as a witness at the trial. All this, taken together, seems to point to Stanton's involvement in a high-level conspiracy.[4]

In the power vacuum immediately after Lincoln's death Stanton was virtual dictator of the United States, but President Johnson soon showed his mettle. A few months later, when he discovered that General Baker had the White House under surveillance, Johnson forced Stanton to sack his Secret Service chief, though the replacement of the corrupt Baker by the equally unscrupulous Wood made no effective difference. Baker, who owed his meteoric rise from ordinary gumshoe to general entirely to Stanton, was privy to his master's secrets. While Allan Pinkerton was sidelined on account of his close connections with McClellan, Baker was appointed to the command of the 1st District of Columbia Cavalry, actually a paramilitary force recruited from known criminals and men of dubious character. Suspects were seized without warrant and often held for weeks on end in the cellars of the Treasury Building, where they were grilled and tortured at Baker's whim. He came to be known as 'the Czar of the Underworld' and was one of the most feared and hated men in the land.

Unlike the Pinkerton operatives, the 1st DC Cavalry were notorious for their corruption and thuggery. Believing that the end justified the means, Stanton turned a blind eye, but could not save Baker in the long run. In enforced retirement, the general busied himself with his monumental history of the Secret Service, published at Philadelphia in 1867. This massive volume caused intense embarrassment to Stanton and probably precipitated the general's death. Over the ensuing months Baker was tailed and harassed by unidentified agents, and several attempts on his life were perpetrated. On one occasion he was severely beaten in an alleyway; on another a bullet shattered a window frame, missing his head by inches. Then, on 3 July 1868, he died in mysterious circumstances, at the age of forty-two. The newspaper reports gave typhoid as the cause of death, though his death certificate said meningitis. His physician was puzzled by symptoms that reminded him of arsenic poisoning, but naïvely dismissed this suspicion as he could not imagine who would want to do such a thing.

In October 1872 there was a two-day hearing at Philadelphia City Hall into a codicil in Baker's will, contested by some of his relatives, though the matter was not settled till January 1879. Buried in the transcript of the hearing were some remarkable details. In the first place Baker was found to have left a strong-box containing $458,299, a remarkable sum for an unemployed detective to have accumulated. Then there was the wrangle over Baker's books and papers which had been left to Laura Duvall (a one-time operative) which were promptly impounded by John P. Smallwood, an agent of the War Department. An inventory of these books was later made, but two bound volumes of *Colburn's United Service Magazine* for 1864 were omitted from a run covering the years from 1860 to 1865. In 1957 a volume containing the numbers for the second half of 1864 was purchased by Ray Neff from Leary's second-hand bookshop in Philadelphia and found to contain long messages, either in a complex sliding code, or simply in the form of dots under certain letters on the printed pages. Neff took the book to a professional cryptographer and had the messages decoded. What they amounted to was a detailed indictment of Edwin Stanton for the murder of Abraham Lincoln. The signature of Lafayette C. Baker was subsequently discovered by ultra-violet examination; it had been written in a ferro-cyanide compound such as was commonly used during the Civil War by agents for invisible writing, revealed later by the application of heat.

These lengthy statements implicated Major Thomas Eckert as Stanton's right-hand man. Baker seems to have stumbled on the plot, 'But now I know the truth and it frightens me no end. I fear that somehow I may become the sacrificial goat.' Baker went on to state that:

> There are at least eleven members of Congress involved in the plot, no less than twelve Army officers, three Naval officers and at least twenty-four civilians, of which one was a governor of a loyal state. Five were bankers of great repute, three were nationally known newspapermen and eleven were industrialists of great repute and wealth. There were probably more that I know nothing of.
>
> The names of these known conspirators is presented without comment or notation in Vol one of this series. Eighty-five thousand dollars was contributed by the named persons to pay for the deed. Only eight persons knew the details of the plot and the identity of the others.
>
> I fear for my life.
>
> L.C.B.[5]

Baker was not the only bit-player in this drama to come to a tragic end. Major Rathbone married his Clara, but later murdered her and tried to commit suicide, ending his days in an insane asylum. Mary Todd Lincoln and Boston Corbett were both certified as lunatics, though the President's widow was released from an asylum and died in her Springfield house in 1882. Stanton, whose career waned after 1866, died in 1869. Miraculously, all of Paine's victims recovered from their horrific injuries, William Seward going on to negotiate the purchase of Alaska from Russia in 1867, his most notable and lasting achievement, and died of natural causes five years later, at the age of seventy-one; but his invalid wife died from shock only weeks after the incident, and Fanny Seward died a year later at the age of twenty-one. In August 1867 yellow fever erupted in the Dry Tortugas, killing the prison doctor. Samuel Mudd volunteered to combat the disease, saved many lives and, on the recommendation of prison officers, was granted a free pardon by President Johnson in 1869. He returned to his farm in Maryland and died there, in 1882.

Thomas Eckert, on the other hand, rose to the rank of general, became president of several commercial telegraph companies, and served as presiding judge of the Texas Court of Appeal before he died in 1910. John T. Ford, who had the bad luck to own the theatre where Lincoln was assassinated, was held in prison for forty days and had his theatre confiscated. When he sued the government he agreed to let the building for $1,500 a month until June 1866 when he sold it to the government for $100,000, for use as a store for Confederate archives. In 1893 three floors of the old theatre collapsed under the weight of paper, killing twenty-two government employees and injuring sixty-eight. Today it is the Lincoln Museum. In the same year John Wilkes's brother Edwin died. He, too, had been one of American's leading actors but after the assassination he had left the stage, vowing never to return. A year later, however, he made a triumphant comeback as Hamlet at the New York Winter Gardens, and was a greater hit than ever, vast audiences flocking to see the assassin's brilliant brother. It was not till 1871, however, that Edwin Booth could bring himself to play Brutus in *Julius Caesar* again. Edwin was appearing on a Chicago stage in 1879 when a madman shot at him and missed.

Almost a million people lost their lives during the Civil War, at a cost of twelve billion dollars to the North and four billion to the South. In its aftermath came economic depression and widespread unemployment as the Union armies, numbering over a million men in March 1865, were disbanded. By the end of the year a permanent force numbering about 50,000 was left, mainly to keep the recently rebellious Southern states in order.

On the other hand, the long-term gain was incalculable. The value of good communications had been forcibly demonstrated during the war, and in the post-war years the telegraph system and railroad networks developed at a meteoric pace. In the world of telecommunications the Sanfords were joined by Colonel Anson Stager, a colleague of Allan Pinkerton who, during the war, had become chief of the Federal military telegraph network and who, in the postwar period, would help to create a virtual monopoly for Western Union. George McClellan was not the only wartime general to carve a fief from the burgeoning railway system; Ambrose Burnside and John Dix also became presidents of important railroad companies before turning to state politics. While McClellan became Governor of New Jersey, Burnside was Governor of Rhode Island and Dix of New York. Robert Todd Lincoln, son of the late President, also became a leading railroad executive. In the wake of railway expansion Adams and American Express spread their freight lines across the continent. The mushroom growth of express and freight lines, railroads and telegraphs brought an immense amount of business to the National Detective Agency through the useful contacts which Allan made during the war. In 1866 he opened an office in New York and another in Philadelphia the following year. Robert Pinkerton was put in charge of the New York office, with responsibility for the eastern and southern sectors of the Agency's business, while his elder brother William, working from Chicago, supervised business in the midwest and west. Allan, of course, was in overall command, though he still enjoyed the rough and tumble of field work.

In September that year the Agency was approached to supply men to guard mining property at Braidwood, Illinois, when the workforce went on strike. Allan was reluctant to take on this assignment, and eventually gave way only on the strict understanding that his men were there to protect the mining equipment. The guards were given stringent instructions not to interfere with the strikers themselves. Over the ensuing quarter of a century Pinkerton operatives were employed as guards in some seventy other strikes. Pinkerton men were never supplied to take the place of workers on strike, and the Agency insisted that if it were necessary for its guards to be armed, they must be properly deputised by the county sheriff. In that quarter of a century, Pinkerton agents shot two men dead, either by accident or in self-defence. Both incidents, however, occurred some time after Allan's death, and paled into insignificance alongside the Homestead steel strike when 200 Pinkertons fought a mob ten times larger; on 11 July 1892 four Pinkerton agents were killed and over a hundred injured, while one striker was killed outright and eleven wounded, seven fatally. On that tragic occasion Pinkerton agents were acting legally to protect property from a violent mob, but the grim body-count left a bitter legacy.

Vast fortunes were made in the communications and transport boom after the Civil War, but inevitably it attracted its share of fraudulent and criminal operators. In 1867 Allan was retained by William Orton, head of Western Union, to investigate a group of criminals who were tapping the company's wires somewhere on the western frontier, and either using the information thus gained for insider trading, or transmitting false messages to the eastern newspapers which had an adverse effect on the New York stock market. Many companies, notably the Pacific Steam Navigation Company, were driven to the edge of bankruptcy, and fraud on a massive scale was estimated to run to many millions of dollars. The knock-on effect was appalling, with suicide and murder commonplace. The task of breaking the wiretapping syndicate came to Allan through Anson Stager, then Western Union's General Manager, and he immediately set to work with George Bangs.

Good, old-fashioned methods paid off. Allan himself went to New York and started with the brokers of Wall Street in an attempt to track the disinformation back to its source. He soon located a broker who had made a fortune by buying up the vastly depreciated stocks of companies named in the more sensational disaster stories in the newspapers. This led Allan to San Francisco and two brothers employed by Western Union. Weeks of patient detective work, shadowing the suspects, eventually yielded the desired result. The wiretappers were apprehended just after they transmitted a story about the sinking of Pacific's flagship, with the loss of 800 lives and a two-million-dollar shipment of gold from Wells Fargo. The ringleaders were prosecuted while a number of crooked messengers and telegraph operators across the country were dismissed. On Allan's recommendations, Orton reorganised the company's codes and tightened security procedures. Allan also drafted a twelve-page document outlining the case for Federal legislature to protect and control the telegraph lines – a matter which was never implemented, and has been hotly debated right down to the present day. 'The lines must be protected by Congress so that a man who stole communications from the wires was equally guilty as the man who stole letters out of the mail and opened them.'

This episode was characteristic of the man. If William and Robert thought they had a free hand in their respective spheres they were soon brought up sharp before paternal interference. Allan's inability to delegate responsibility was bad enough before the war, when the Agency was mainly concerned with cases in Illinois and the north-west, but Allan failed to grasp that times had changed and the business had moved on. His voluminous letter-books show only too vividly how he tried to retain a firm control, demanding to know the details of every case and insisting that reports on investigations from the branch offices be sent to him regularly, no matter how trivial the case. George Bangs was at that time superintendent of the New York office, but long years of faithful service did not save him from his boss's irascibility. Allan's letters in this period were increasingly bitter, and often irrational in their criticism. Bangs and Robert Pinkerton, however, evolved a method of deflecting Allan's ire and quietly getting on with their work.

On the evening of Saturday, 6 January 1866, thieves broke into the armoured boxcar on the Boston and Albany Railroad containing two safes belonging to the Adams Express Company. At New Haven, Connecticut, the Adams messenger, riding in the baggage car, checked the boxcar and found the door swinging open. Inside, the safes had been rifled and some $700,000 in cash, bonds and jewellery had been taken. This was the biggest train robbery up to that time. Edward Sanford, president of Adams Express, immediately called Allan who set off with William to join Robert in New York. There he interviewed Moore, the messenger, who admitted that he had only checked the lock on the door facing the platform at Bridgeport, but had not bothered to look at either of the two doors after that stop. Allan saturated the area with his agents who went about the slow but painstaking procedure of questioning the residents of towns and villages along the line, as well as all railroad employees.

The robbery was soon pinpointed to Cos Cob when a Pinkerton detective recovered a bag containing $5,000 in gold coins, which the thieves had dropped by accident in bushes at the trackside during their getaway. The enquiry concentrated on the Stamford area, and at a livery stable Allan learned that two men had tried to hire a horse and buggy on the night of the robbery but had been turned down because the ostler did not know them. They apparently stayed at a local hotel, before taking an eastbound train the following morning. Robert and William got an accurate description of the men and trailed them to Norwalk. One man was identified as John Grady, a railroad brakeman at Norwalk, but he had suddenly vanished.

The investigation led to an old man named Tristam, and Robert learned that he had taken a trip to New York City with a large parcel which he kept on his lap 'hugging it as he would a child'. In New York Pinkerton agents shadowed Tristam to a tenement on the Lower East Side where his married sister lived. The detectives raided the apartment and found $113,762, still in Adams Express bags. Tristam was arrested in a saloon and confessed to William Pinkerton. He implicated several others, including Grady. When one of the gang escaped to Canada, Allan sent his sons to Montreal and Quebec in pursuit and they chased him back to New York, where he was arrested. It later transpired that the gang had originally planned to roll out the safes after pulling the emergency cord, but finding that the cord in the boxcar was encased in a steel tube they forced open the safes, filled two suitcases with loot, and then jumped out at Cos Cob. Failing to get transport, they were forced to bury some of the bags, which were afterwards unearthed by Pinkerton agents. This case was widely publicised and considerably enhanced the Agency's reputation.

In this case the thieves were rank amateurs. By contrast, the gang of bond forgers arrested later the same year were skilled professionals. They actually opened a real estate office in Philadelphia and carried on some legitimate business as a front for their crooked operation. In this instance the case was cracked by Robert Linden, the assistant superintendent of the Philadelphia office, who discovered a vital scrap of blotting paper with a faint New York address which led to more clues. In the resulting operation Allan himself took to the open road once more, travelling all over the eastern states, often on horseback, to shadow the chief suspect. It was a classic example of dogged detection, the sort of case in which Allan revelled.

On 2 March 1867 President Johnson, increasingly at loggerheads with the radical Republicans in Congress, had a showdown with his opponents – and lost. On that date the Tenure of Office Act was passed, forbidding the President to sack civil officers without the consent of the Senate. Another Act, passed the same day, required him to issue military orders only through the General of the Army, Ulysses S. Grant, whom the President was forbidden to remove from his command. These extraordinary invasions of presidential power were engineered by Edwin Stanton. It has never been explained why Johnson, who was all too well aware of Stanton's duplicity, allowed him to remain in his Cabinet, but when he eventually moved against his double-dealing Secretary of War he found himself out-manoeuvred. Johnson bided his time, waiting for an opportunity to get even. He sought to test the validity of the Act before the Supreme Court and get rid of Stanton at one fell swoop. Johnson decided to dismiss Stanton and replace him by General Grant, without obtaining the consent of the Senate; but his plan to bring the matter before the Supreme Court miscarried when the House of Representatives brought articles of impeachment against the President. As usual, the wily Secretary was one jump ahead. On 5 March 1868 the sordid impeachment proceedings began and ended on 16 May, the radical Republicans failing by just one vote to gain the two-thirds majority in the Senate necessary for conviction. The remainder of Johnson's term as President was comparatively uneventful but he demitted office on 4 March 1869, a beaten and embittered man. Five years later he returned to national politics as a Senator for Tennessee but he died suddenly after his maiden speech.

Stanton's dreams of power were shattered by the failure of the impeachment and thereafter his political standing declined. His last ambition was to be appointed to the Supreme Court, but he was a dying man by the time the appointment came through in 1869.

The impeachment itself was preceded by a lengthy investigation by the House Judiciary Committee which met in camera to examine charges that the President had been implicated in Lincoln's assassination. The first witness at this secret tribunal was none other than Lafayette C. Baker who set the tone by testifying that Andrew Johnson had conspired with Jefferson Davis to betray the Union. Johnson himself was neither present, nor represented, at these hearings, and in order to gain vital information of the charges being concocted against him he turned to Allan Pinkerton and 'through his instrumentality, the President and his friends were informed every day as to the secret deliberations of the men trying to impeach him'.[6] Allan's 'instrument' was a pretty young lady who flirted with the Committee's stenographer and wormed out of him transcripts of each day's hearings which were sent on to Pinkerton in Chicago for immediate retransmission to the White House.

❖ 11 ❖

Diplomatic Incident
1868

And naked to the hangman's noose
The morning clocks will ring
A neck God made for other use
Than strangling in a string.

A.E. HOUSMAN, *A SHROPSHIRE LAD*

The pulp novel and the silver screen have romanticised the Wild West and made heroes out of the thugs, hoodlums and psychopaths who robbed banks, held up trains and terrorised whole prairie communities. In general, the forces of law and order come off second best in these fables, while 'the Pinkertons' are regarded as a shadowy, often sinister, element. The thieving idylls of Butch Cassidy and the Sundance Kid, for example, as depicted by Robert Redford and Paul Newman, are interrupted only by the persistence of those nameless, faceless guys who doggedly pursued them. In the aftermath of the Civil War lawlessness was rife right across the middle-western states. County sheriffs were ineffectual or corrupt or both, and in the resulting vacuum lawlessness combated lawlessness. This was the golden age of the vigilante and the lynch mob. Justice was dispensed by the gun rather than the gavel. The breakdown of law and order served as a grim backdrop to material progress, as thousands of new migrants from Europe poured into the prairies. In 1869 the first transcontinental railroad was completed, and in the five years after the war the rail network expanded as never before, opening up the wilderness. Flourishing farming communities developed along the railroad lines and construction camps were transformed almost overnight into towns and cities. The trains were infinitely faster and more reliable than the stage-coaches, while their steel-plated armoured cars offered infinitely better protection against highway robbery.

The complacency of the railroad companies was shattered on 6 October 1866 when three masked men boarded the Ohio and Mississippi train as it pulled out of Seymour, Indiana. Three miles east of the town they overpowered the Adams Express messenger and pushed two safes out of the armoured car. One held $15,000 in cash, the other $30,000 in cash and gold. The thieves managed to open the first safe but the second, of much more robust construction, was abandoned unopened. The express company contacted Allan Pinkerton and he set off immediately for Indiana. He had not been long in Seymour before he realised that it harboured a gang of ruthless desperadoes headed by the Reno brothers, Frank, John, Simeon and William. It was John and Simeon, together with Franklin Sparks, who had held up the train, the first formal train hold-up in American history. Seymour, in 1866, was described as 'a carnival of crime' by one writer, for the Reno gang robbed, pillaged, tortured and murdered with impunity. Realising that the problem was much greater than a simple attack on an armoured car, Allan in time-honoured fashion infiltrated three of his best operatives into the town. Dick Winscott, posing as a rather shady customer who had left the East when things got too hot for him, opened a saloon in the town, a dingy, smoke-filled dive which soon became the favourite haunt of the Renos and their hangers-on. During one of the wild parties with which the Renos celebrated their latest coup, Winscott persuaded John Reno and Franklin Sparks to pose for a photographer. Reno and Sparks, foaming tankards in their hands, leered drunkenly at the camera. In due course their mugshots were on their way to Chicago, to join Pinkerton's Rogues Gallery. Two other agents, whose names are not known, posed as a riverboat gambler and a depot storeman at the railroad station.

The spectacular raid on the train triggered off a copycat crime. Two young punks held up another train near Seymour, robbing the Adams Express car of $8,000. The Renos were outraged that others were muscling in on their territory, called out their gang and set off in pursuit. Catching up with the 'two young men from Jackson County', they gave them a severe beating, seized the loot, and then turned over the pair to the sheriff of Jackson County. In his autobiography John Reno added that one of these boys had been 'making up' to his girlfriend; robbing a train in Reno territory merely added insult to injury.[1]

Showing their versatility, the Reno gang next robbed the county treasury in Daviess County near Gallatin, Missouri, netting $22,065. L.C. Weir, general manager of Adams Express, notified Allan of this robbery and asked him to investigate it also. Winscott confirmed that the Renos were responsible for this crime, but counselled against any attempt by Allan and his posse to seize the Renos in Seymour itself, as innocent lives would be lost in the resultant shoot-out. Allan and William Pinkerton came to the conclusion that the only way to bring John Reno, the leader of the gang, to justice would be to kidnap him.

Allan telegraphed the sheriff of Daviess County to meet him in Cincinnati with an arrest warrant for Reno. At the same time Allan hired a special train in Cincinnati and set out with six of his burliest detectives. Having got the arrest warrant, Allan wired Winscott to get Reno on to the station platform on some pretext and notify the exact time. For two days the locomotive and car stood at Cincinnati with steam up. Then the telegram arrived: John Reno would be on the platform at a particular time, waiting for a friend who would be expected on the regular express train. Allan's special chugged into Seymour only minutes ahead of the express. Seeing Winscott on the platform chatting to a husky, dark-haired man, Allan bellowed 'That's our man' and led his team as they swiftly alighted from their car, moved through the crowd which had gathered, as usual, to await the arrival of the mail train, and unobtrusively ringed the outlaw. Too late, John Reno realised that he was surrounded, but as he tried to draw his revolver his arms were pinioned. Before the throng realised what was afoot, the Pinkertons had the shouting, screaming bandit bundled into the car. Allan brought up the rear, signalling to the engine-driver to get moving. Reno was handcuffed and trussed with ropes before the train was clear of the station. In vain, the rest of the gang mounted up and rode off after the train, but the wood-burning loco hauling a single car soon outdistanced the pursuers.

The following morning, the heavily manacled Reno was arraigned at Gallatin before a judge who did not mince his words: 'You're the one who did this work and we're going to hang you from the highest tree in Grand River Bottoms if that money isn't returned!' Reno was dumped in the condemned cell with a twenty-four-hour armed guard. In his autobiography John recalled how 'The natives began coming from all directions with their shotguns and coonskin caps and with their hair hanging down to their shoulders. Some of them had not taken the mess from their backs that had grown there during the war.' On the morning of Monday, 18 January 1868, John Reno, under heavy guard, was taken to the Missouri state penitentiary. Later he wrote: 'When we arrived at the prison gate I looked up and read in large letters over the entrance: the way of the transgressor is hard; admission twenty-five cents. But I was on the deadhead list and went in free.'

In John's absence, brother Frank headed the gang which now went on an orgy of robberies across the Mid-Western states, holding up trains, county treasuries and post offices in Indiana, Missouri and Iowa. In February 1868 they robbed the Harrison County Treasury at Magnolia, Iowa, of $14,000 – 'a public calamity', as the local newspaper reported it. Allan now sent William to Iowa to investigate this case. At Council Bluffs William enquired if there was 'a disreputable place' in town owned by a former resident of Seymour. This led him to a saloon run by a former counterfeiter who had once lived in Seymour and this haunt was placed under round-the-clock surveillance. This produced one unexpected result; a regular habitué was Michael Rogers, one of the town's leading citizens and 'a pillar of the Methodist Church'. On receipt of this information Allan checked the Iowa police files and found that Rogers had been in some trouble before the war. Tracing the man's movements, William discovered that he had called at the county treasury to pay his taxes shortly before the robbery took place. Rogers was suspected of having cased the joint and tipped off the Renos.

For several days Pinkerton agents shadowed Rogers and on the fourth day a man answering Frank Reno's description was seen to visit the Rogers' home. At dawn the following day four men, led by Frank Reno, entered the house by the back door, shortly before news broke that the Mills County Treasury had been burgled and $12,000 stolen from the safe. William had the greatest difficulty convincing the local sheriff that Rogers was implicated in these robberies. Only when a rail handcar used by the gang in their getaway was found did the sheriff reluctantly issue a search warrant. Shortly after dawn a day later the Pinkertons surrounded the Rogers' house. William himself crashed down the door to find Frank Reno with Albert Perkins and Miles Ogle, two of the country's most notorious counterfeiters, having breakfast. While the Pinkertons searched the house William suddenly noticed smoke coming from the kitchen stove; yanking off the lid, he was just in time to save the $14,000 stolen at Magnolia from going up in flames. Reno, Ogle, Rogers and Perkins were arrested and detained at Council Bluffs, but the following day, 1 April, they broke out. Scrawled in chalk above the hole breaching the brick wall, the detectives found the words APRIL FOOL.

After that, there was no holding the gang. That summer they had their greatest success when, on 22 May, they robbed the Marshfield Express of $96,000 in government bonds and gold on its way to the United States Treasury. After this spectacular robbery the twelve-man gang split up. Frank Reno, Albert Perkins, Michael Rogers and Miles Ogle fled to Windsor, Ontario, the home of their accomplice Charlie Anderson, a notorious Canadian safecracker. Simeon and William Reno holed up in Minneapolis, while Frank Sparks, Henry Jerrell and John Moore high-tailed it to Coles County, Illinois, twenty-seven miles west of Terre Haute, Indiana. On 16 July, Allan Pinkerton, accompanied by Dick Winscott and four other agents, rode out from Chicago to Mattoon, the Coles County seat, and joined the local lawmen in scouring the countryside after a tip-off. Sparks was apprehended in a barn, while Moore and Jerrell were caught in a saloon at Aetna. The three bandits were taken to Indianapolis, ironically, in the same baggage car they had held up, still riddled with bullet holes from the robbery.

At Indianapolis they were transferred to a southbound express for the journey back to Seymour. Now Allan's problems of holding the three desperate criminals were compounded by acts of sabotage. The train was subject to mysterious and unaccountable delays and Allan suspected that the railroad employees, so long terrorised and victimised by the Renos, were hand in glove with the vigilantes who were also determined to root out the gang. The train, after innumerable delays, eventually pulled into Seymour around midnight; to his consternation, Allan found that the westbound Ohio and Mississippi Valley train, with which they should have connected, had departed over an hour previously. Now they were stranded in the middle of the night, in Seymour of all places, a town that was bitterly divided between those who aided and abetted the gangsters and those who were hostile to them. Allan managed to hire a wagon to transport the prisoners and their escort to Brownstown where the sheriff, John Scott, could be relied on to give assistance. Sparks, Jerrell and Moore, handcuffed and leg-ironed, were forced to lie on the floor while the six Pinkertons sat over them, armed with Winchester rifles and Navy Colts.

Three miles west of Seymour, however, the wagon was ambushed by over two hundred men wearing red flannel masks – the badge of the vigilante. The detectives were taken completely by surprise, swiftly overpowered, disarmed and told to 'get along and trot for Seymour'. The three robbers were hauled to their feet and nooses tightened round their necks. Only Moore was defiant, shouting at the mob that they were 'a pack of mossback hoosiers'. A minute later he was dangling at the end of a rope. Later the bodies were cut down and the verdict 'hanged by persons unknown' closed the case. Their funeral in Seymour became a carnival, special trains being chartered to bring in ghoulish crowds from far and near to view the purple-faced corpses in their open coffins.

Now the race was on between the Pinkertons and the vigilantes to get to the rest of the gang, and advertisements began appearing in the Indiana newspapers appealing for funds to give the Renos the grand public hanging they deserved. On 22 July Simeon and William Reno were arrested by William Stiggart, a Pinkerton agent, at Lexington in Floyd County in the extreme south of Indiana. Laura Ellen Reno, afraid that vigilantes would easily storm the flimsy shack that served as a gaol in Lexington, offered to pay the costs of transferring her brothers to the infinitely more secure gaol in New Albany. Meanwhile, Allan Pinkerton was receiving threats from vigilante groups: any attempt to move the prisoners by rail would be met with extreme force and the derailment of all trains in the vicinity. In the end Allan arranged with Thomas J. Fullenlove, sheriff of Floyd County, to have the prisoners taken by steamboat fifty miles up the Ohio River to Madison. When word of this ruse got out the whole of southern Indiana erupted and Governor Baker was forced to mobilise the state militia. From Madison Pinkerton and a veritable squadron of heavily armed agents on horseback took the prisoners back to Lexington by a circuitous route in time for the preliminary hearing on 30 July. Two companies of state militiamen ringed the tiny courthouse, fearful of the 'army of hangmen' which the newspapers confidently predicted would arrive at any moment. Thousands of morbid sightseers crowded into the little town to watch the fun. With the greatest difficulty Judge P.H. Jewett presided over the packed courtroom, heard the charges and took the pleas of not guilty to a warrant signed by Allan Pinkerton. At that point the courtroom erupted. Men leaped over benches, clawing and kicking at the militiamen, who fought them off with rifle butts. Shouts, screams and hoots rent the air as Judge Jewett jumped on his chair crying, 'Take those men back to jail quickly! At once! Clear the courtroom!' For twenty minutes pandemonium reigned supreme, as the howling mob wrestled with detectives and militiamen. Eventually, however, the prisoners were led out of the room ringed by bayonets. Four days later the Reno brothers, guarded by the militia and several heavily armed deputies, left Lexington in the dead of night for New Albany.

The following month there was an attempt by vigilantes to besiege New Albany when there was a rumour that the prisoners were about to be moved. On this occasion Allan only narrowly averted disaster when he wired Governor Baker, saying that he had now located Frank Reno and his accomplices in Canada, and pleaded for a delay in moving Simeon and William for the time being. Cannily he suggested that it would be more economical to try all of the gang members together, rather than waste taxpayers' money on separate trials. The red-masked vigilantes had a fruitless wait as they lay in ambush covering every road out of New Albany.

Originally known simply as Ferry, the chief port of Essex County, Ontario, was renamed Windsor after the accession of Queen Victoria in 1837. Thirty years later it had become the terminus of several Canadian railways, connecting with important American railroads through the ferry-boats that plied the river. Though even then overshadowed by the sprawling city of Detroit just across the water, Windsor had an unenviable reputation as a frontier town where the scum of the American underworld congregated beyond the writ of US county, state or Federal laws. The Windsor Turf Club, despite its high-sounding name, was a saloon and pool-hall where the cream of America's safecrackers, burglars, conmen and stick-up artists socialised. Slightly lower down the scale were Manning's and Rockford's, two saloons on the waterfront. While investigating the robbery of a Union Express safe on a train near Garrison, New York, Pat O'Neil, a fresh-faced young operative who came to be nicknamed the Pinkerton Kid, recognised Jack Friday, the Reno getaway driver, in Rockford's saloon. When he accosted the bandit, young O'Neil was felled by a pool cue. Friday leaped through the window, 'taking the

General George McClellan

George McClellan and his wife, Ellen

Major E.J. Allen (Allan Pinkerton) with the Army of the Potomac (1861–62)

OPPOSITE

(top) Pinkerton detectives Seth Paine, Gus Thiel, George Bangs with William Pinkerton (far right), in their capacity as members of the first US Secret Service with the Army of the Potomac, Harrison's Landing, Virginia, July 1862

(bottom) Allan Pinkerton (bearded and standing next to the tent pole) with his agents at field headquarters, 1861

Lincoln visits the Pinkerton camp with Major-General
McClernand (right)

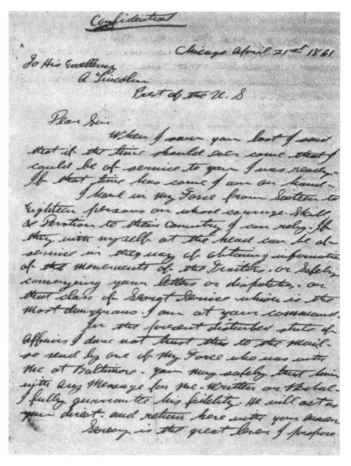

Letter from Allan to Lincoln, 21 April 1861

This photograph of Abraham Lincoln
was taken shortly before his assassination

John Wilkes Booth, actor and assassin

Edwin McMasters Stanton

David Herold (left) and Lewis Paine were both executed for their alleged part in the assassination of Abraham Lincoln

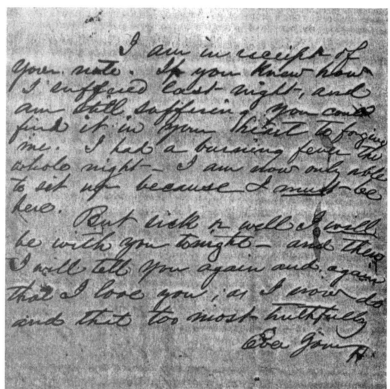

One of the infamous 'H' love letters, from Senator Henry Wilson to Rose Greenhow

Brigadier-General Thomas Jordan of Virginia, to whom Rose Greenhow passed vital Union military secrets

The Old Capitol Prison, where Rose Greenhow was held during part of the Civil War

General McClellan and his staff

Major-General Ambrose Burnside, who was asked to take over
from McClellan as commander of the Army of the Potomac

panels with him' as O'Neil reported to Allan. The other customers, as desperate a band of ruffians as one could imagine, set upon Pat and would have beaten him to death had Tom Manning, the saloon-keeper, not intervened, saying that Pinkerton would never rest until he ran them all down.

Acting on Pat's tip, Allan and a posse of operatives descended on Windsor and raided the gang's hideout, a small frame house on Windsor Avenue and Brant Street. Frank Reno, Albert Perkins, Charlie Anderson and Michael Rogers were arrested and arraigned. Anderson, being a Canadian subject, was apparently immune, while Rogers, making an effective plea of mistaken identity, was released and fled that night back across the border to Detroit. This left Frank Reno and Albert Perkins to be dealt with. While they were held in the Windsor gaol Allan rushed back to Cincinnati to obtain an extradition order. From the Adams Express office in Cincinnati on 9 August Allan wrote to Fred Seward in Washington. The young man whose skull had been fractured by Lewis Paine had made a good recovery – contrary to Stanton's prediction – and was by this time serving as Assistant Secretary of State under his father. Allan had known young Fred since 1861 and got on well with him, sharing the same anti-slavery views. Fred passed the papers to William Hunter who was then deputising for William Seward, and a few days later he wrote to Edward Thornton, the British ambassador. The following day Thornton forwarded the extradition request to Lord Monck, the Governor-General of Canada.[2]

Allan then returned to Windsor with L.C. Weir, the Adams general manager, to attend the extradition hearing. In the interim, however, Frank Reno had gathered a formidable array of character witnesses, and even produced his mother to swear that he had been at home at the time of the Marshfield robbery. While the hearing dragged on, Thornton dropped the bombshell that the Foreign Office in London had cabled him, saying that the correct procedure, under the treaty of August 1842, had not been followed. On further examination it was found that the Privy Council had only recently revised the criteria on extradition, without bothering to communicate them to the embassy in Washington. There was an exchange of diplomatic notes by transatlantic cable, and the matter was deadlocked. Meanwhile the criminal fraternity of Windsor decided that something would have to be done about 'that pesky Pinkerton' and Dick Barry, a notorious safebreaker and crack shot, was given the hit. He followed the detective when Allan boarded the ferry to Detroit; on the American side of the river, as Allan walked down the passenger ramp, Barry aimed a revolver at the back of Allan's head. Hearing the hammer being cocked, Allan spun round, hooked his finger in the trigger guard, and yanked the pistol from Barry's hand. After a fierce struggle, Allan beat his assailant to the ground and handcuffed him. At pistol point he marched him off to the Detroit police station.

A few days later there was a second attempt on Allan's life. This time a train robber named Johnson fired at him but narrowly missed. Allan gave chase, felled his attacker and handed him over to the Wayne County police. Two hours later Allan was told that Johnson had escaped, the sheriff blandly admitting that the train robber had got away 'while taking a buggy ride about the city'. When Allan notified the State Department of these attempts on his life, and the fact that the Canadian authorities were giving him the runaround, Fred Seward ordered a US Navy gunboat to Windsor. The warship anchored off the Canadian side, its guns trained on the port. There it remained for ten days and only weighed anchor when the Governor General sent a stiff protest from Ottawa to Washington. Viscount Monck was now stung into action; he travelled down from Ottawa to Windsor and interrogated Frank Reno in person, eventually obtaining a confession that he was one of the Marshfield robbers. Even so, there were further delays. Then Reno's lawyer obtained a writ of habeas corpus on the grounds that train robbery was not an extraditable offence. This matter was the subject of more wearisome courtroom wrangling but was finally thrown out.

The case took a curious twist when Lord Monck informed Allan that he had received a sinister warning from Colonel Wood, head of the US Secret Service, that the Renos should remain in Canada, as they would be lynched as soon as they were brought back to Indiana. This was an incredible admission from a high official of the American government. In issuing such a threat, Wood was sailing very close to the wind. His involvement with the Reno gang became apparent when, at the trial of Dick Barry for the attempted murder of Allan Pinkerton, the defendant claimed that he had been put up to it by William P. Wood. In Washington, of course, Wood hotly denied the allegation, but Barry from the witness stand stuck to his story. To crown all, Judge McMickum, the Windsor magistrate presiding over the hearing, announced publicly that Frank Reno had tried to bribe his sixteen-year-old son by offering the boy $6,000 in gold 'to influence his father in their behalf'.[3]

This was the last straw as far as Monck was concerned, and he told Allan that he could have the Renos, 'and bad luck to them all'. Allan jubilantly cabled William Pinkerton that they had won the extradition they had sought so long. With Pat O' Neil, Allan drove in a buggy to Monck's office to claim his prisoners. There, however, they were told that, under the new extradition regulations, there was a seven-day waiting period before prisoners could be claimed by law officers of another country. A week later Allan returned to Windsor to pick up the wanted men. This time he was informed that the Foreign Office had wired fresh instructions. Now Allan was required to produce written authority from the State Department, countersigned by President Johnson. Allan, now in a towering rage, telegraphed William Seward at his home early on Monday, 15 September. Seward was about to accompany Fred to Albany to attend the funeral of George Wharton (father of the celebrated novelist Edith Newbold Wharton), and it was from New York City *en route* that he wrote at great length the following day to William Hunter, reviewing the case and Allan's part in it. Hunter prepared the necessary documents and had them signed by President Johnson. Hunter had the papers sent by special messenger to General Averill, US Consul-General in Canada, at his residence in Montgomery, Vermont. When Averill advised Allan that the documents were ready, he took the train to Vermont, collected them, crossed the border to Montreal and thence to Ottawa where he delivered them personally to Lord Monck. The Governor General finally signed the extradition order, but warned Allan that the Canadian authorities would no longer be responsible either for his protection or the safety of the prisoners.

Allan wired William who ordered a sea-going tug to Windsor. Aboard were Chief Patrick Foley, head of the Pinkerton Guard Service, and John Curtin (later one of San Francisco's most celebrated detectives) as well as a number of other Pinkerton agents, all heavily armed. The manacled prisoners were escorted to the dock by Allan, his hand resting on the butt of his Navy Colt. As dawn broke on 7 October the tug edged out from the quayside. It was a beautiful autumn day, the river as calm as a millpond. The detectives sat in the tiny galley, smoking and chatting with the outlaws. Suddenly there was a horrendous crash and the tug heeled over; Allan looked out to find a lake steamer looming over them, its bows badly dented where it had sheered through the hull of the tug. The smaller vessel, holed below the waterline, rapidly went down. The detectives and their heavily chained prisoners floundered in the icy water but were picked up by the steamer which then crawled over to Detroit. There, a large crowd and a formidable posse of Pinkerton agents greeted them.

Having changed out of their wet clothing Allan, Curtin, Foley and other agents escorted the prisoners on to a steamboat bound for Cleveland, whence they travelled in a cavalcade of armoured wagons and buggies to Louisville. The following day, Allan, now choked up with a severe cold, handed over his prisoners to Sheriff Fullenlove who had them committed to the New Albany prison. Allan inspected the gaol and considered its walls not strong enough to withstand a vigilante assault. He urged the sheriff to have the Reno gang transferred to Indianapolis. While the vigilantes of southern Indiana were perfecting their plans, Reno sympathisers were threatening to raze Seymour to the ground if their heroes were hanged. A few days later the Democratic Party held a convention in New Albany, and Fullenlove was offered $1,000 to 'let the Seymour Committee get the Renos'. Fullenlove was an honest and courageous lawman but perhaps overconfident when he refused the bribe and announced publicly 'There will be no murder for any amount of money . . . The law must take its course.'

For two months feelings ran high and Reno gangsters and other desperadoes stepped up their campaign of terror and intimidation. Then, on 7 December, the engine-driver Flanders, who had been wounded in the train hold-up, died. As the harsh winter ensued and the temperature dropped to thirty below, an unnatural air of tranquillity settled on southern Indiana. At midnight on 12 December New Albany was asleep, the only sign of life being the dim light in the window of the guardhouse at the gaol where deputy Tom Matthews was dozing by the fire. Outside, warming himself by a brazier, crouched deputy Luther Whitten with his rifle at the ready. Shortly after midnight a special train of the Jefferson, Madison and Indianapolis Railroad glided silently into the station, its lights dowsed and its bell muffled. Before it had come to a halt red-masked men, armed to the teeth, were disembarking and heading off purposefully to predetermined positions. The telegraph wires were cut and New Albany was completely isolated. The leader, with a large numeral one chalked on the back of his coat, raised a hand and said, 'Ready men – *Salus populi suprema est lex.*' Whether he thought that saying it in Latin gave it greater legality, the tag that 'the safety of the people is the supreme law' justified subsequent actions.

The vigilantes, now numbering several hundred armed men, formed up and marched down State Street to the gaol. Whitten heard the measured tread of boots and ran towards the guardhouse to raise the alarm, but he was tackled and pistol-whipped. Fullenlove came out of his house shouting, 'I am the sheriff, the highest peace officer in the county! You must respect the law!' As he reached the gate, several shots rang out and Fullenlove fell, his arm shot in three places. He was carried, bleeding copiously and barely conscious, into his house and laid on a couch. His wife strenuously refused to hand over the keys of the gaol, but then she, her stricken husband and deputy Whitten were bundled into a bedroom and locked up. By now the keys had been found so the vigilantes headed off towards the gaol. Matthews barricaded himself behind the door leading to the cells and threatened to shoot anyone who dared to step inside. The vigilante leader ignored him and tried the keys, one by one, in the lock. When none worked, Number One coolly gave Matthews the option: either he opened the door of his own accord, or they would batter it down and hang him along with the gang. Reluctantly, the terrified deputy complied.

Frank, Simeon and William Reno, along with Charlie Anderson, were dragged from their cells, nooses placed about their necks and slowly hauled up to the beams. Charlie's rope gave way and he plummeted to the stone floor to lie screaming and begging for mercy. This time the vigilantes tightened the noose more carefully and then gently lowered him from the beam so that the weight of his body tugged the noose and he slowly strangled. Simeon Reno also had a slow, agonising death. He had been strung up with the tips of his toes touching the ground. So long as he kept on his toes he could stay alive but as he weakened, so he strangled. He fought desperately to cling on to life, at one point partially reviving, but after a struggle lasting forty minutes his body ceased thrashing around and he hung limply like the others. The vigilantes were long gone by that time, Number One primly surrendering the gaol keys to the frightened stationmaster before calmly reboarding the train. The wintry sky was lightening when city officials rounded up a posse and scurried along to the gaol with a doctor for Sheriff Fullenlove. In the gaol itself they found Matthews with the ten other prisoners who, at one point, were about to be hanged for good measure. And then there were the four slowly swinging bodies, eyes popping, tongues lolling, puce faces turning to blue.[4]

Subsequently Governor Baker telegraphed Allan Pinkerton, and he and William hurried to Indianapolis for consultation. As a result, resolute warnings against vigilantes were published, but the gesture was empty. Investigation of the lynching by the county attorney was perfunctory, and secretly both state and county officials heaved a sigh of relief. The power of the Renos had been broken, that was the main thing. There was a minor sensation a day or two later when Laura Reno was summoned from her ladies' finishing school in Louisville, Kentucky, to identify her brothers' bodies. When she removed the handkerchief covering Simeon's hideously swollen face she rushed to the window and, unladylike, screamed at the crowd thronging outside, shaking her fist at them and saying that the blood of her brothers was on their heads. That afternoon the doors of the gaol were opened to let thousands file past the open coffins of the gangsters. In the Missouri penitentiary news of his brothers' deaths was broken to John Reno. 'That awful news came near dethroning my reason,' he later wrote, 'but I was kept hard at work which may have saved me.'

On the morning of 21 December the citizens of Seymour, fifty miles farther north, awoke to find the town plastered with vigilante posters naming the remaining members of the gang and promising them a necktie party if they did not depart at once. There was utter chaos when local officials believed to be sympathetic to the Reno gang were beaten, tortured and threatened, and there was a wave of thefts, burglaries and beatings by crimson-flannelled thugs masquerading as vigilantes. To make matters worse, the State Department in Washington received a stiffly worded note of protest from the British government, via Lord Monck, demanding an apology for the 'shocking and indefensible lynching'. Anglo-American relations were at their lowest ebb since 1861 when the USS *San Jacinto* had stopped the British mail packet *Trent* off the Bahamas and seized the Confederate commissioners to Britain and France, James Mason and John Slidell. While the British government seriously considered abrogating its extradition treaty with the United States, Congress rushed a bill through both houses giving Federal protection to extradited criminals. William Seward sent a copy of the Act, hot off the press, with a diplomatic letter of apology to London.

The Reno case, on account of its diplomatic repercussions, was widely reported on both sides of the Atlantic and brought the Agency international recognition. Shortly afterwards Allan was retained by banks in Massachusetts, New Hampshire and Pennsylvania to solve major robberies. Over a million dollars were rifled from the vaults of the Beneficial Savings Fund of America in Philadelphia, by far the biggest bank robbery up to that time. When the Agency solved these cases and recovered most of the stolen money, numerous other commissions came flooding in. The maxim 'nothing succeeds like success' was never truer.

While Allan was waging war on the Renos, George Bangs in New York was quietly getting on with the more routine business. One of his greatest coups, as 1868 drew to a close, was to solve a difficult murder case in Edgewood, New Jersey. It was a classic case, using well-tried Pinkerton techniques of infiltrating an operative to befriend the chief suspect, and it paid off handsomely when the suspect, confronted with the dead man's watch and jewellery, broke down and confessed. Bangs had no reason to suppose that he had not done a good job – until he received a blistering, fifteen-page letter on 23 December 1868. It was an astonishing document, violent and bitter of language, extremely abusive in parts, as Allan Pinkerton reviewed the progress of the New York office over the previous two years since it was established. This near-hysterical tirade had been precipitated by an admission from Bangs that he had been having trouble with some of his New York staff. Allan tersely told him to give those 'incompetents the boot. Show your fist, let them be kicked downstairs as quickly as possible'. One passage, in particular, must have given Bangs cause for concern, as his employer, whom he had known so well for twenty years, went incoherently off at a tangent:

> You know my policy in such cases, it is no delaying the fight; if a fight has to come, let it come and let it come the sooner the better for all concerned – at all events at least for me. Delay no fight one moment – make all the attacks you can. Keep yourself right upon the attack with hands clean and with clear conscience you are sure to win . . . no power in Heaven or on earth can influence me when I know I am right . . . the right is mighty and must prevail and all we have to do is to manage our own affairs with discretion, with honor, with integrity and we must and we shall win.[5]

As we read between the lines, the picture of a man at the end of his tether emerges. After his involuntary dip in the Detroit River in October Allan had been plagued with a heavy cold which dragged on for weeks. He was assailed with blinding headaches which made him stop in the middle of dictating letters and reports, close his eyes and grip his fevered forehead. The incessant travelling, by rail, steamer, buggy and horseback over six states of the Union and two Canadian provinces in his relentless pursuit of the Renos, his utter contempt for physical or mental limitations, and the overweening belief in his own principles were now driving this man to the edge of destruction.

• 12 •

Intimations of Mortality
1868–77

But the fair guerdon when we hope to find,
And think to burst out into sudden blaze,
Comes the blind Fury with th'abhorred shears,
And slits the thin-spun life.

JOHN MILTON, *LYCIDAS*

As the church bells of Chicago rang in the New Year of 1868, thirty-five-year-old Kate Warne, Allan's first female operative and latterly superintendent of the Female Detective Bureau, died in her sleep after a long and painful illness. The man who had valued her services for almost twelve years was at her bedside to the very end. A few hours later George Bangs received a melancholy telegram and observed sadly that 'the old group' was slowly dying off. Five months later Allan's elder brother died. Robert Pinkerton is a shadowy figure. Horan thought that he had accompanied his mother, Isabella Pinkerton, to America but from the absence of his name from the Scottish registers after 1840 it seems probable that he emigrated before Allan. No record of his wife Elizabeth has ever been traced, so it is not known when, where or how she died, or if she bore any children. It seems that Robert lost his wife and therefore probable that he lived with his widowed mother until her death in 1854. Thereafter he certainly moved in with Allan and his family. Horan's epitaph is singularly apt: 'He died a middle-aged man, indistinct, completely lost beneath the dominant shadow of his famous brother.'[1] Robert, four years older than Allan, never had anything to do with the Agency, and there is no record of a trade or occupation. Perhaps the best one can say is that he may have been good company for his sister-in-law when Allan was away from home so often.

Two personal tragedies and at least two attempts on Allan's life that momentous year of 1868 did not deflect him from his relentless crusade against crime. For the first time the annual operating costs of the Agency passed the million-dollar mark. On the other hand, the Agency letter-books indicate that Allan was tempted with a change in his career. At forty-eight he was in the prime of life and by far the most experienced detective in the country. In 1868 he was approached by a number of prominent figures, including congressmen, civic leaders and Commodore Cornelius Vanderbilt no less, urging him to accept the position of Superintendent of the New York City Police Department, an organisation which was riddled with vice and corruption. Allan politely declined all these offers, even though this was the very year that Police Chief John Kennedy had chosen to denounce the Baltimore Plot of 1861 as a figment of Pinkerton's vainglorious imagination. Why Kennedy went public on this matter, and in this manner, has never been explained.[2] With remarkable self-control Allan wrote to Vanderbilt praising Kennedy as a good police officer, but to George Bangs he later admitted, 'Political influence would only prevent the operation of the department in the manner in which I would want to conduct it, making necessary changes for the interest of efficiency.'[3]

About the same time, however, Allan was writing another of his paranoid letters to his long-suffering general superintendent. After savagely excoriating Bangs for the slackness he had found in the New York office, Allan went on:

The year 1868 has been marked by a determined fight against us; at the close of that year that fight still continues but I tremble not before it. I feel no power on earth is able to check me, no power in Heaven or Hell can influence me when I know I am right. I think it cannot be long ere our enemies flee – that they are vanquished, it cannot be long if we persevere in the right and they are continually in the wrong.[4]

The hubristic tone seems ironic in hindsight, for a few months later Allan was suddenly struck down. He was seated at his desk in Chicago one day, dictating letters to his secretary, when he was assailed by a blinding headache and collapsed. A physician was instantly summoned and Allan, paralysed by a stroke, was rushed home. In a remarkable piece of damage limitation, William and Robert intimated to employees and clients alike that the boss had suffered a mild shock and carefully cultivated the impression of their father's physical resilience. They parried all enquiries with bland statements; after all, was not their father the Eye that Never Slept? How they succeeded so well is nothing short of miraculous, but their task was probably made easier by virtue of the rather secretive nature of the business and its rigidly hierarchical command structure. Far from being 'a mild shock', Allan was suffering a severe stroke which almost killed him. His recovery was very slow and painful, and only by his iron will did he eventually overcome his severe disability. For two years he was completely paralysed down his right side and virtually unable to speak. Although he began to regain the use of his limbs in the summer of 1870, it was years before he was able to write his name. Though he dictated letters, his signature would ever afterwards be a laborious scrawl, the letters hardly formed. His right side would remain partially crippled and when he was emotionally distraught or moved to anger his stocky frame shook uncontrollably – 'with the palsy', he described it – and his speech became slurred.

The dour determination of Pinkerton to confound the best medics in the country (who said that he would be confined to a wheelchair for the rest of his life) drove him just as relentlessly as he had pursued criminals. For more than a year he underwent a variety of treatments in New York. When he was sent back to Chicago as incurable, he turned in desperation to a medicinal spring near St Louis, Michigan, which had been discovered by men drilling for salt. For six months, from March till September 1870, he lived in this village, subjecting himself to a punishing daily regimen of mineral baths in a crude mud-hole, followed by a torturing course of therapy which he had devised for himself. Slowly, excruciatingly, he regained the use of his legs and on sticks he took his first tentative steps. Gradually he extended his range, forcing himself to walk distances that became longer day by day, until he was tramping twelve miles daily. To a friend he boasted, in a letter dictated in September 1870 shortly after his return to Chicago, 'I can now talk very well but have to be slow and cautious. I walk every day, eight, ten and twelve miles.' The spidery signature at the foot of this letter belied his boasting.

Another twelve months would elapse before Allan began to resemble his old self. Though he was physically handicapped, Allan's mind was as sharp as ever and he chafed at the weakness of the body which kept him from returning to work. In the long period of convalescence he began to busy himself with other projects. In January 1864 he had purchased some 254 acres of land from the Illinois Central Railroad for $4,067.52 but it was not until his stroke that he began developing his estate. In his mind's eye he had an image of a baronial mansion which he had seen from afar when he travelled round Scotland as a journeyman cooper; now he passed the time translating a half-forgotten dream into 'The Larches' near Onarga, eighty-three miles due south of Chicago. Typically, he threw himself wholeheartedly into the job, designing the magnificent villa down to the last detail and planning the landscaping of the grounds. Having chosen a name for the estate, Allan then set about clothing the bare acres with the trees he had loved as a tramp cooper.

Already snowed under with work, George Bangs was ordered to find larch trees – thousands of them – for the estate. When Bangs discovered that these trees did not exist in the United States, he received a laconic telegram from his boss: 'Then cable Scotland and order them.' Dutifully, Bangs wired Scotland and an entire shipload, 85,000 saplings no less, arrived in February 1871. George Bangs personally inspected the cargo with the New York agent of the shipping company, and made arrangements for them to be freighted to Chicago by train the following day. The agent, however, neglected to get the precious cargo under cover. Overnight the temperature dropped to a record low, and in the morning when Bangs hurried down to the windswept dockside he found that the trees had perished with severe frost. He cabled the bad news to Chicago and back came the response: 'Fire the agent. Send to Scotland for another boatload of trees'.[5]

In due course the second consignment arrived and was shipped to Chicago without further mishap. In the spring the trees were planted along the long driveway leading up to the mansion house itself. Later, neighbours would reminisce about the sturdy, stocky little man with the grey beard and beetling brows who stumped around, leaning heavily on his stout blackthorn stick, supervising stone-masons and carpenters and bawling them out in his thick Scottish brogue. In place of a simple clapboard farm steading, there slowly arose a palatial mansion, not without grim reminders of the dangerous life lived by its chief occupant. 'The Larches', in fact, was constructed like a fortress, with guardhouses at each of its three entrances, manned by Negroes in smart blue uniforms and gold buttons. Joan's province was the garden and its immense flowerbeds. Like the trees, the flowers were planted on a lavish scale and their heady scent would perfume the air all over the estate. There was also a racetrack, a fishpond, a large open campground which was used for religious revivalist meetings, and, unusually, a large wine pavilion known as the Snuggery which, a few years later, Allan had linked to the main house by a deep tunnel. This was not the harmless whim of an ageing eccentric as some contemporary reports suggested, but rather the carefully planned escape route of a man whose life had often been threatened. Years later, even after the Irish terrorist group known as the Molly Maguires had been crushed, the threat of reprisal bombings was ever present. At the heart of the estate was the Villa, a fortress of a building with a square tower surmounted by a glazed cupola where riflemen with powerful field-glasses continually scanned the surrounding estate for would-be assassins. A wide hall ran the full length of the house, lit all night by four huge crystal chandeliers.

The high point of Allan's career had been the eighteen months he spent in the field with Little Mac. At great expense, therefore, he brought out from Scotland the artist Paul Loose whom he commissioned to paint a series of murals depicting episodes from the war, as well as landscapes. In the fullness of time the rich and famous, the socialites and celebrities, were entertained at

'The Larches' and admired the epic paintings of 'McClellan and his Staff', 'Bull Run', 'The Battle of Gettysburg', 'Sherman's March to the Sea' and best of all, 'Secret Service Staff of the Army of the Potomac' showing Allan in his characteristically flat bowler hat, surrounded by fifteen of his best operatives. Over each door on the ground floor were oil portraits of the men Allan admired most from that period: Lincoln, Grant, Sherman and, of course, George McClellan.

As he slowly regained his health Allan began to live a little. Hitherto he never had any time for the social graces, but now he and Joan began to entertain on quite a lavish scale. Many years later the local people would still reminisce about the weekend parties in the late 1870s and early 1880s when Allan would bring his house guests down from Chicago by private Pullman car:

> It was the big event of the town and we all used to troop down to see the gay crowd of men and women troop off the train. Pinkerton's carriage with four horsemen and a coachman in livery would be on hand and everything would be shined up.[6]

To this secluded mansion came the great and the good: Henry Sanford, now president of Adams Express, Commodore Vanderbilt in his eighties, August Belmont, Ambrose Burnside, Fred Seward, Chief Justice Salmon P. Chase and even the President of the United States himself, Ulysses S. Grant.

From this relatively tranquil period belongs one of the few extant photographs of Allan and Joan together. His hair is thinning but his keen eye is as alert as ever. Joan, a few inches shorter, is a dumpy little woman, her dark hair drawn back severely in the fashion of the time to accentuate the roundness of her face. One old resident of Onarga recalled running across the fields of the estate as a small boy and seeing Allan and Joan walking slowly along the winding paths, the summer dusk heavy with the fragrance of the flowers that lined the gravelled paths and lawns. It was recalled that Allan loved horses and dogs, and always had colts and thoroughbreds in the paddocks beyond the mansion. He had a soft spot for the tough western Indian ponies and he enjoyed watching a good rider breaking these mustangs to the saddle. He also imported several Shetland ponies for his grandchildren and their little friends to ride. One of these children would recall sixty years later how they would ride around the estate in a pony cart, while the old man entertained them with vivid stories about Abraham Lincoln and his adventures at the battlefront. In the evening, when Allan brought out meat to the kennels, the yelping and barking of the hounds echoed across the countryside. Later on, there would be a little cemetery in the corner of a field where favourite dogs and horses were interred, each with its tiny headstone.

The Snuggery was Allan's den, where the very favoured male guests would be taken for a glass or two of fine wine and an opportunity to relive the battles and campaigns of the war or review the relentless battle against crime. Its walls were adorned with maps and diagrams, some dating from the Civil War, but others tracing the movements of the outlaw gangs, such as the Renos and later the James brothers. The impression is often given, especially in magazine articles written long after the event, that Allan was living in the past at 'The Larches'; but it is more probable that high-level conferences on strategy to combat organised crime in the late 1870s were held here.

The severe stroke that almost killed him was a grim warning to Allan to take things easy. Fortunately for him, he heeded it, up to a point. William and Robert were effectively running the show from the middle of 1869 onwards, but Allan never put this into formal effect. By the end of 1871 he felt fit enough to return to work. After all, he was only fifty-two and had many years of hard work left in him. He came back to his office, slower in speech but quicker to anger, more irascible than ever, but still 'A.P.', the Founder.

He had only been back at his desk a few weeks when disaster struck again. By 1871 Chicago had a population of 306,000 and was a commercial centre of considerable importance, but two-thirds of its buildings were of wood, and that summer had been excessively dry. On the night of 8 October fire broke out near the lumber district on the west side and a high and veering wind off the lake fanned the flames. The conflagration leaped the river and by the time it was brought under control it had totally razed an area of three and a half miles, destroying 17,450 buildings and property valued at $196,000,000. Over 100,000 people lost their homes, though only twenty-five lost their lives. Thousands of people fled before the flames and rushed into the lake to escape the firebrands. Robbery, pillage, extortion and orgies of crime added to the general mayhem. The fire raged unchecked for twenty-seven hours before it was halted by gunpowder and a providential thunderstorm.

At that time Allan and Joan lived in a grand mansion on West Monroe Street which fortunately escaped the holocaust, but the National Detective Agency, with its priceless Rogues Gallery and archives, was reduced to ashes. A particularly cruel blow was the destruction of Allan's Civil War files which he was about to sell to the government for a reputed $100,000. In February 1872 he wrote at length to his old friend Salmon P. Chase, describing how he and his staff had tried to drag records from the Washington Street building, only to run for their lives before the rapidly advancing inferno. Everything was incinerated within fifty minutes, 'including four volumes of my records of the Army of the Potomac, from the time McClellan took over the Army of the Ohio until he retired from the field . . . among these the history of Cameron and Stanton was fully portrayed.' The last reference is particularly intriguing and one cannot help wishing that Allan's record of the strange episode in which Edwin Stanton ousted Simon Cameron from the Secretaryship of War had been preserved.

Undefeated by this latest blow, Allan was soon hard at work rebuilding his offices. A team of carpenters was engaged as soon as the walls had cooled down from the fire, 'and was soon made pretty comfortable with some lumber'. Every cloud has a silver lining, for in the aftermath of the blaze the Agency was busier than ever. As Allan confided to the Chief Justice, he had obtained contracts to guard 'all the burned district and so I have done very well'. To Chase, however, he also admitted that he was still suffering the debilitating effects of his illness:

Sometimes I am troubled by an impediment in my speech but not all the time . . . bad weather troubles my limbs.

But upon the whole I am better amazingly. In the morning at five o'clock I am up and into a cold bath from ten to eighteen minutes, then rub myself dry and by six out in the air for a walk for probably three quarters of an hour or an hour. Breakfast ready by seven, then walk to the office. In this manner I am beating all the doctors.

Still partially handicapped, and sickened by the stench of burned-out buildings, Allan doggedly fought on, working harder than ever to rebuild his shattered business. To Bangs in New York he wrote in trenchant mood, 'I will never be beaten, never. Not all the Furies of Hell will stop me from rebuilding *immediately*.' The last word was heavily underlined.

Continuing ill health and the devastating setback of the fire were bad enough; but in 1872 the United States was hit by a severe economic downturn. Business was generally bad that year and things were just beginning to pick up again when, in September 1873, a slump was triggered off by the spectacular failure of Jay Cooke, the financier of the Northern Pacific Railway. For more than five years the nation underwent a drastic cutback; railroad construction virtually ceased and as late as 1877 over eighteen per cent of the railway mileage was in the hands of receivers. The iron and steel industry was prostrated, and mercantile failures for four years amounted to $775,000,000. During this tumultuous period partnerships and the individual control of businesses gave way to corporations. Inevitably the Agency was hard hit by the great depression, but by strict budgetary controls and drastic pruning of staff, Allan somehow weathered the storm.

Paradoxically, there was more work than ever. The agents operating out of New York and Philadelphia were dealing with robberies running to millions of dollars, which made the activities of the Renos look like chickenfeed. Despite the severe setback in the railroad companies, they continued to provide Pinkerton with the bulk of his business. Nevertheless, the thefts of the gangs who held up the trains were as nothing compared with the larceny on a grand scale perpetrated by Credit Mobilier, a construction company controlled by Union Pacific stockholders. This scandal broke in 1873 and led to a Congressional investigation which damaged the reputations of several leading Republicans, notably the Vice-President, Schuyler Colfax, and Henry Wilson, whose love letters to Rose Greenhow Allan had seized.

While Allan gloated over the discomfiture of Wilson, his old enemy, he was alarmed by the panic in the business sector. In May 1873 he wrote to Bangs, 'I can scarcely tell which way to go, and many a time I am perfectly bewildered what to do . . . I am afraid.' To Willie, however, he struck a defiant note: 'I will come out all right, by'n bye . . . My idea is never to lose heart, never think for a moment of giving up the ship. I am bound to go through sink or swim. Hold your head up. I will back you at all eternity.'

There are copious references to belt-tightening in the Agency's letter-books for 1872 and 1873. The Agency was doing a thorough job in apprehending train robbers and exposing dishonest railroad employees, but with the savage downturn in business the railway companies were taking a long, hard look at the costs of such security. Bangs reported to Allan on one occasion that the New York Central 'was contemplating having us but after they heard what it cost the Hudson River road to keep their conductors honest it was claimed that our bill was more than the conductors would steal in three years'. Bangs even speculated a few dollars of the Agency's money in wining and dining an executive of the railroad at Delmonico's on Broad Street, in the vain hope of winning the security contract.

In desperation Allan took on work which stretched his operatives to the limit. In May 1872 he was retained by the Spanish government to investigate the activities of Manuel de Cespedes, a wealthy Cuban sugar planter. On 10 October 1868 he had begun an insurrection at Yara and this gradually engulfed the island's eastern provinces, dragging on for ten years. Cespedes demanded the emancipation of the island's slaves, together with the grant of free and universal suffrage. Allan must have had a hard time swallowing his scruples to take on this case. The brutally repressive policies of the Spanish colonial administration were so contrary to all his long-held principles, and his natural sympathies should have been with the rebels. When Spanish troops were turned loose to commit the most horrible atrocities on the rebel districts, however, Allan withdrew his agents from the investigation.

Back in the United States Allan suffered severe cash-flow problems. On 15 August 1872 he wrote despairingly to Bangs, 'I suppose there is no hope for anything paying in New York. God knows what I am to do two days from this date.' The same day he wrote to Captain Fitzgerald, one of his chief Chicago operatives, complaining that his business

> is in great want of money, on every hand I am in debt . . . It is nearly Saturday and you know I have to pay everyone. I must have money for they must have money. I would not for anything allow them to go without their wages, but how am I going to get the money unless you and the others do your duty and bring in the money?

Somehow or other Allan obtained sufficient cash to pay his staff. The immediate crisis passed but the long-term problem remained and by the autumn Allan was facing financial ruin. On 17 October he wrote despairingly to Bangs, imploring him to

> collect all your bills without one moment's delay, things are coming right on us. Let business stand for the moment – go to work and collect bills, sacrifice everything to get money, discount at any price . . . Any day whatever there may be a crash around us that we little suspect.

Operatives were taken off cases and sent on the rounds to collect money owing to the Agency. Adams Express coughed up various sums, ranging from $75 to $1,200 which Bangs promptly remitted to J.G. Horne, Allan's penny-pinching accountant in Chicago. This cash enabled Allan to meet the wage bill that month, but the prospects seemed bleak. To raise sufficient money to cover the expenses of an assignment offered by the Atlantic and Great Western Railroad Allan was even obliged to liquidate a substantial block of railroad stock. Henry Sanford, president of Adams Express, was himself very hard-pressed and tried to collect money from Allan which the detective had borrowed some time previously. When Allan said that he could not repay the loan Sanford became very abusive 'and has insulted me in every way lately', as Allan confided to Bangs on 16 November. Somehow business began to pick up again and the Agency struggled through, but it was a pretty close-run thing.

During this period, as his health gradually returned and he sought some distraction from his mounting money worries, Allan turned for the first time to writing. Over the years he had written, or dictated, thousands of letters and reports running to many millions of words. Now he began writing for posterity. In 1873 the fruits of this labour saw the light of day as *The Bankers, their Vaults and the Burglars*, published in Chicago. This rare book, part reminiscence, part manual of instruction, was sufficiently well received for Allan to be encouraged to embark on a sequel. The following year, *The Expressman and the Detective* was likewise published at Chicago.

Subsequently he was approached by G.W. Dillingham of New York with an intriguing proposition; if Allan would be prepared to submit an outline, together with the relevant case histories, Dillingham would employ a 'ghost' to generate the text of a book which would be published under Allan's name. In 1875, therefore, Dillingham published three books: *The Detective and the Somnambulist*, *The Murderer and the Fortune-teller* and *Claude Melmotte as a Detective, and Other Stories*. On 29 February 1876 Allan confided to his son Robert that he currently had 'seven writers working on my stories'. Most of these books have all the marks of being put together by literary hacks; in particular the highly coloured dialogue owes much to the crude melodramas so fashionable in the mid-nineteenth century. But three of the later books, from internal evidence, were Allan's own work. *The Spy of the Rebellion*, published in 1883, was provoked by Allan's desire to tell his side of the story of President-elect Lincoln's journey to Washington, while *Thirty Years a Detective*, published the following year, was Allan's autobiography. The other book which differs radically from the lurid style in most of the Dillingham publications was *The Molly Maguires and the Detectives*, published in 1877, which adhered faithfully to the transcript of the trial. In all, the eighteen books bearing Allan's name on the title page ran to more than three million words; of these only five may be regarded as wholly or largely his own work. Although these works have autobiographical elements, they are far less revealing of Allan's character than the letters to his sons or to George Bangs.

In the closing phase of Allan's active career, two cases dominated the Agency. Both were spread over several years and have become epics of American folklore, spawning millions of words, endless novels, plays, ballads and films. Jesse Woodson James, born in Clay County, Missouri, in September 1847, a psychotic drug-addict and ruthless killer, has become the world's most famous outlaw; even President Theodore Roosevelt called him America's Robin Hood. The bare facts of his life are well known. His family were Southern sympathisers, persecuted during the Civil War. At fifteen Jesse joined the guerrilla band led by C.W. Quantrell. When Quantrell's band surrendered in 1865 they were treacherously shot and wounded, and Jesse took his revenge on society by turning bandit. For sixteen years, from February 1866 till 1882, the gang robbed and killed its way across the Mid-West. At its height, the James band included elder brother Frank, as well as Jim, John and Cole Younger, Cell and Ed Miller and the Ford brothers, Bob and Charlie. In the end the Fords would turn traitor and shoot Jesse in the back for the $10,000 reward. Frank James surrendered soon afterwards, but was never brought to trial and lived on until 1915, working quietly on his farm. Cole Younger eventually shot himself; at the post mortem a surgeon removed no fewer than twenty-nine bullets which had been lodged in various parts of his body as a result of gun battles over the years.

Allan's operatives had a brief but bloody encounter with the James gang in 1871 but financial constraints prevented the Agency resuming its campaign against these desperadoes until 1874. At the beginning of that year William Pinkerton sent a young agent named John W. Whicher to Missouri to infiltrate the gang. In March his hideously mutilated body was found at the roadside near Independence; he had been bound, then shot in the head and body, several times, at very close range. Allan was outraged at this brutal, cold-blooded murder and a few days later sent in two of his best men. Louis Lull had been a captain in the Chicago Police Department before joining the Agency. Now he travelled to Missouri under the name of W.J. Allen, uncannily close to Allan's own wartime alias. Lull was accompanied by John Boyle, a former St Louis policeman, using the alias of James Wright. At St Clair County they were joined by a deputy sheriff, Edwin B. Daniels. The three men, posing as cattle dealers, met John and Jim Younger on Chalk Hill Road on 16 March. The outlaws called them to halt and then opened fire. Wright galloped off as the gunslingers shot off his hat; but Daniels and Lull were stopped and disarmed. When Lull drew a hidden Smith and Wesson revolver and shot John Younger, brother Jim shot the detective several times. Lull was found the following day and rushed to a hotel in Roscoe where he died of his wounds after making a detailed statement. Allan wanted to hire a special train to bring Lull back to Chicago but the local doctor, D.C. McNeil, wired that Lull was too ill to be moved. Mrs Lull, accompanied by Robert Linden, assistant superintendent in the Philadelphia office, went to Roscoe to be with the wounded detective at the end.

After this débâcle Allan wrote bitterly to Bangs in New York:

> I have no soldiers but all officers in my regiment – all are capital men to give orders, few will go forward unless someone goes ahead. I know that the James Youngers are desperate men, and that if we meet it (*sic*) it must be the death of one or both of us. They must repay . . . There is no use talking, they must die. Mr Warner [Frank Warner, superintendent of the Chicago office] and William refused to go with the men to Missouri, both declared they were not to be made a notch to be shot at . . . Consequently I made no talk but simply say I am going myself.[7]

In January 1875 a group of heavily armed men descended from the train at Union Station in Clay County, Missouri and, assisted by 'ten trustworthy Clay County citizens', surrounded the rough log cabin which the local people had dubbed Castle James. The outlaws, forewarned of the raid, slipped quietly away to another hideout, leaving behind the James boys' mother Zerelda, her second husband Dr Samuels and their two children. An incendiary device was lobbed into the house but Samuels pushed it into the fireplace where it exploded, sending white-hot shards of metal around the room. Zerelda's arm was torn to shreds and Jesse's eight-year-old half-brother Archie was fatally wounded. At the boy's funeral three days later huge crowds turned out to vilify the Pinkertons. For the first time in the Agency's quarter-of-a-century existence, Allan found himself and his men on the wrong side of popular opinion. Press coverage and editorial comment were uniform in condemning the Pinkertons. Allan had not taken the field himself, as he had intended, but it is highly probable that William was implicated, at least in so far as he directed operations from his hotel in Kansas City. When the sheriff of Clay County was goaded into seeking indictments for first-degree murder against the Agency's detectives, Allan wrote angrily to Robert in New York on 12 September:

I have but little to say about this subject: the fact is they are trying their best to get indictments against some of my men for the operation in Clay County where James' mother had met with a merited and fearful punishment. Also into West Virginia, Texas, Arkansas where they will undoubtedly try to get indictments against my men who have gone to these places to fight the battle.

Oddly enough, Allan was convinced that the gang had been wiped out, an assumption that was very wide of the mark. Referring to those Mid-Western police chiefs who had been widely quoted in the newspapers as highly critical of the Agency's ruthless methods, Allan continued:

I will gladly allow these people to go into Clay County or St Clair County or Monegaw Springs as my men have done. I paid the penalty of having lost my men but I will not bandy words regarding those great men in the detective business at the present time . . . 'Tis enough I must say I ask nothing from the Adams Express Company. I must say I spent money freely and I ask no reward. I must say my end is accomplished and in that I am content.

Allan hotly denied that his son William had led the raid on the Samuels place, though he never revealed the names of those operatives who were involved. As a result, the allegation that William had been involved stuck, and gathered credence with the passage of the years, coming back time and time again to haunt the Agency. Similarly, the device lobbed into the cabin, an iron-based copper sphere filled with cotton soaked in turpentine, had been intended merely to smoke out the inmates; it was singularly unfortunate that Dr Samuels should have pushed it with his stick into the fireplace, with such tragically devastating results. Soon after the event Augustus C. Appler, editor of the Osceola *Democrat* rushed out his book on the James family, and thus let loose the floodgates. Since 1875 it is estimated that upwards of two hundred books on Jesse James have been published. As Jesse James became a legend in his own lifetime, the image of the National Detective Agency was tarnished for the first time.

In the very year that Allan and Joan left Scotland there was organised in Ireland a secret society called the Molly Maguires. Its members were drawn from the lowest class of the peasantry, desperate men who had been evicted from their land, and it hit back at the instruments of their oppression, the bailiffs, process-servers and agents of the landlords. The Molly Maguires of Pennsylvania, founded in 1854, consisted of similar classes of Irishmen but there was no connection between the two societies. In the coal-mining districts of Pennsylvania the organisation came under the control of a lawless element which created an élitist, inner order of Molly Maguires with the object of intimidating the English, Welsh and German miners, and of ridding the region of any mine superintendents, bosses and police who should make themselves objectionable to members of the order. Any member who had a grievance would report it to his 'body master' who would confer with the officers of neighbouring divisions and arrange for the murder of the offending person by men drawn from a distance. These contract killings by total strangers baffled the state and county authorities, and in the chaotic period following the end of the Civil War the society grew enormously in power. By 1875 it completely dominated the miners and even forced a general strike.

After repeated attempts to bring the criminals to justice had failed, Franklin Benjamin Gowen, president of the Philadelphia and Reading Coal and Iron Company, despairingly tossed the matter over to Allan Pinkerton. Interestingly, it was not Gowen who made the first move. As early as 17 May 1872, when he was up to his eyes in debt, Allan had written to George Bangs, urging him to call on Gowen, then president of the Reading Railroad, 'to suggest something to Mr Gowen about one thing or another which could be feasible and I have no doubt he would give us work'. This was no cold call, for Allan had previous worked with Gowen in rooting out dishonest conductors and other railroad employees. Now crime connected with the railroad was taking a sinister turn; freight-cars were being sabotaged or derailed. These and other violent acts were being laid at the door of the Molly Maguires, and when the giant coal-tip at Pottsville mysteriously caught fire Gowen could no longer leave matters to get out of control. Posterity would seek to sanctify the Mollies, and in much of the literature on trade unionism and organised labour they have been transformed into martyrs, hounded to the gallows by union-busting capitalists. From this premise it was but a short step to condemning the Pinkerton detectives, as agents of those capitalists, 'the serfs of capitalism who secured the convictions of honest men by fabricating evidence'. Much of the opprobrium heaped on the Pinkertons in the aftermath of the Homestead strike of 1892 would rake up the affair of the Molly Maguires, to denigrate the memory of Allan Pinkerton.

In that year Matthew Mark Trumbull, who had been a physical force Chartist like Allan and who had likewise taken an emigrant ship to Montreal one jump ahead of vengeful authorities, wrote a blistering attack on his one-time comrade. Trumbull, incidentally, had enlisted in the Mexican War and was made a sergeant. Later he was chased out of Richmond, Virginia, for voicing abolitionism; he practised law in Chicago, rejoined the army at the outbreak of the Civil War and rose to the rank of brigadier-general. After the war he returned to his Chicago law firm and specialised in labour disputes. He was a lifelong friend of Julian Harney, with whom he corresponded regularly for many years, and also maintained a close friendship with James Charlton, a physical force Chartist whom Allan Pinkerton had known in Newcastle. Charlton also resided in Chicago where, in 1870, he became the general manager of the Chicago and Alton Railroad, a company which used the Pinkerton Agency on a long-term basis. Trumbull, a close friend of Ulysses Grant from before the Civil War, was inevitably well acquainted with Allan Pinkerton, whose political outlook had once been more or less identical to his own. In 1890 Trumbull published his memoirs, but two years later, in the aftermath of the Homestead strike, he felt impelled to rush out a second edition to which he appended a fiery postscript:

> In the days of my hot youth, I was a revolutionary Chartist, eager to fight for the overthrow of the British monarchy and the erection on its ruins of a British republic; and there were enough of those who aspired as I did to cause the Government alarm.
>
> Among the prominent Chartists of the north was a young man whose name was Allan Pinkerton: and when the Government was busy fining, imprisoning and transporting Chartists, Pinkerton made his escape to the United States where, in bitter irony, grim fate made him establish the most dangerous order of spies that ever preyed upon social freedom in America; and it became his unlucky destiny to give his name to an army of illegal soldiers not under the command of the nation or the state, an impudent menace to liberty: an irresponsible brigade of hired banditti, equipped with rifles and threatening every American working man.[8]

To be sure, this was penned in the white heat of the moment, long after Allan himself was dead, but it is probably not an inaccurate expression of the view that developed in socialist circles in the 1870s and 1880s after the Molly Maguires were brought to justice. It was an unfair view, nonetheless. Even if some of the Molly Maguires also happened to be members of the miners' union, this did not mitigate the brutality of their crimes. They were ruthless thugs and heartless killers who terrorised the mining community for many years. Nor should it be overlooked that after their power was broken in 1877 the outrages ceased and the mining industry enjoyed a period of comparative tranquillity.

In the previous decade, however, the Pennsylvania coalfields seethed with discontent. Unchecked immigration during the postwar depression forced down wage rates and the conditions in which the miners – men, women and children – laboured were barbaric. Into this unstable situation were thrown old hatreds and new enmities. Protestants and Catholics from Ireland imported their traditional mutual antipathies, but racism and Copperhead sympathies also played their volatile part. Coal-mining was dirty, dangerous, frequently fatal, and it bred a generation of hard men. In this explosive atmosphere murder and violent crime were commonplace, and inevitably the Molly Maguires were blamed for everything, whether they were the perpetrators or not. Gowen, scion of a wealthy Philadelphia family, had impeccable capitalist credentials. The law and Democrat politics were in his blood, and a combination of luck, good connections and courtroom skills brought him to the presidency of the Reading Railroad. In 1871 he doubled the freight rates on coal, upsetting both the mine-owners and the nascent trade union. A year later, operating through various front men, he purchased vast tracts of coal-bearing land and also manoeuvred a bill through the state legislature giving the Reading a virtual monopoly in the coalfields. Gowen was later charged with bribery but the case collapsed for lack of evidence. By the beginning of 1875 the Reading owned 100,000 acres of prime coal country, more than twice as much as its nearest rival.

Only one thing threatened Gowen's meteoric progress, and that was the Molly Maguires. Allan Pinkerton conferred with Gowen and agreed to take on the crusade against the Irish terrorists. Although Allan's classic ploy of infiltration had failed tragically in the case of the James gang, it was a proven method which, in this instance, would yield spectacular results. In his book, published in 1877, Allan described how he set about this tricky assignment:

> It is no ordinary man that I needed in this matter. He must be an Irishman and a Catholic, as only this class of person can find admission to the Mollie Maguires. My detective should become, to all intents and purposes, one of

the order, and continue so while he remains in the case before us. He should be hardy, tough and capable of laboring, in season and out of season, to accomplish unknown to those about him, a single absorbing subject.[9]

No one appreciated better than Allan, the old physical force Chartist, how informers were detested. The job called for someone of outstanding qualities. While mulling over this problem, Allan found the solution. He was travelling to his office on a West Side streetcar in Chicago one day when he spotted one of his operatives, James McParland, acting as conductor during a routine check on pilferage. McParland had emigrated from Ulster to Chicago, holding down a wide variety of jobs before the great fire of October 1871 had wiped out his liquor store and saloon. He had previously had some police experience and joined the Agency after the fire. He was twenty-nine years of age. Allan left a brief note for McParland at his home, asking him to call privately. Then Allan outlined the assignment, saying that he would not hold it against him if he refused. McParland thought for a moment and then accepted.

On 23 October 1873 McParland, posing as James McKenna, a fugitive from a murder charge in Buffalo, set out for the coalfields. Dirty, unshaven and clad in rags, he was hired as a miner and for two and a half years engaged in a desperate undertaking which 'was of such a nature that even the most calm recital of his deeds had all the aspects of the wildest fiction'.[10] Throughout this period even Gowen did not know McParland's true identity. Only six men were privy to the details: Allan and his two sons, George Bangs, Benjamin Franklin (superintendent at Philadelphia) and Robert Linden (assistant superintendent at Chicago). Tall, red-haired, possessed of a fine tenor voice and a large repertoire of Irish ballads, and handy with his fists and boots in a scrap, Jim McKenna soon made his mark in the Irish community. Eventually he won the confidence of Pat Dormer, a Molly who ran the Sheridan saloon in Pottsville, who gave him an introduction to Muff Lawler, the body master in Shenandoah twenty miles north. From there, McKenna went to Girardsville where he met Jack Kehoe, owner of the Hibernian House and one of the leaders of the order. During this time, McParland was working a punishing twenty-hour shift at the coal-face for a miserable ten dollars a week. It was not until 13 April 1874 that he was inducted into the secret society, paid three dollars entrance fee and took a sacred oath on his knees. When McKenna disarmed a gunman who tried to kill Lawler his stock in the Molly Maguires rose dramatically.

He was put to the test when Kehoe nominated him to kill Gomer Jones, a Welshman who had shot a young Molly, but somehow he wriggled off the hook. He was appointed lodge secretary, a position that made it easier to send reports to Franklin, although his cover was almost blown when a Pinkerton clerk mistakenly sent a letter to the Pottsville post office, addressed to James McParland instead of McKenna. Tension mounted in the coalfields over the winter of 1874–75 as the coal-owners combined to reduce wages still further. Members of the Workingmen's Benevolent Association, the miners' union, went on strike in January 1875, while the owners retaliated by bringing in non-union workers from Wyoming, prepared to take the pay cuts. In his despatches to the Agency, forwarded to Gowen, McParland reported objectively. One report trenchantly informed Gowen that 'all classes of persons in the coal regions are very much embittered toward your company and openly denounce the course you have taken'.

The strike dragged on for several months, and became increasingly violent. In April the Shenandoah lodge came to McParland with a plan to blow up the railway bridge between Catawissa and Williamsport, to prevent the shipment of 'scab' coal. Now McParland faced a dilemma. If he agreed, he would be committing a serious felony; if he refused, he would come under Molly suspicion. The nimble-witted operative divulged that he had 'absolute knowledge' that the railroad police had the bridge under constant surveillance and that any attempt to dynamite it would lead to instant arrest. Persuaded by the vehemence of his arguments the Mollies finally gave way. A few days later a wagon loaded with iron slag was uncoupled and only narrowly missed collision with a passenger train. McParland eventually got admissions from two Mollies that they had been responsible and in due course they were tried and convicted, the first break in the case.

Getting to that point, however, was a slow and hazardous operation which risked breaking McParland's cover. At a meeting with Gowen in April 1875 Allan proposed streamlining and accelerating communications by setting up a flying squad of police to cover the coalfields. This force, comprising six Agency operatives and six hand-picked railroad men, would be under the command of a Pinkerton lieutenant who alone would have contact with McParland. The man chosen for this risky task was Robert Linden, then aged about forty. Linden and McParland had their first rendezvous on 7 May, at Ashland twenty miles west of Shenandoah. Now McParland had an ally, but this also doubled the risk of exposure.

Ten days later McParland found himself propelled into the top position as Shenandoah body master. Soon afterwards Kehoe decided to step up the campaign of terror against the English and Welsh in Mahanoy City. When the strike collapsed at the end of May the Molly Maguires began a campaign of intimidating the Wyoming blacklegs and a week of violent rioting ensued, culminating in the attack on William 'Bully Bill' Thomas, who was shot by three gunmen on the night of 27 June. At the subsequent trial McParland was severely criticised by the defence lawyers; if he were not actually an *agent provocateur* then he was implicated in the crime by failing to warn Linden, Franklin or Allan Pinkerton that the murder was imminent. Some historians have taken the view that Thomas was cold-bloodedly sacrificed in order to get a conviction of murder against the plotters rather than the lesser felony of assault and conspiracy; but in all honesty McParland (who was seriously ill at the time of the crime) was powerless to warn his superior officers. His own survival was on the line, with Molly gunmen breathing down his neck at all times. In fact, Thomas miraculously survived the triple shooting, but others were not so lucky. Benjamin Yost, a German who acted as community policeman, was shot dead, and shots were fired at Barney McCarron, his deputy. The attempt on a fellow Irishman, however, hardened community opinion against the Molly Maguires. Over the ensuing months murders and mayhem escalated. McParland submitted a lengthy and thought-provoking report analysing labour conditions in the coalfields, implying that Gowen himself was largely responsible for the ugly situation. To his everlasting credit, Allan insisted that Gowen receive this report without cuts.

The strain of this undercover work took a heavy toll on McParland who had several bouts of serious illness; but he doggedly remained at his post and continued writing reports which would eventually send the principal Mollies to the gallows. It was a difficult time for Allan also. There were many other cases, perhaps not so important, that required his urgent attention while the Molly Maguire investigation continued. A blow which Allan took very badly was the defection of Gus Thiel, one of his longest-serving and most trusted lieutenants, who left the Agency to set up in business on his own account, a move which Allan never forgave. Thiel was by no means the only man to 'desert' as Allan put it strongly. These defectors were roundly condemned, their long records of sterling service swept aside. He brooded over the unfavourable publicity which had arisen over the bombing of the Samuels cabin, and fretted as the Molly Maguire case dragged on, McParland and Linden seemingly unable to get sufficient evidence for a wholesale arrest of the ringleaders.

The situation in the coalfields was not unlike that in Clay County where, by this time, the James gang were being lauded as heroes. But time was against the Molly Maguires; the Irish community was divided in its loyalties, and the other ethnic groups were violently hostile. The spirit of vigilantism was in the air, as Allan noted approvingly in a letter to Bangs on 17 August in which he likened the Molly Maguires to the *thugs* of India. After expressing serious doubts whether a jury in the coalfields would ever convict the terrorists, even if brought to trial, Allan went on:

The only way then to pursue them as I see it is to treat them as the Renos were treated in Seymour, Indiana. After they were done away the people improved wonderfully and Seymour is quite a town. Let Linden get up a vigilante committee. It will not do to get many men, but let him get those who are prepared to take fearful revenge on the M.M.'s. I think it would open the eye of all the people and then the M.M.'s would meet with their just deserts. It is awful to see men doomed to death, it is horrible. Now there is but one thing to be done, and that is, get up an organization if possible, and when ready for action pounce upon the M.M.'s when they are in full blast, take the fearful responsibility and disperse.

This is the best advice I can give you. I would not keep this letter in Philadelphia, but if you want to preserve it send it over to New York. Place all confidence in Mr Linden, he is a good man, and he understands what to do.

If you think it is advisable, bring the matter before Mr Gowen but none other than him.

Fortunately, the saner counsels of George Bangs and Robert Pinkerton prevailed, and Allan's extraordinary (and highly illegal) proposal was not followed up.

Ironically, McParland was now reporting to Linden that he himself had been targeted as 'a bad Molly' and was getting threats from local vigilante groups. By October 1875, following a further wave of violence in and around Shenandoah, McParland slipped off to New York where he reported personally to Bangs and compiled a massive report, naming no fewer than 374 persons implicated in Molly crimes. A list of the names was subsequently printed as a handbill which Linden circulated in the coal towns, possibly with a view to encouraging 'leading citizens as to who the parties are who have committed the recent assassinations' to take the law into their own hands. Very early in the morning of Friday, 10 December, masked men broke into the home of Charles O'Donnell in Wiggins Patch, shot Ellen McAllister, severely injured her mother Margaret O'Donnell, and pumped fifteen bullets into Charles O'Donnell's head. Other members of the family were beaten or shot but escaped death. When a garbled and exaggerated account of this attack reached Pottsville (claiming that all the O'Donnell men had been murdered) McParland immediately dashed off an indignant letter to Franklin, tendering his resignation. 'I am not going to be accessory to the murder of women and children.' Hitherto the 'Sleepers' (Molly gunmen) had confined their attacks to men, but McParland feared that this vigilante action would lead to total war.

Franklin immediately sent a covering letter to Allan:

This morning I received a report from 'Mac' of which I sent you a copy, and in which he seems to be very much surprised at the shooting of these men; and he offers his resignation. I telegraphed 'Mac' to come here from Pottsville as I am anxious to satisfy him that we had nothing to do with what has taken place in regard to these men. Of course, I do not want 'Mac' to resign.

McParland's emotional reaction to the shootings implies that he was aware of Allan's instructions to Linden, and the latter's questionable activities in circulating the handbill listing the 374 suspects. In fairness to Allan, however, it should be noted that there were others openly advocating vigilante action. The local newspapers were uniformly vociferous on the issue and the Tamaqua Citizens' Committee had been whipping up mob violence against the Irish community. At the inquest into the murder victims, Mrs O'Donnell was asked if she could identify her assailants. At that moment Jack Kehoe jumped to his feet saying, 'This business will be settled in another manner.' John Slattery, one of the Molly Maguires who later turned state's evidence, testified that the 'vigilantes' were actually some of Kehoe's men. Kehoe, suspecting that Charles O'Donnell was turning traitor after feeling remorse over a double slaying, decided to pre-empt his betrayal. Even before Slattery's damning evidence was produced there were rumours that the affray had been a 'clan fight'. The Boston *Pilot* of 18 December actually reported that the shooting 'grew out of a previous shooting affair, the facts of which the O'Donnells were aware of, and it is thought the murderers found it necessary to silence them for fear of damaging evidence in their possession'.

Allan convinced McParland that the Agency was not implicated in the murders and persuaded him to remain at his post, but McParland's position was becoming more and more difficult by the day. Kehoe, confronted with the incriminating handbill, deduced that the Mollies were being betrayed by someone who was singularly well informed. It would only be a matter of time before his suspicions alighted on the lanky, red-haired McKenna.

Matters took a fresh turn a few days later when Mrs O'Donnell testified that the leader of the vigilantes was Frank Weinrich, a Mahanoy City butcher who was a first lieutenant in the Pennsylvania National Guard and a widely respected citizen. Weinrich was arrested, charged with homicide, and released on bail. When Kehoe whipped up Irish mob violence against the luckless butcher he was taken into protective custody and spirited off to the gaol at Pottsville. Several days later, during a habeas corpus plea by Weinrich's attorney, Mrs O'Donnell was cross-examined by the district attorney who demanded to know if she had made the identification on Jack Kehoe's orders. The frightened widow reluctantly whispered 'Yes' and Weinrich was promptly released. This strengthened the view that Kehoe, who had tried to send an innocent man to the gallows, was implicated in the murder of the O'Donnells, to whom he was actually related by marriage.

Eventually sufficient rock-hard evidence had been amassed for charges to be brought. Jimmy Kerrigan, Mike Doyle and other Mollies were arrested and arraigned for the murder of John Jones, a mine superintendent, on 3 September 1875. In prison Kerrigan sang like a canary, and as a result four other Mollies were arrested for the murder of mine superintendent Thomas Sanger and his lodger, William Uren, on 1 September 1875. McParland, who was courting Mary Ann Higgins, a cousin of Kerrigan, called at the Kerrigan house in January 1876 to find the family actually plotting the murder of their own son Jimmy in reprisal for his betrayal of his comrades.

On 23 February 1876 Frank McAndrew, the Shenandoah body master whom McParland had befriended, came to him and, in a troubled voice, let slip that Kehoe was laying bets that he, Jim McKenna, was the informer they had been looking for. Instead of fleeing for his life, the courageous McParland went to Girardsville and confronted Kehoe in his own bar. Angrily he demanded to know who had been putting the finger on him, and Kehoe admitted that he had got his information from a railroad conductor. McParland strenuously refuted the allegation and demanded that the Mollies hold a trial to exonerate him. Kehoe said that the trial would be held the following month in Ferguson's Hall, Shenandoah. He tried to write the letters summoning the other body masters to a council but his hand shook so much that he let McParland write the letters instead. To cap all, McParland even stayed the night with Kehoe. Back in Pottsville the following day, however, another Molly leader accused McParland of being the informer. By now McParland realised that time was running out. At great risk he contacted Linden and begged him to keep out of sight for a while till things calmed down again. Incredibly, he told Linden to let Allan Pinkerton know that he was confident of getting the better of Kehoe and his cohorts.

On his return to Shenandoah, however, McParland realised that Kehoe had no intention of giving him a trial. Again McAndrew tipped him off that at least a dozen men had been assigned to the job of killing him with axes and iron bars. McParland bluffed his way out of trouble; having eluded his ambushers, he went straightaway to Kehoe's bar, accompanied by McAndrew whom Kehoe had ordered to have the job executed. In this second confrontation Kehoe ended lamely by advising McParland to see Father O'Connor, the parish priest, who had warned Kehoe that McKenna was a detective. With courage bordering on the reckless, McParland went to the priest to find out who had betrayed him, but this time Linden and his operatives maintained a discreet surveillance as he did so.

When confronted by McParland, Father O'Connor denied everything, saying that he had never seen or heard of McKenna before and that if he were indeed a member of the Molly Maguires, 'the curse of God was on my head and every possible member', as McParland later reported.

The following day, 7 March 1876, instead of returning to Pottsville as arranged, and probably to certain death, McParland boarded a northbound train, 'with Captain Linden shadowing me in the same car'. That spring there began the series of trials which would eventually bring the Molly Maguires to justice. Gowen, who had been district attorney of Schuylkill County ten years previously, was now working as a special prosecutor aiding his successor in that office, George Kaercher. He contacted Allan Pinkerton and urged him to let McParland take the stand, even though this was contrary to their agreement. Such a decision would put McParland's life in jeopardy; but without his personal testimony it was feared that the case against the Mollies would collapse.

Against his better judgement Allan consented to approach McParland. At first the latter refused point blank, but Allan persisted and eventually pressured him to take the stand. The trial opened at Pottsville on 4 May 1876 and after the jury was sworn in the district attorney stunned the courtroom when he announced that James McParland, a Pinkerton detective known as Jim McKenna, would be the chief witness. Early that very morning Linden's squads had struck simultaneously in a series of dawn raids. Eleven high-ranking Mollies were taken into custody, a heavily manacled Jack Kehoe being the most prominent, and added to those already on trial. On Saturday, 6 May, McParland took the stand – no longer the unshaven disreputable character but a well-groomed young man, dressed in the height of fashion. McParland proved to be a model witness, unflappable and unshaken by the lengthy and at times very provocative questioning by the defence lawyers. The series of trials dragged on for several months, during which Linden continued to round up other members of the society. Muff Lawler turned informant and the noose gradually tightened around Kehoe. On 16 April 1877, almost a year after his arrest, Kehoe was convicted of murder and sentenced to hang. Two months later, nineteen of the Mollies went to the gallows, ten being executed at one go. Kehoe fought a desperate legal battle, appealing against his sentence, but in the end he, too, mounted the steps to the scaffold. Unluckily for him, the hangman placed the knot incorrectly (whether by accident or design was never determined) and instead of instant death from a broken neck, Kehoe slowly strangled, a hideously agonising end for a brutal and ruthless killer.

Gowen was forced to resign from the railroad company when it was on the verge of bankruptcy, and returned to private law practice. Called to Washington to plead in a case against Standard Oil, he shot himself in his bedroom at Wormsley's Hotel. At first it was suspected that Gowen had been the victim of a Molly hit, and Linden, now superintendent at Philadelphia, was sent by Allan to investigate the death. Suicide was the verdict, although surviving Mollies maintained that Gowen's conscience had at last got the better of him.

Despite the posturings of left-wing writers of a later generation who sought to blacken the character of the one-time Chartist militant, the exploitation of the miners in Pennsylvania was a red herring. Allan Pinkerton was up against a ruthless mob of hardened killers whose crimes were not motivated by social injustice at all. The murders, beatings, arson and dynamite attacks were often racially inspired, with the principal aim of intimidating miners of other ethnic origins, and there was abundant evidence of brutal assaults on fellow-Irishmen who crossed them. F.P. Dewees, whose scholarly but objective account of the Molly Maguires was published at the conclusion of the trial, and is still in many respects unsurpassed, summed up the era of the Molly Maguires as 'a reign of blood . . . they held communities terror bound, and wantonly defied the law, destroyed property and sported with human life'.[11]

And *The American Law Review* of January 1877 fulsomely extolled the work of Allan Pinkerton and his agents: 'The debt which the coal counties owe to these men cannot be overestimated, nor can the personal qualities of untiring resolution, daring and sagacity, in both principal and agents be too highly praised.'

Last Years
1876–84

Thou Eye among the blind,
That, deaf and silent, read'st the eternal deep
Haunted for ever by the eternal mind

WILLIAM WORDSWORTH, *INTIMATIONS OF IMMORTALITY*

On 4 July 1876 Chicago, along with the rest of the country, celebrated the centenary of the Declaration of Independence. Although the jubilation was marred by the news, received that day, that George Armstrong Custer and 264 men of his Seventh Cavalry had been totally wiped out by the Sioux at the Little Bighorn a few days earlier, Chicagoans had much to celebrate. Their city was now the fourth largest in the country. In 1840 it had had a population of 4,479; in June 1876 it was estimated at 420,000, a growth without parallel. This was even more remarkable considering the appalling devastation of October 1871. At that time it was predicted that it would take at least ten years to rebuild the city. In fact, such was the resilience and exuberance of its citizens that Chicago arose from its ashes more splendid than ever, in under five years. In place of the endless narrow streets of clapboard houses there were fine apartment buildings and office blocks of iron and steel clad in Lake Superior brownstone, Ohio sandstone and that pure white sandstone known as Athens marble. During the nationwide panic of 1873 the Chicago banks alone were not compelled to issue certificates of deposit, but continued to pay out current funds. Compared to the eastern cities, there were few failures, although the National Detective Agency, among others, came perilously close to collapse. Allan Pinkerton had the satisfaction at least of seeing the land which he had purchased in the city for $50 an acre in 1868 rising in value to $1,500 an acre only five years later.

Allan also had the satisfaction of seeing both of his sons making excellent marriages. In 1866 William, barely twenty but matured far beyond his years by his experiences in the war, married Margaret Ashland, one of the city's wealthiest heiresses, and moved into the palatial mansion built for them on the appropriately named Ashland Boulevard near the city centre. William had two daughters, both of whom also married well. Robert likewise made a good match, marrying Elizabeth Hughes of Denver, member of an old and prominent middle-western family. She was the sister of Thomas P. Hughes, president of the Colorado Lead Works, and Hendrick Hughes, manager of the famous Keeley Institute of Denver. Robert and his family lived on Brooklyn's fashionable Eighth Avenue in what the New York *World* once described as 'the handsomest mansion in Brooklyn'. Robert's two daughters married millionaires and occupied leading positions in New York society in the early years of the twentieth century. The only person to carry on the family name was Robert's son Allan II, born in 1876. On news of his first grandson's birth, Allan wrote to Robert saying, 'I hope he is worthy of the name.' Twenty years later, Allan II would join the Agency and carry it to even greater heights in the period after the First World War in which he was a major in Military Intelligence, like his famous grandfather before him. He would serve his detective apprenticeship, like his father and uncle, in various parts of the country under the Agency's most renowned superintendents, such as James McParland of Molly Maguire fame, and George D. Bangs, son of the Agency's first general superintendent.

George Henry Bangs himself gave thirty years' service to the Agency before his death in 1883, but he actually came close to dismissal on a couple of occasions. On 2 September 1875 Allan received a telegram from Henry W. Gavinner, a senior executive of the Pennsylvania Railroad and one of the Agency's most prestigious clients. The telegram from Philadelphia read:

I have just passed Mr Bangs on Third Street between Walnut and Wellings Alley, drunk as a lord, reeling and staggering from side to side, trying hard to retain a cigar in his mouth, sustaining himself from falling by wildly catching all posts and rails and finally landing on a pile of building debris. He came out of a saloon near Wellings Alley, nine a.m. Mr Boyd [another railroad executive] said this is the second time he has seen Bangs in this condition and he reported to the offices of the company.

Allan was furious and immediately dictated a letter to his son Robert in New York, enclosing a copy of the telegram. Robert was peremptorily ordered to pay Bangs his wages up to that Saturday and 'not to give him another penny except as when you know it is necessary'. Robert was also instructed that, if Bangs had not returned to the office, he must go to the general superintendent's residence and confront Mrs Bangs with the facts. Later that day, still fuming, Allan loosed off a stinging broadside to Bangs himself:

My God, I was horror struck when I had finished reading [the telegram] . . . Oh, I cannot tell you what my feelings were; I was almost driven mad. George Bangs, I have known you for years and now what does all this mean? When is this going to end? Think of the railroad officials in Philadelphia who saw you 'drunk as a lord'. Oh, my God, I cannot stand this. Think of the General Superintendent of this Agency so miserably drunk as you were. And at nine a.m.! Yes, at nine a.m. I thought it might have been nine p.m., but no, it was nine a.m.! It was at a time when railroad officials were going to work!

Allan was stung by Gavinner's remark that Bangs had been seen in a similar condition before, and felt that he had been betrayed by Benjamin Franklin, the Philadelphia superintendent, as well as his own son. 'You must look me square in the face, George – you were drunk as a lord once before and neither Franklin nor my son, Robert, saw fit to inform me. What is going on?' This diatribe went on and on for several pages, as Allan ranted and raged over Bangs and his 'terrible condition'. He cast up all that he had done for Bangs over the years, and reviewed their long and close association, the heroic efforts of Bangs to keep the business going during the war and their fight through the depression years to keep the Agency from going under. Not content with flaying his general superintendent, Allan wrote long letters that day to Franklin and Robert, bitterly attacking them for covering up Bangs's previous lapse. When Franklin replied defensively and tried to put the matter in perspective he made the mistake of saying that Bangs had been drunk on 31 September. Back came the instant rejoinder from Allan, not half labouring the point that Bangs could not possibly have been drunk on that day 'because there is no such day in the year . . . I said he was drunk as a lord on August 31st!' For several days letters and telegrams flew back and forth between Chicago, Philadelphia and New York. Bangs himself wrote a dignified but suitably contrite letter, with the promise that he would never take another drink. Eventually the matter blew over and Bangs was forgiven, but it rankled with Allan ever afterwards that the man on whom he had always relied most of all had let him down so badly. In fairness to Bangs, he had been under considerable pressure for upwards of three years. The wonder is that he did not take to the bottle sooner.

As general superintendent, George Bangs was Allan's right-hand man and technically in command of the superintendents (including William and Robert) who ran the offices. He had a roving commission, spending much of his time on tours of inspection. Allan himself, when his health permitted, could never remain long in his Chicago office, but made frequent forays to New York and Philadelphia. These visits from 'the old man' were dreaded almost as much as his letters, which became increasingly paranoid. Whenever his sons seemed to be stepping out of line Allan came down on them hard. There is little correspondence to this effect regarding William, whom Allan saw virtually every day, but Robert was frequently on the receiving end of his father's petulance. On 29 February 1876, for example, Allan had occasion to deliver a stinging rebuke to Robert, concluding with a reminder that the National Detective Agency belonged to him 'and I mean to be the Principal of the whole and will continue to be until Death claims me as its own'.

The increasingly harsh tone of Allan's letters upset Benjamin Franklin, whose wife kept nagging him to ask for a substantial increase in salary. In March 1876, therefore, Franklin wrote to Allan, demanding a fifty per cent increase, from $2,000 to $3,000 per annum. This interesting letter recounted his career with the Agency, particularly his key role in the Molly Maguire case.

Allan's immediate response was a long letter to Robert on 8 March discussing the problem. Allan reviewed Franklin's record as head of the Philadelphia Police Detective Bureau, his long period of sickness 'when no one would hire him' and the five years he had been employed by the Agency. 'You, Robert Pinkerton, and I are the only ones who know what I have done for Benjamin Franklin,' wrote Allan. 'When he was sick only I could control him . . . Mrs Franklin had no more control over him than a child . . .' Allan was not minded to raise Franklin's salary and if he resigned as a result, 'Willie will take over the Philadelphia office and you two will make a good team.' Then, blithely overlooking Bangs's recent lapse, he concluded defiantly: 'I can always count on George Bangs; he will never leave me, he will stand by me and I will stand with him.'

Evidently Robert contacted Franklin and tactfully explained the situation for Franklin let the matter of an increase drop. Instead, he wrote a long, conciliatory letter to his Principal, but this only provoked a cold response in which Allan stated, for the record, that only one man deserved credit for breaking the Molly Maguires, and that was James McParland.

In the summer of 1876 Allan was in the Chicago general office one day when a client entered and asked for an immediate shadow to tail someone. Allan looked on dumbfounded as the clerk at the reception desk immediately called over an operative and assigned him to the task in front of the client. After reading the riot act to the hapless clerk, Allan busied himself drawing up a new code of conduct, reminding all employees that

the principles of this Agency mean everything is to be kept secret and all persons doing business with the Agency must do it through the General

Superintendent, Superintendents, Assistant Superintendents or Chief Clerks, and the Patrons must not be allowed to speak to or see the operatives . . . The business must be done strictly through the above parties.

And to George Bangs Allan wrote forcibly on 23 June 1876 reminding him that 'The executives of the various branches are to read again my *General Principles* where they will find their duties broadly set forth.'

In September that year Robert Pinkerton collaborated with Bangs and Franklin in urging Allan not to hire female detectives. Soon an avalanche of letters, telegrams and memoranda were cascading around their unrepentant shoulders. To Robert in New York Allan wrote bluntly:

It has been my principle to use females for the detection of crime where it has been useful and necessary. With regard to the employment of such females I can trace it back to the time I first hired Kate Warne, up to the present time . . . and I intend to still use females whenever it can be done judiciously. I must do it or falsify my theory, practice and truth.

Getting to the bottom of this extraordinary matter Allan discovered that Franklin's jealous wife was pressuring her husband against the use of females in his office. Allan exploded with wrath and loosed off a furious tirade to George Bangs on 29 September:

I cannot tolerate that a female should be consulted about this and under no circumstances will I allow any argument to be brought up on this subject . . . with me the question is whether I am right or I am wrong . . . I think I am right and if that is the case, female detectives must be allowed in my Agency.

As for Mrs Franklin, I hope that Mr Franklin will realize what he is drifting into . . . I don't like to lose Mr Franklin but if I am driven to it I must discharge him. I shall be very sorry for it.

To reinforce his policy Allan sent Angela Austin to Philadelphia to work along-side Franklin. She was a handsome Texan widow who had once been an actress. The glamorous Mrs Austin had a considerable impact, but inevitably her presence did not end the scheming. The Franklins prevailed on Robert to send a blunt memo to his father saying that he did not want Mrs Austin, or any other female, under his jurisdiction. This provoked a sharp response from Allan:

I return your letter as it is disrespectful to me as the Principal of this Agency.

It is doubly so, yea, triply disrespectful to me as your father, therefore I return it to you . . . If Mrs Franklin is to become Superintendent of the Philadelphia office then I shall put another man in the place of her husband . . . this you can rely upon . . . if Mrs Franklin is to be jealous of her husband this is nothing to me. I simply wish to extract from him the fulfilment of his duties, nothing more nothing less. For the last time I shall tell you that you have no right to interfere with the employment of any Agency, except those of New York, of which you are Superintendent. As for any trouble that may occur between me and my Superintendents leave that for me to settle. After I am dead and the sod is growing over my grave you will then learn that someone must take the management of everything, but while I live I mean to be the Principal of this Agency and I question much if you will prove to be a better Principal than I have been . . . I am at work from half past four in the morning to nearly nine o'clock at night, and I have enough to do without getting any complaints from you.

A recurring problem that year was dishonesty which, in Allan's book, was by far the deadliest of sins. For years he had prided himself not only in his own personal incorruptibility, but in that of his employees. The Agency stood out as a beacon of rectitude amid a morass of corrupt policemen, crooked politicians and dishonest railroad conductors. When Allan's penny-pinching accountant, Horne, discovered that the fiddling of expense sheets was rife, and that even George Bangs himself was guilty of inflating his claims, Allan wrote to his general superintendent, more in sorrow than in anger; but simultaneously wired a memo to Robert curtly ordering him to cut back on bills. This was bad enough, but in the autumn of 1876 it came to Allan's attention that the men in the uniformed security service were stealing from the property they were supposed to be protecting. This scandal came to light when Allan received a tip-off that some of the security guards were living well beyond their apparent means. To compound the larceny, the head of the department was working a fiddle of his own, by putting new clients on the so-called 'dead beat list' and pocketing the monthly fees.

Allan's reaction to this evidence of widespread dishonesty at the heart of his organisation seems curious, but perhaps it owed much to his residual Chartist philosophy. Despite the damning evidence produced by Horne, Allan refused to sack any of the men, believing naïvely that a good talking-to from himself would show them the error of their ways. He knew only too well that if he fired them, their chances of subsequent employment would be very slim. Instead, he got Bangs to send two operatives from New York to Chicago to make a thorough shake-up of the Patrol Service. Subsequently, the command structure and operating regulations were tightened up and safeguards instituted to minimise temptation. It was a humane solution to a serious problem which,

Allan admitted, was costing him 'ten thousand dollars some way or another'.

All these problems of alcoholism, sexism, insubordination, fiddling and downright thieving by people whom Allan thought he could trust were as nothing to the sense of betrayal he suffered at the very heart of his own family. When it came, it was from a quarter that Allan had least expected. Of his four daughters, only one grew to maturity and probably for that reason she was the apple of her father's eye. In July 1876 Joan, the second daughter to bear her mother's name, celebrated her twenty-first birthday. She was pretty, lively and spirited, and while her brothers seem to have inherited their mother's docility, Joan had the fire and mettle of her father. To Allan she was 'Pussy', an old Scottish term of endearment which found expression in many of the letters he wrote to her from the battlefront or his many travels, the pages copiously decorated with whimsical sketches of kittens in human situations. When William and Robert married and left home Allan drew even closer to young Joan, who had inherited her mother's fine soprano voice and a deep love of good music. Joan had the best education that money could buy and, as one of Chicago's belles, was much in demand at the many Centennial balls and banquets that momentous summer.

At first there was no sign of the conflict to come, in Allan's frequent letters to Robert, though in these letters Allan was often revealed as a rigid martinet, pernickety, obstinate, irascible, egocentric, self-willed and dictatorial, brooking no opposition even in the most trivial of matters. Whether his wife had ever complained or stood up to him seems unlikely. She herself had been raised in the dour, Calvinist tradition in which women unquestioningly accepted the will of their lords and masters. Allan's iron régime, of cold baths and long walks before breakfast, of rising at four-thirty and retiring to bed by nine, must have affected the entire household. Young Joan, fresh from her exclusive ladies' college, was hardly likely to endure such spartan conditions all her life. Yet, incredibly, Allan seems to have assumed that his adored Pussy would always be at home, carrying on the unquestioning obedience and loving self-sacrifice of her mother.

One of Joan's classmates had a brother named William Chalmers, to whom she was introduced at a party that spring. They had a great deal in common; they were both first-generation Americans born of Scottish parents and William's father was already a prominent financier and industrialist. It was love at first sight and during the summer and autumn the romance blossomed. William, handsome, well educated and cultured, shared Joan's passion for music. It was the sort of match that mothers dream of for their daughters, and Joan senior certainly gave the young couple every encouragement. William became a regular caller at the Pinkerton Homestead, the vast, rambling mansion set in spacious grounds, at 554 West Monroe Street. Allan, out all day at his office from sun-up till late in the evening, invariably found 'young Chalmers' on his return.

At first the young man's presence does not seem to have registered with Allan, though he frequently mentioned it, in passing, in his letters to Robert. But by midsummer 1876 the tone of the letters began to change as it dawned on Allan that Chalmers was paying court to his beloved daughter. The very idea that another man could replace him in Pussy's affections horrified Allan. In vain he sent her off on an extended tour of Britain and Europe in the hope that she would soon forget the boy, but absence truly made the heart grow fonder, and as soon as she returned Joan resumed her association with Chalmers. On 22 November Joan sought her father's permission to marry William. Allan refused vehemently and there was, as he admitted to Robert, 'quite a scene'. One can imagine the ugly situation, the stocky paterfamilias trembling with rage, his speech slurred with emotion, as he battled with his headstrong daughter. Allan, at this period, was an enthusiastic devotee of phrenology, a pseudo-science which, before the advent of psychology, sought to determine a person's character from the shape, size and contours of the skull. Allan's reports of the period frequently referred to 'bumps on the head' as evidence of criminal tendencies or heroic traits. Allan was convinced that his own skull put him in the highest class of brilliance, but he had also come to the conclusion that the shape of Chalmers' skull showed that the young man lacked the necessary brain power to make him a good husband.

In the end young Joan backed down. Through the ensuing winter there was an unnatural calm, with mother Joan desperately trying to keep the peace. Allan casually mentioned to Robert that young Joan was 'listless and pale, caring only to stay in her room'. Christmas came and went with no change in the tension, but on 19 January 1877 friends came to dinner and Allan reported smugly the following day to Robert 'They vied with each other to please me and make me happy'.

Allan and Joan retired to bed at eight o'clock as usual, but some hours later his slumbers were disturbed. On awakening shortly after one in the morning he thought he heard voices and crept downstairs to the dimly lit living-room to investigate. On turning up the gas-lamp he was astounded to find his daughter and William Chalmers on the sofa. According to his letter to Robert on 20 January, Allan, barely controlling his anger, said, 'What does this mean, Mr Chalmers? You must leave this house at once and never enter this door.' Chalmers bowed in embarrassed silence and wordlessly made a hurried exit, but Joan was made of sterner stuff and rounded on her father. Voices raised, the two of them battled it out, until the noise wakened Joan senior and she tried desperately to calm her husband and daughter. Joan junior was adamant. She was twenty-one, old enough to know her own mind, and she refused to let her unreasoning tyrant of a father browbeat her. She and William were deeply in love and nothing would prevent their marriage. Allan riposted tersely that he would make her a present of some money, but that he would not attend the ceremony to give her away. 'If necessary, your mother and I will travel about Europe until it is all over.' In tears, Joan stormed out of the room and began packing her bags. In the morning, despite her mother's tearful entreaties, she left Chicago and went to New York to live with Robert and his family in Brooklyn until her father came round.

For months Allan bombarded poor Robert with self-pitying letters harping on about the wicked ingrate. Joan's desires for marriage were ignored; Allan could not see beyond the betrayal, the lack of loyalty, above all the defiance of his rules and regulations. Allan's side of the correspondence is known from the copies in the Agency letter-books, but we can only speculate on Robert's responses. Gradually the old man calmed down, and the initial anger was replaced by the pathetic refrain, 'Joan must know the door is always open, all she has to do is walk in'. The girl's mother suffered in silence, but the strain told on her. In the spring of 1877 she took to her bed with some unspecified, but undoubtedly stress-induced, ailment. At first Joan's illness was only mentioned fleetingly, but by March Allan was reporting to his son that he had cut down on evening work 'to stay at your mother's side, listening to her every word'. Allan kept hoping that Robert would eventually show Joan the error of her ways and pack her off back to Chicago, but Robert appears to have handled the matter very diplomatically. By June 1877 Allan had assumed the role of the sorrowing father, ready to forgive his wayward daughter and see her 'at any hour' should she return.

While his rage against young Joan was at its height Allan found yet another target for his wrath. Dwight Lyman Moody had been a seventeen-year-old shoe salesman in Boston when he 'saw the light' in 1854. Two years later he had moved to Chicago to become a successful businessman, but at the same time started a Sunday school which, as a result of his boundless enthusiasm, soon became a church. He gave up business in 1860 to devote himself entirely to evangelism and, in his mission to the young soldiers during the Civil War, he found many converts. In the postwar period he headed the Chicago YMCA, but in 1870 he was joined by Ira David Sankey, whose stirring hymns soon revolutionised the movement. In that decade Moody and Sankey toured Britain and America, holding spectacular revival meetings which 'reduced the population of hell by a million souls'. At first Allan tolerated the activities of the revivalists, even allowing them to use his fields at 'The Larches' for their meetings, but his attitude changed completely when he discovered that the staff of the Philadelphia office had become infected with religion. His letter of 23 January 1877 to Benjamin Franklin shows him at his unreasonably domineering worst:

What is this? I should never have dreamt for a moment that the evil preachings which are spread throughout the U.S. by Moody and Sankey and others should have at length come into my Agency . . . I would have hoped that my employees would have known better . . .

This incredible diatribe rambled on and on for several pages in similar vein, then went off at a tangent about 'the general principles of my Agency'. Then he concluded with one of the most extraordinary orders he ever issued. Instead of wasting their time, praying and singing hymns of a Sunday, his operatives would be required to report for duty:

They are to give their whole time to my business without any reservation whatsoever. The men are to remain on duty on Sunday until the Superintendent sees fit to excuse them . . . none of them shall in any way undertake to attend church on Sunday but shall be at the office at 9 a.m.

Franklin's reaction to this outrageous demand is not recorded. Two months later the Philadelphia superintendent had the temerity to raise the matter of his salary again. This time he not only sought an increase to $3000 per annum, but argued that the raise should be retrospective to cover the previous three months in which his work-load had vastly increased. This not unreasonable request precipitated another shoal of confidential letters to Robert and Bangs, in the course of which Franklin's career, past performance, domineering wife, frequent illnesses and stiff-necked attitude towards female operatives were thoroughly ventilated. Allan's solution was to replace Franklin by Robert Linden whose star, in the aftermath of the Molly Maguire case, was now in the ascendant. In the end, however, Franklin caved in, and retained his position.

By June 1877 young Joan was sufficiently concerned for her mother's failing health to overcome her repugnance about her father. Wearily she broke her silence and informed Allan that she would shortly be returning to Chicago. Allan was jubilant, and wrote immediately to Robert, crowing at the imminent return of 'my favorite child, the only girl I have'. A few days later, however, he complained to Robert that the matter had not been resolved. Pussy was demanding that 'she have company' till eleven in the evening. Allan, the heavy father, was as obdurate as ever. 'I cannot see how it can be done . . . as the slightest sound will awaken me and your mother, then it is hard for us to fall asleep again . . . I cannot see any reason for Pussy having company later than 10 p.m.' Robert persuaded his sister to concede the point and she, anxious for her mother's poor state of health, finally returned to Chicago that autumn. Thereafter there was an uneasy truce; young Joan would bide her time, but her passion for William Chalmers was undiminished.

The one bright spot in this troubled year came in November when George McClellan was elected Governor of New Jersey. Allan wrote on 13 November to congratulate his old commander and concluded:

The thousands of old soldier and soldiers' children who have loved and still love you will someday put you into the White House . . . You must be sure as I, that I have no axes to grind, no favors to ask. I merely come to you with these things as a friend, whom you know and trust and as that friend I only ask that you shall place yourself in the hands of able friends and their friends, so that all these things may be consummated.

That year, the Pinkertons celebrated their thirty-fifth wedding anniversary. How they celebrated – if at all – is not recorded but Allan may actually have overlooked the date. Some days later, however, he must have remembered, for he broke the habit of a lifetime by dictating a letter to his 'bonnie wee lass' on 28 March. The three-page letter beginning 'My Dear Little Wife' recounted their life together from that momentous day in 1842 'when we had pledged our faith, sailed from Scotland and wondered if we should ever look at fair Scotia again as we sailed down the Clyde'. He tenderly recalled their adventures and wanderings in the early years, the birth of their wee ones and the tragic death of Belle and others: 'We both remember the days of their birth as well as the last day we had them on earth . . .' Then he ended poignantly:

I know, since you were eighteen[1] years of age you have been battling with me, side by side, willing to do anything, to bear our children and work hard, yet you never found fault, you never said a cross word but was always willing to make our home cheery and happy . . . Now Joan, on this day, I wish you to take things easy. When I can get home I will come and sit by you and talk to you and cheer you . . . this is a dark and gloomy day but wait, it will get to be brighter days and you will be able to go out again . . . Let us wish we may be spared a few more years . . . enjoying happiness and health ourselves, our children and our friends . . .

The letter was written by an amanuensis, but at the end the palsied hand had appended the spidery name 'Allan'.

In July 1879 Allan celebrated his sixtieth birthday, but his health was poor and he was increasingly concerned about Joan. By now much of the old pugnacity had gone out of him. Not only did he tacitly agree to young Joan's marriage, but he began handing over the running of the Agency to William and Robert. The change was slow and subtle, and not without a fierce rearguard action at times. At first he reluctantly gave up meddling and interfering in every case that passed through the Agency, then the frequency of his visits to the branch offices decreased. Finally he took to staying at home sometimes, sitting quietly in the garden with his ailing wife, rather than walking to the office every day. When Franklin was stricken by a serious illness Allan wrote a sympathetic memo to Bangs decreeing that Franklin was to be kept on full salary as long as possible, and that, if his illness should prove to be so serious that he had to retire, he should receive a lump sum of $1,000, 'or whatever sum you think I would be justified in paying'.

Occasionally there was something of the old spark. Early in 1879 the Agency was involved in the negotiations for the ransom of the body of A.T. Stewart, a New York tycoon, which had been seized by grave-robbers. When the case reached a dead-end Robert turned to his father for help. From his office fifteen hundred miles away on 24 March the old man considered the report, then made his own deductions:

> The fact is, Robert, from all this seeming correspondence I think the body is not far away. You will notice they talk about the annoyance of the Custom House officers in having the body brought from Canada, but they forgot to mention any annoyance to them whilst taking the remains to Canada. No, I do not think this story of the body being taken to Canada hangs well together; I think the remains may be in New Jersey or at farthest in Pennsylvania . . . This man says he is in Montreal, although you have not been there, I think by your correspondence it has been clearly shown that no letters were ever delivered to this man at Montreal, as purported were sent to him.

It was a re-run of the Maroney case of twenty years earlier. Allan was proved right and the case was broken soon afterwards.

William and Robert had effectively taken control of the Agency by the end of 1877, but Allan thought that he was still firmly in command. In May 1879, after his father had behaved in his customary pigheaded fashion, Robert gave up in exasperation. What provoked him to rebel is not recorded for certain, although it has been suggested that Robert, seeing how the Agency was flourishing as never before, demanded a share of the profits rather than a superintendent's salary. When Allan turned this down, Robert announced that he was resigning. Furthermore, he intended to change his name.

There was an ominous silence, and Robert waited with bated breath for the response. In due course he received a long recriminatory epistle in which the old man pulled out every stop, applied every last ounce of emotional blackmail and ended with the anguished cry 'You are my children . . . I love you . . . soon you will have everything'.

Robert backed down, but after that Allan let his sons have their way more and more. From time to time he fought back, tenaciously clinging to his old, proven methods. In 1881, for example, he resumed his campaign for female detectives and wrote at great length to Bangs on the subject, although it is not known what the outcome was.

Old friends were dying, and the world was changing rapidly. Allan had been quick to adopt new technology, and in the 1860s boasted his own private telegraph lines linking the Chicago headquarters to the offices in Philadelphia and New York; but in 1876, at the Centennial Exposition of the Industry of All Nations in Philadelphia, he had seen a fellow Scot named Aleck Bell demonstrate a gadget called the telephone and dismissed it as a toy without a future. Five years later Allan was finally induced to install this newfangled aid to communications, but never used it himself.

By 1882 the old man was still going in to the office from time to time, though he preferred to go by carriage rather than walk. By now the Agency, under the dynamic direction of William and Robert, was branching out in all directions. William, in particular, was responsible for overseas business, with representatives in France, Spain, Germany and Turkey as well as Britain. On 8 July 1882 Allan dictated one of his last business letters, addressing it personally to William Ewart Gladstone. In the wake of the Fenian terrorist outrages, which culminated in the assassination of Lord Frederick Cavendish, the Irish Secretary, and his chief official Burke, in Phoenix Park, Dublin, Scotland Yard had sought the help of the Pinkertons in getting information on the Irish-American fund-raising groups who were believed to be behind the terrorists. A tentative enquiry from London provoked a three-page letter from Allan, telling the Prime Minister that the Pinkerton detectives were 'honest, bold in the truth, sleepless in energy and loyal in thought and act . . . It will be very difficult to find investigators possessing such qualifications for it requires great caution to select these men and women'. Allan promised to recruit an army of informers 'from men of leisure or the labouring Irishman with the dudeen in his mouth'. Interestingly, this letter alluded to 'other matters' in which the Agency had assisted the British police, but unfortunately no details are recorded. The importance of this letter was emphasised by Allan appending his own, now extremely shaky signature.

At the end of August 1882 Mrs John Brown, widow of the celebrated Abolitionist, was fêted in Chicago, the highlight of her visit being a grand reception in Farwell Hall, under the chairmanship of Judge James B. Bradwell. On the platform with Mrs Brown was the widow of John Jones, Allan's Negro friend. Allan himself was too ill at the time to attend in person, but he dictated a memoir of his associations with John Brown, and in ringing tones this was read out by Judge Bradwell. Mrs Jones then added her own comments, recalling how

> Mr Brown greeted Mr Pinkerton that of friend to friend, yea, more than brother to brother. Then the three of them, my husband, Mr Brown and Pinkerton had a talk together. I don't think I should divulge the secrets of that meeting even now of twenty-five years ago. Only one thing I will repeat. I remember Mr Pinkerton saying 'There's a Democratic meeting in town today. I will go right down and make them give enough money to send those slaves to Canada'.

George Henry Bangs retired as general superintendent in 1881. Six years earlier his son George D. Bangs Jr joined the Agency and in the eventful year of 1892 took over his father's old position, giving sterling service in that role until his death in 1923. George Henry, however, did not live long to enjoy his retirement. On 14 September 1883 William Pinkerton brought Allan a telegram announcing the sudden death of his old associate. William later recalled how his father took the tragic news, 'staring straight ahead, hands gripped tightly over the head of his cane, tears rolling silently down his cheeks'.

It is appropriate that the last recorded letter dictated by Allan Pinkerton was sent on 31 October 1883 to C.E. Chapman, a former Negro slave, then residing in Boston, Massachusetts. He had written to William Pinkerton to say how much he admired his father's fight against slavery, and he wondered whether Mr Allan Pinkerton would favour him with an autograph. In due course Allan dictated a reply:

> Your letter to my son, asking for my autograph, has been received. I am not in the habit of giving my autograph to any persons, for particular reasons to myself, but in this instance for the purpose you wish it, I forward it to you. I have always been a friend to the colored man and will do anything to secure him his rights.

This letter was signed with a barely legible scrawl, to which William appended a postscript: 'The tremulousness observed in my father's signature is caused by the effects of a paralytic stroke.'

Allan was bedridden for much of the ensuing winter but with the return of summer in 1884 he began to get up and about again. One day in early June he went out for a short walk, but tripped on the sidewalk, fell and bit his tongue. Gangrene set in, followed by general septicaemia, and after three weeks of intense pain he died on the afternoon of 1 July, twenty days short of his sixty-fifth birthday. Although he had been in poor health for fifteen years, the suddenness of his passing shocked his family, friends and business associates alike. Obituaries appeared in all the American and Canadian newspapers, followed in due course by tributes farther afield, in Britain and Europe, where the reputation of the Agency was now well established.[2]

Allan's will, filed for probate in the Cook County Surrogate Court on 10 July, contained no surprises. Most of his money, shares and property valued at about half a million dollars went to his wife, who survived him by only two years. After Allan's death, life ceased to have any real meaning for her. Even the birth of Pussy's children failed to console her. The gentle lady who had made that terrible voyage from Scotland with her firebrand of a husband, who had survived shipwreck and untold hardships, who had risen from humble housewife in Dundee to chatelaine of an imposing mansion in Chicago, simply gave up the will to live. She lingered on for many months, now completely bedridden. When the end was in sight, William, Robert and Joan were summoned to her bedside, and shortly before dawn on 13 May 1886 she whispered to William that she was going to join his father, then closed her eyes and slipped peacefully away.

William and Robert inherited the Agency which they operated as a co-partnership. As the century drew to a close the Pinkerton brothers opened new offices across the United States and diversified into wholly new areas of business. Some, like their brilliant organisation of the retail jewellery trade to combat the increase in jewel thefts, had long-term beneficial effects. Others, however, like their tragic involvement in the bitter Homestead Steel dispute of 1892, tarnished the Pinkerton name unjustly and took many years to live down.

In his will, Allan made provision for $15 a week to be paid to George Bangs's widow by way of a pension, and he also ordered that the graves of Tim Webster, Kate Warne and other Pinkerton agents buried near him in Graceland Cemetery 'never be sold, graveled or aliened in any manner whatsoever'. He also requested that 'The Larches' be maintained in its present condition for seven years, then another seven, and if possible to remain in the family forever. Sadly, later generations did not have Allan's deep attachment for the place. A century later the grounds were largely given over to the cultivation of corn, but belatedly the Iroquois County Historical Society attempted to restore the Villa and prevent the Loose murals from further deterioration. Sadly, this campaign failed through lack of funds and Allan Pinkerton's proud country seat is now a ruin.

As regards his headstrong, wilful daughter, Allan relented in the end, although he went to his grave convinced that her husband would never amount to anything more than a clerk in his father's counting-house. To young Joan was assigned the copyright in his eighteen books which continued to sell strongly and went into numerous editions till the end of the century. Not that Joan ever needed the royalties, for her William eventually became one of the Mid-West's leading industrialists and a multi-millionaire noted for his business acumen. Joan and William, in fact, became the undisputed leaders of Chicago society, playing a prominent part in organising the Chicago Opera Company and numerous charities. Joan Pinkerton Chalmers, dubbed 'the Queen of the West Side', ruled her own family with an iron fist and, when moved to anger, her violet-blue eyes would flash with the same brilliance as the diamonds in the tiara she habitually wore to the Opera. Yet this autocratic *grande dame* had a surprisingly flippant side to her nature; one newspaper in the 1930s reported how the octogenarian socialite could unbend, by dancing a cakewalk.

For a man who had created a vast organisation that combated crime and violence at all levels, from petty pilfering to grand larceny, from street mugging to wholesale murder, and made his name a household word around the world, the modest size of Allan's estate may seem surprising. Indeed, barely a decade before his death, Allan had almost gone bust. He enjoyed the good things of life, but his lifestyle was by no means lavish by the standards of the time. The smallness of his estate, however, was a mute testimony to his honesty and integrity. It was but a fraction of the fortune which he might have amassed had he stooped to taking bribes, pay-offs and kick-backs, as so many of his contemporaries in the regular law-enforcement agencies so often did. He lived in a world where the law was often flouted with impunity[1] and lawlessness prevailed in its most brutal and savage forms. He had grown up in a country where people frequently took the law into their own hands, where brawls often ended in fatal shootings and where the lynch mob reacted with horrific savagery. Within a few years of Allan's death the Mafia would be operating, from New York to New Orleans, in a manner that made the Molly Maguires look like choirboys. The Agency succeeded in infiltrating the Mob and was the first body to challenge its criminal activities, bringing several of its leaders to justice. At the turn of the century the Pinkertons relentlessly pursued Butch Cassidy and the Sundance Kid. In 1911 Home Secretary Winston Churchill asked his old friend William Pinkerton to provide protection for King George V at his coronation. Later the Agency would furnish bodyguards for the Prince of Wales (later King Edward VIII) and investigate the Lindbergh baby kidnap.

Remarkably Pinkerton's remained very much a family concern for many years. Robert Pinkerton died in 1907 and his elder brother William in 1923. Under his nephew, Allan Pinkerton II, the Agency was incorporated in 1926. He died in 1930 at the early age of fifty-six and was succeeded as president by his twenty-six-year-old son Robert Allan Pinkerton II, a Harvard law graduate and Wall Street stockbroker. In 1965 he changed the name of the Agency to

Pinkerton's Inc. to reflect the shift away from the detective work which had been the company's traditional role. With his death in 1967 the family connection ended. Edward Bednarz, who had joined the Agency as a racetrack detective and risen over the years to general manager and executive vice-president, took over the top job.

Until the advent of the Federal Bureau of Investigation in 1908 the Pinkertons operated as a *de facto* national police force, investigating and solving many of the great interstate crimes. Long before Interpol, the Pinkertons were fighting the fraudsters and gangsters who knew no national boundaries. The force that Allan created helped to tame the Wild West, and would one day hunt down outlaws from the frozen wastes of Canada to the tropical rain forests of Bolivia. Security had become big business by the 1890s, but has since grown out of all recognition. By 1965 Pinkerton's had 13,000 employees and forty-five offices in Canada and the United States. The security aspect, which had begun with the six men of Pinkerton's Protective Patrol more than a century earlier, had assumed much greater importance and accounted for eighty per cent of the company's business. Thirty years later, when the company had grown to 250 offices worldwide, with 50,000 employees, security services accounted for ninety-six per cent of the company's global business. Were he to return today, Allan might marvel at the electronic wizardry, the sophisticated surveillance equipment and the powerful computers employed by Pinkerton Security Services in their global fight against crime, but he would heartily approve.

He would also be heartened to discover that the general principles of detection which he enunciated almost a century and a half ago still hold good, and have been emulated by criminal investigation forces all over the world. Little did he realise, as a barefoot cooper in Dundee investigating his first cases of counterfeiting, that his technique of infiltrating gangs would be fundamentally unchanged 150 years later.

Today Pinkerton Security Services is a billion-dollar worldwide organisa-tion, with offices in twenty countries, from Canada to the People's Republic of China. Following the death in 1967 of Robert Pinkerton II, great-grandson of the founder, the company went public and subsequently moved its world head-quarters to California, first to Van Nuys and latterly to Encino, Los Angeles.

In May 1993 a regional office was opened in Glasgow, to provide the full range of the company's services throughout Scotland, from the security of factory premises to anti-terrorist measures in the North Sea oil rigs. The ghost of the militant Chartist from the Gorbals must be chuckling, now that the wheel has come full circle.

Notes

1. The Gorbals, 1819–38

1. *Statistical Account*, 1793
2. James Cleland, *Annals of Glasgow* (Glasgow, 1816), vol. I, p.65
3. John Carrick, *Glasgow, Past and Present* (Glasgow, 1884), vol. I, xix
4. *Glasgow Herald*, 20 November 1848
5. Govan parish registers
6. Senex, *Glasgow Past and Present* (Glasgow, 1851), vol. I, p.235
7. For this and subsequent genealogical data, see the Gorbals parish registers
8. Testimony of Allan Pinkerton to William Pinkerton, letters, 1879
9. No record of a marriage exists in any parish register of Scotland. Even had William Pinkerton married Isabella McQueen in an establishment other than the parish church, such a marriage would automatically have been registered in the parish records. On the other hand, irregular marriages such as this were commonplace at this period, and were regarded as legally valid as late as 1939, when the position was regularised by the passage of the Irregular Marriages (Scotland) Act. The stigma of bastardy did not attach to the children born of such irregular unions.
10. See, for example, the entries in the *Encyclopaedia Britannica*, *Encyclopaedia Americana* and the *Dictionary of American Biography*, and the biographies by Sigmund Lavine and James D. Horan, all of which give 25 August as the date of birth.
11. James D. Horan, *The Pinkertons: The Detective Dynasty that Made History* (New York, 1967), p.2; hereafter referred to as Horan.
12. *Dictionary of American Biography*, vol. XIV (1934); Sigmund Lavine, *Allan Pinkerton, the First Private Detective* (New York, 1963), p.3; hereafter referred to as Lavine.
13. *New Statistical Account* (1835), p.214
14. Horan, p.4
15. *Dictionary of American Biography*, op. cit.
16. Lavine, p.3
17. Pinkerton MSS, Library of Congress
18. The records of the Mechanics' Library of Glasgow reveal that, in 1831, average

borrowings were 20 books per person, per annum

19. *Glasgow Directory*, 1803

20. Allan Pinkerton himself gave his name erroneously as William McCauley. Correct details extracted from the Gorbals registers and *Glasgow Directory*. By 1840 this business was in the hands of William's son, Alexander.

21. Records of the Coopers' Guild of Glasgow

2. The Young Militant, 1839–42

1. The belief that Sir William Wallace was born at Elderslie, Renfrewshire, had only arisen in recent years. In fact, he was born at Ellerslie, near Kilmarnock, Ayrshire. See James Mackay, *William Wallace: Brave Heart* (Edinburgh, 1995), pp.16–22.

2. David Urquhart, writing in *Diplomatic Review*, July 1873, based on Chartist documents published in the Sheffield *Free Press* in 1856

3. Thomas Devyr, *The Old Book of the Nineteenth Century* (London, 1882). Devyr in 1839 was sub-editor of the extreme radical *Northern Liberator* and an active participant in the Northumberland movement.

4. R.G. Gamage, *The History of the Chartist Movement* (London, 1854), p.17

5. Horan, p.5

6. David Williams, *John Frost: A Study in Chartism* (Newport, 1939), pp.195–239

7. Autobiographical letters of Allan Pinkerton to Robert Pinkerton, 1879, Pinkerton MSS, Library of Congress

8. *Scottish Patriot*, 7 December 1839

9. *Northern Star*, 2 September 1843

10. *Northern Star*, 26 June 1841

11. G.J. Holyoake, *Sixty Years of an Agitator's Life* (London, 1893), vol. I, p.106

12. A.R. Schoyen, *The Chartist Challenge* (London, 1958), p.104

13. Census returns, Glasgow, 1841

14. Neilston parish registers show that Joan was born on 7 January 1827. The Carfraes were the only family of that name in Renfrewshire.

15. Pinkerton MSS, Library of Congress

16. Lavine, p.4

17. Horan, p.11

18. Ibid., pp.518–19

19. *Clyde Bill of Entry and Shipping List*, Vol. I, No. 50, in Strathclyde Regional Archives, Glasgow

20. *Acadian Recorder*, Halifax, Nova Scotia

3. Emigrant, 1842–47

1. Shipping News, in the *Glasgow Herald*

2. Lavine, p.2, assuming that the ship's destination was Halifax, Nova Scotia, to explain why she was so far off course

3. *Chicago Daily News*, 27 May 1931

4. *Chicago Democrat*, 30 March 1849

5. No copy of *Old Country Ballads* appears to be now extant. Many books under the imprint of Robert Fergus & Company have been recorded from 1850 onwards.

6. Edgar L. Wakeman, in an interview with Joan Pinkerton, 1889. Unfortunately, his

version of her conversation in what purported to be a Scottish dialect does not bear reprinting verbatim.

7. Horan, p.14
8. Allan Pinkerton, *Professional Thieves and Detectives*, published posthumously (New York, 1890). See also the *Chicago Tribune*, 1 July 1890, for an account of the affair by George Renwick, Superintendent of Streets in Dundee, Illinois.

4. Chicago, 1847–59

1. *Chicago Democrat*, 4 May 1849
2. *Illinois State Register*, 28 January 1863
3. *Chicago Press*
4. Horan, p.25
5. Pinkerton letter-books
6. Oliver Wendell Holmes, in *Dictionary of American Biography*, op. cit.
7. *St Louis Globe Democrat*, 5 June 1846
8. Hilary Draper, *Private Police* (Harmondsworth, 1978), pp.13–14
9. Charles Ledru, *La vie, la mort et les derniers moments de Vidocq* (Paris, 1857)
10. *Daily Democratic Press* (1853)
11. Allan Pinkerton, *Reminiscences*
12. *Dictionary of American Biography*, p.622
13. William Starr Myers, *General George Brinton McClellan* (New York, 1934), p.3. The ruin of McClellan's Castle is the principal landmark of Kirkcudbright to this day.
14. McClellan's papers, running to 153 bulky scrapbooks, diaries and letter-books, are preserved in the Library of Congress. They contain numerous letters from Allan Pinkerton and copies to him, mainly from the period 1857–64 though extending to the 1880s.
15. Horan, p.36
16. Ibid.
17. Ibid., p.38
18. Allan Pinkerton, *The Spy of the Rebellion*
19. Myers, op. cit., p.236
20. This account was given in a paper by Major Allan Pinkerton, at Chicago on 1 September 1882, in honour of Mrs John Brown. A detailed account appeared in the Chicago *Times*, 1 September 1882. See also H.O. Wagoner in Spokane *Review*, 2 September 1892, and letters from Kagi to Charles P. Tidd, Detroit, 13 March 1859.
21. Lloyd Lewis, 'Pinkerton and Lincoln' in *Illinois Historical Journal* (1948), p.376
22. *The Spy of the Rebellion*, preface, p.xxvi; Lloyd Lewis, op. cit., p.376

5. The Road to War, 1859–61

1. Allan Pinkerton, *The Expressman and the Detective* (Chicago, 1874); Alvin F. Harlow, *Old Way Bills* (New York, 1934), pp.326–28
2. I.N. Arnold, *Lincoln and Slavery* (New York), p.vii
3. Verbatim account in P. Schouler, *Massachusetts in the Civil War*, (Boston, 1890), vol. I, pp.59–65
4. N. Edwards, *Life of N.B. Judd*, (Chicago, 1867), pp.11–17

5. Ward Lamon, *Life of Lincoln*, (New York, 1872), pp.511–26. Horan's account (chapter 7, 'The Baltimore Plot') is marred by his usual cavalier approach to dates, placing the incident in April 1861, two months later.
6. Pinkerton letter-books, 1861.
7. Evidence before the Select Committee of Five, pp.133–37
8. The Pinkerton reports, now in the Huntington Library, San Marino, California, were edited by Norma B. Cuthbert and published as *Lincoln and the Baltimore Plot 1861* (San Marino, 1949). See also John G. Nicolay and John Hay, *Abraham Lincoln: A History* (New York, 1890), vol. III, pp.289–316.
9. In fact, this first appeared, in written form, in a letter from Norman Judd to Allan Pinkerton, dated 3 November 1867
10. To this day controversy rages over Lincoln's disguise. The first paper to publish a description of the strange garb of the President-elect on his arrival in Washington was the New York *Times* which reported: 'He wore a Scotch plaid cap and a very long military cloak, so that he was utterly unrecognizable.' The story was picked up by other papers and was repeated worldwide in news items, cartoons and editorial comment. The *Times* story was telegraphed from Washington by Joseph Howard, a freelance journalist who had been guilty of perpetrating hoaxes. For this reason the story has often been disputed, though no alternative mode of dress was ever suggested. Allan Pinkerton himself maintained that Howard's description was accurate.
11. During the Congressional hearings in the aftermath of the Homestead Strike of 1892, when Robertson, the assistant general superintendent, was giving testimony, one of the House Committee sarcastically asked, 'The reason for organising the Pinkerton National Detective Agency was not wholly charitable or humanitarian?' 'No,' retorted Robertson, 'but there was a good deal of charity with the old gentleman.'

6. Setting Up the Secret Service, 1861–62

1. Judd to Lincoln, 21 April 1861
2. *The Spy of the Rebellion*
3. McClellan Papers, vol. I, p.11
4. For the popular, but inaccurate view, see, for example, the entry in the *Encyclopaedia Britannica*
5. William Starr Myers, *General George Brinton McClellan* (New York, 1934); H.J. Eckenrode and Bryan Conrad, *George B. McClellan: The Man who Saved the Union* (Chapel Hill, 1941).
6. Horan, p.66
7. Lincoln Cabinet Papers, Library of Congress
8. Myers, p.180
9. Buckner (1823–1914) had a distinguished war record, ending as a lieutenant-general. He was Governor of Kentucky in 1887–91 and in 1896 was a Democratic nominee for the vice-presidency of the USA. He outlived all his contemporaries, dying at Mumfordville, Kentucky, on 8 January 1914
10. Horan, p.67
11. The manuscript of Pryce Lewis's adventures was assigned by his daughter Mary to

the Davis and Elkins College and serialised in the college's *Historical Magazine*, March-May 1949. See also Allan Pinkerton, *The Spy of the Rebellion*, pp.203–26.

12. Horan (p.80) quotes a telegram from Carnegie to Allan Pinkerton without appreciating its significance

13. Joseph F. Wall, *Andrew Carnegie*, p.192–93

7. The Wild Rose of the Confederacy, 1861–62

1. G.F. Milton, *Abraham Lincoln and the Fifth Column* (New York, 1942), p.52; Lafayette C. Baker, *History of the US Secret Service* (Philadelphia, 1867); William Seward's Secret Service Letter-book, 1861, Library of Congress

2. New York *Herald*. For a detailed account of Mrs Greenhow's life, see Ishbel Ross, *Rebel Rose* (New York, 1954)

3. John A. Marshall, *American Bastille* (London, 1872)

4. Most notably in the film *Rose of the Confederacy* (1994), in which Allan Pinkerton was played by Christopher Reeve – a fine piece of miscasting!

5. Pryce Lewis, *Memoirs*, op. cit.

6. William E. Doster, *Lincoln and the Episodes of the Civil War* (New York, 1915), p.104

7. Thomas Russell, *The Life and Public Service of Henry Wilson* (Boston, 1876)

8. Allan Pinkerton to Thomas Scott, Assistant Secretary of War

9. Ishbel Ross, op.cit.

8. Behind Enemy Lines, 1861–62

1. Henry McTier Warfield was the paternal grandfather of Bessie Wallis Warfield, later Duchess of Windsor. S. Teakle Wallis was his best friend, after whom Bessie's father was named Teakle Wallis Warfield.

2. Allan Pinkerton to William Seward, National Archives, Washington, DC

3. John B. Jones, *Diary of a Rebel War Clerk* (Richmond, 1868)

4. Ibid.

5. Pryce Lewis, *Memoirs*

6. *The Spy of the Rebellion*, p.544

7. Ibid., p.551

8. Richmond *Examiner*, 1 May 1862

9. Major Allen, 1862–64

1. For a more balanced view of McClellan see Myers (1934) and Eckenrode and Conrad (1941), op. cit. See also *McClellan's Own Story*, edited by Ellen McClellan and W. Prime and published in 1886 soon after McClellan's death. John Hay wrote to John G. Nicolay, his collaborator on the ten-volume biography of Lincoln, on 10 August 1865, while the book was in progress: 'I have toiled and labored through ten chapters over *McClellan*. I think I have left the impression of mutinous imbecility, and I have done it in a perfectly courteous manner . . . It is of the utmost moment that we should *seem* fair to him, while we are destroying him.'

2. McClellan to Allan Pinkerton, 21 May 1862

3. Horan, p.114. An entire chapter ('Too Many Bayonets') supports this contention.

4. Ibid., p.117

5. Correspondence of Major E.J. Allen to the Chief of Commissary and Assistant Secretary of War, in Library of Congress

6. R.B. Warden (ed.), *War Diaries of Secretary Chase* (Cincinnati, 1874); J.W. Shuckers, *Life and Public Services of Salmon Portland Chase* (New York, 1874), p.488.

7. Pinkerton letter-books, 22 September 1862: E.J. Allen to General McClellan

8. *McClellan's Own Story*, p.33

9. Bennett Papers, Library of Congress

10. Horan, p.134

11. *McClellan's Own Story*, p.628

12. Joseph C.G. Kennedy to General R.B. Marcy, 30 December 1885

13. See for example *Life and Letters of George Gordon Meade* (New York, 1913), vol. I, p.320

14. *McClellan Papers*, vol. I, p.91

15. Colonel E.H. Wright to George Ticknor Curtis, 28 December 1886, in *McClellan Papers*, vol. II, p.39

10. Aftermath of War, 1865–68

1. Pryce Lewis, *Memoirs*, op. cit.

2. R.J. Atkinson to George McClellan, Orange, New Jersey, 7 July 1863

3. John Cottrell, *Anatomy of an Assassination* (London, 1966), p.158

4. Otto Eisenschiml, *Why Was Lincoln Murdered?* (Boston, 1937)

5. Cottrell, op. cit., pp.212–13, with a great deal of supporting forensic evidence

6. George Fort Milton, *The Age of Hate: Andrew Johnson and the Radicals* (New York, 1930), pp.411, 732

11. Diplomatic Incident, 1868

1. John Reno, *His Life and Career* (New York, no date)

2. Reno extradition papers, in *Records of the Department of State*, Notes to Great Britain, vol. XIV, in National Archives, Washington. Seward's letter to Hunter makes it clear that extradition applied only to Perkins and Reno. It is not clear at what point it was decided by the Canadian authorities to hand over Charlie Anderson as well.

3. New Albany Independent Weekly Ledger, 26 August 1868

4. Horan, with customary carelessness, placed New Albany gaol in Seymour, although they are 53 miles apart. For a graphic account of the lynching, see the New Albany *Independent Weekly Ledger*, 19 December 1868 to 12 January 1869. The Indianapolis *Journal* of 18 December 1868 published the gruesome report of the county coroner on the death of Simeon Reno.

5. Allan Pinkerton to George H. Bangs, 22 December 1868, Library of Congress

12. Intimations of Mortality, 1868–77

1. Horan, p.180

2. John Cottrell, op. cit., pp.27–28 states (without giving his source) that 'unknown to Pinkerton and Lamon, another armed detective had taken a berth on the last car. This conscientious New York police officer was hurrying to Washington to warn the

authorities that the President-elect was in danger of assassination on his journey through Baltimore the next day. The officer's name was John Kennedy.' Kennedy's help was also enlisted by Stanton following Lincoln's assassination.

3. Allan Pinkerton to George H. Bangs, 5 January 1869

4. Undated fragment of a letter from Allan to Bangs, the beginning of which, with the date, is missing. From internal evidence it appears to belong to early in 1869, after the previously quoted letter.

5. Dorothy M. Long, 'The Pinkertons of Onarga', in *Iroquois County Historical Society Journal* (Winter 1969)

6. *Illinois Central Magazine* (January 1946), p.22

7. Allan Pinkerton to George H. Bangs, 17 August 1874

8. Matthew Mark Trumbull (under the *nom de plume* of 'Wheelbarrow'), *Open Court* (New York, 1892), vol. VI, p.3316

9. Allan Pinkerton, *The Molly Maguires and the Detectives* (New York, 1877), p.17

10. J. Walter Coleman, *The Molly Maguires* (New York, 1936)

11. D.P. Dewees, *The Molly Maguires* (Philadelphia, 1877), pp.239–50

13. Last Years, 1876–84

1. Joan was actually fifteen at the time (see p.240), but it is not improbable that she misled Allan as to her age

2. See, for example, the obituaries in the Glasgow *Herald* and the London *Times*.

Select Bibliography

Arnold, I.N., *Lincoln and Slavery* (New York, n.d.)

Arnold, Samuel, *The Lincoln Plot* (Baltimore, 1902)

Baker, Lafayette C., *History of the United States Secret Service* (Philadelphia, 1867)

Bancroft, Frederic, *The Life of William H. Seward* (Boston, 1900)

Boston, Ray, *British Chartists in America* (Manchester, 1971)

Boyer, Richard, *The Legend of John Brown* (New York, 1973)

Broehl, Wayne J., *The Molly Maguires* (Cambridge, Mass., 1964)

Carrick, John, *Glasgow, Past and Present*, 3 vols. (Glasgow, 1884)

Cleland, James, *Annals of Glasgow* (Glasgow, 1816)

Cole, Arthur Charles, *Centennial History of Illinois*, 5 vols. (Springfield, 1919)

Cole, G.D.H., *Chartist Portraits* (London, 1941)

Coleman, J. Walter, *The Molly Maguires* (Richmond, Virginia, 1936)

Corliss, Carlton J., *Main Line of Mid America: the Story of the Illinois Central* (New York, 1950)

Cottrell, John, *Anatomy of an Assassination* (London, 1966)

Cuthbert, Norma B. (ed.), *Lincoln and the Baltimore Plot* (San Marino, California, 1949)

Devyr, Thomas A., *The Old Book of the Nineteenth Century* (London, 1892)

Dewees, F.P., *The Molly Maguires* (Philadelphia, 1877)

De Witt, David M., *The Impeachment and Trial of Andrew Johnson* (New York, 1909)

Dictionary of American Biography (New York, 1930–35)

Doster, William E., *Lincoln and Episodes of the Civil War* (New York, 1915)

Eckenrode, H.J., and Conrad, Bryan, *George B. McClellan: the Man who Saved the Union* (Chapel Hill, North Carolina, 1941)

Edwards, N., *Life of Norman Buell Judd* (Chicago, 1867)

Eisenschiml, Otto, *Why Was Lincoln Murdered?* (Boston, 1937)

Gamage, R.G., *The History of the Chartist Movement* (London, 1854)

Gobright, L.A., *Recollections of Men and Things in Washington During Half a Century* (Philadelphia, 1869)

Greenhow, Rose O'Neal, *My Imprisonment and the First Year of Abolition Rule at Washington* (London, 1863)

Holyoake, G.J., *Sixty Years of an Agitator's Life*, 2 vols. (London, 1893)

Horan, James D., *The Pinkertons: the Detective Agency that Made History* (New York, 1967)

Horan, James D., and Swiggett, Howard, *The Pinkerton Story* (London, 1952)

Johnston, David, *Autobiographical Reminiscences of an Octogenarian Scotchman* (Chicago, 1885)

Lamon, Ward, *Recollections of Abraham Lincoln, 1847–1865* (New York, 1896)

Lavine, Sigmund, *Allan Pinkerton: the First Private Detective* (New York, 1963)

Ledru, Charles, *La vie, la mort et les derniers moments de Vidocq* (Paris, 1857)

Lomask, Milton, *Andrew Johnson, President* (New York, 1960)

McClellan, Ellen (ed.), *McClellan's Own Story* (New York, 1887)

Marshall, John A., *America's Bastille* (Philadelphia, 1872)

Milton, George Fort, *The Age of Hate* (New York, 1930)
    Abraham Lincoln and the Fifth Column (New York, 1942)

Myers, William Starr, *General George Brinton McClellan* (New York, 1934)

Nicolay, John G. and Hay, John, *Abraham Lincoln: A History*, 10 vols. (New York, 1890)

Pinkerton, Allan, *The Bankers, Their Vaults and the Burglars* (Chicago, 1873)
    The Molly Maguires and the Detectives (New York, 1877)
    Criminal Reminiscences and Detective Sketches (New York, 1879)
    The Spy of the Rebellion (New York, 1883)
    Thirty Years a Detective (New York, 1884)

Pratt, Fletcher, *Stanton* (New York,1933)

Reno, John, *John Reno, Life and Career* (New York, n.d.)

Ross, Ishbel, *Rebel Rose* (New York, 1954)

Rowan, Richard W., *The Pinkerton Detective Dynasty* (New York, 1931)

Sandburg, Carl, *Abraham Lincoln: the Prairie Years and the War Years* (New York, 1954)

Schoyen, A.R., *The Chartist Challenge* (New York, 1958)

Schuckers, J.W., *Life and Public Services of Salmon Portland Chase* (New York, 1874)

Seward, Frederick W., *Recollections of a War-Time Statesman and Diplomat* (New York, 1916)

Swiggett, Howard (ed.), *A Rebel Clerk's War Diary* (New York, 1935)

Villard, Oswald Garrison, *John Brown, 1800-1859: a Biography Fifty Years After* (Cambridge, Mass., 1910)

Warden, R.B., *War Diaries of Secretary Chase* (Cincinnati, 1874)

Welles, Gideon, *Diary*, 3 vols. (Boston, 1911)

Williams, David, *John Frost, a Study in Chartism* (Cardiff, 1939)

Williams, Kenneth P., *Lincoln Finds a General*, 2 vols. (New York, 1949)

Williams, T., *Lincoln and his Generals* (New York, 1952)
    Lincoln and the Radicals (Madison, Wisconsin, 1941)

Williamson, James J., *Prison Life in Old Capitol* (West Orange, New Jersey, 1911)

Wormser, Richard, *Pinkerton: America's First Private Eye* (New York, 1990)

Wright, Leslie C., *Scotland in Chartism* (London, 1953)

Index